Property Notices: Validity and Service

Property Notices: Validity and Service

Tom Weekes
Barrister, Landmark Chambers

JORDANS

Published by
Jordan Publishing Limited
21 St Thomas Street
Bristol BS1 6JS

The case of Mannai Investment Co Ltd v Eagle Star Life Assurance Co Ltd reproduced in Appendix 2 by permission of Reed Elsevier (UK) Limited trading as LexisNexis Butterworths.

Crown Copyright material is reproduced with kind permission of the Controller of Her Majesty's Stationery Office.

British Library Cataloguing-in-Publication Data

A catalogue record for this book is available from the British Library.

ISBN 978 1 84661 029 5

Typeset by Letterpart Ltd, Reigate, Surrey

Printed in Great Britain by Antony Rowe Limited, Chippenham, Wilts

CONTENTS

Foreword	xi
Preface	xiii
Table of Cases	xv
Table of Statutes	xxv

Chapter 1
Identifying the Requirements of a Valid Notice   **1**
Introduction   1
   The 'two-stage approach'   1
   The policy of upholding notices that achieve their purpose   2
'Mandatory requirements' and 'directory requirements'   2
   Statutory notices   2
     How to determine whether a statutory requirement relating to a
       notice is a mandatory requirement or a directory
       requirement   4
     Examples of requirements of notices that have been held to be
       directory (ie where non-compliance with the requirement
       has been held not to invalidate a notice)   5
   Contractual notices   7
'Formal requirements'   8
   Requirements merely to convey a particular meaning   8
   'Formal requirements'   9
   The significance of the distinction between requirements to convey
     a particular meaning and 'formal requirements'   11
Prescribed forms   11
   The general approach of the court: does the inaccuracy or omission
     go to the substance of the notice?   12
   The omission of material that would have been irrelevant to the
     actual recipient   13
   It is irrelevant whether the actual recipient was, in fact, prejudiced   14
   The adoption of a version of a prescribed form that has been
     superseded   14
Inaccuracies in 'particulars'   15

Chapter 2
The Interpretation of Notices   **17**
Introduction   17

The decision in Mannai Investment v Eagle Star 17
  The facts of Mannai Investment 17
  The law before Mannai Investment 18
    The pre-Mannai Investment rule about the interpretation of
      break clauses 18
    The traditional approach to the interpretation of notices 19
  The decision in Mannai Investment 20
    The interpretation of break clauses 20
    The interpretation of notices 21
    The application of the 'reasonable recipient test' to the facts 22
Contractual and statutory notices fall to be interpreted in the same
  way 23
The significance of an obvious mistake 24
The 'reasonable recipient' would have to be in no doubt 25
The test is objective: it is irrelevant how the recipient or the server
  interpreted a notice 25
  The server's subjective interpretation of a notice is irrelevant 25
  The actual recipient's subjective interpretation of a notice is
    irrelevant 26
The 'objective contextual scene' against which notices fall to be
  interpreted 28
  Covering letters 29
  Other notices 29
  Rent demands and litigation 30
  The non-factual background 30
Types of 'defect' amenable to the reasoning in Mannai Investment 30

Chapter 3
Common Issues **33**
Is a written notice required? 33
Fraudulent statements 34
Proposals and requests 35
The server's motivation 39
Signatures 40
  What is a signature? 40
  Signatures in covering letters 40
  Signatures of agents 40
Notices served 'without prejudice' to an earlier notice 41
Notices served 'subject to contract' or 'without prejudice' 42
Inconsistencies 44
Deadlines for the service of notices 45
  The usual rule 45
  Rent review notices 45
Specification of the date of the expiry of a notice 47
The identity of the correct server and recipient 49
  Legal proprietors 49
  An apparent exception to the general rule: service of a notice to
    quit following the death of the tenant 51

Joint owners   52
  The correct server of a notice where a legal estate is jointly owned   52
    The general rule: notices must be served by, or on behalf of, all
      of any joint owners   52
    An exception to the general rule: notices to quit   53
    Another exception to the general rule: Agricultural Holdings
      Act 1923, s 12   55
  The identity of the recipient of a notice where an estate in land is
    vested in joint owners   55
Misidentification of the server   56
  Notices identifying an agent as the server   59
Misidentification of the recipient   61

Chapter 4
Waiver, Estoppel and the Withdrawal of Notices   **65**
Introduction: waiver and estoppel   65
Loss of a right to serve, or to rely upon, a notice   66
Loss of a right to dispute the validity of a notice   67
  Loss by a recipient of an entitlement to dispute the validity of a
    notice   67
    Service by the wrong person   68
    Service after a contractual deadline   68
    Incorrect date for the expiry of a notice   68
    Defective contents   68
  Loss by the server of a right to dispute the validity of a notice   69
Limitations on the application of estoppel and waiver   70
  An estoppel cannot be used as 'a sword' to create a cause of action   70
  Public policy may prevent a waiver or an estoppel from defeating a
    statutory right   71
Withdrawal of notices   71

Chapter 5
Service at Common Law   **73**
Introduction   73
Service by the person entitled to serve the notice (or his agent)   74
  Service by agents   74
  Service by sub-agents   75
  A notice served by the wrong person cannot retrospectively be
    'validated'   75
Service on the recipient (or his agent)   76
  A notice must be received by, or come to the attention of, the
    recipient   76
  The presumed sequence in which notices are deemed to have been
    served   77
  Service on an agent of the recipient   77
    Solicitors   78
    Managing agents   80
    Servants   80

Rent collectors 80
Service on a recipient incapable of understanding a notice 81
'Indirect' service 82
The same person as the server and the recipient 83

Chapter 6
Service Pursuant to Contractual Provisions **85**
Introduction 85
Methods of service 85
  'By post' 85
  At the recipient's 'last known address' 85
Do contractual provisions displace the common law? 86

Chapter 7
Methods of Service Authorised by Statute **87**
Introduction 87
  The purpose of statutory methods of service 87
  Human rights 88
  The statutory provisions do not exhaustively prescribe how notices
    can be served 88
  Can the statutory provisions relating to service be used 'as an
    engine of fraud'? 88
Law of Property Act 1925, s 196 90
  To what types of notice does s 196 apply? 90
    (i) Notices required or authorised by the Law of Property
      Act 1925 to be served 91
    (ii) Notices required to be served by any instrument affecting
      property executed or coming into operation after the
      commencement of [the Law of Property Act 1925] unless a
      contrary indication appears 91
  The methods of service authorised by the Law of Property
    Act 1925, s 196 93
    (i) Leaving the notice at the last-known place of abode or
      business in the United Kingdom of the person to be served 93
    (ii) Affixing or leaving a notice at demised or mortgaged
      premises, or the office or counting-house of a mine 95
    (iii) Sending the notice by registered post or recorded delivery 96
Landlord and Tenant Act 1927, s 23 97
  To what notices does the Landlord and Tenant Act 1927, s 23
    apply? 98
  Methods of service authorised by the Landlord and Tenant
    Act 1927, s 23 98
    (i) Personal service 98
    (ii) Leaving the notice at the recipient's last known place of
      abode in England and Wales 98
    (iii) Sending the notice by registered post or recorded delivery 100
    (iv) Service upon the landlord's predecessor in title 102
  Methods of service not exhaustive 102

Service on the agent of a tenant 102
The relationship between the Landlord and Tenant Act 1927,
    s 23(1) and the Interpretation Act 1978, s 7 103
The Agricultural Holdings Act 1986, s 93 103
    Methods of service authorised by the Agricultural Holdings
        Act 1986, s 93 104
    (i) Delivering the notice to the recipient 104
    (ii) Leaving the notice at the recipient's proper address 104
    (iii) Sending the notice to the recipient by post in a registered
        letter or by the recorded delivery service 106
    Service on agents and servants 108
    Change of landlord 109
Agricultural Tenancies Act 1995, s 36 109
    Methods of service authorised by the Agricultural Tenancies
        Act 1995, s 36 110
Companies Act 2006 111
Other statutes 111

Appendix 1
Directory of Authorities about Property Notices Referred to in the Text 113

Appendix 2
Mannai Investment Co Ltd v Eagle Star Life Assurance Co Ltd 147

Index 181

FOREWORD

It is a well-known feature of life that the human condition is such that everything that conceivably can go wrong sometimes does go wrong, and that, occasionally, even that which could not go wrong does go wrong. And when it comes to property notices a great deal can go wrong, as perusal of the ensuing pages of this book demonstrates. Problems arise most commonly from misinterpretation of the contract or the statute pursuant to which the notice is served, poor drafting of the notice, and failure to serve the notice properly. However, these three categories contain an almost infinite variety of sub-categories, and anyway this is not a mutually exclusive list – or even an exhaustive list – of categories (as chapter 4 of this book shows).

These problems are not new. Even in the very early nineteenth century, when the landlord of *The Bricklayer's Arms* public house served notice on his tenant to quit *The Waterman's Arms* (see *Doe d Cox v Roe*), mistakes got made, and no doubt that was by no means the first time. In the ensuing 200 years, as perusal of the law reports, indeed as perusal of the case index in this book, demonstrates, a remarkable number of problems have been encountered in this field.

Property notices give rise to a remarkable variety of different sorts of issue. Those areas include interpretation of contracts, construction of statutes, drafting of notices, principles of service, and even the inter-relationship of law and equity. The issues can raise important and wide-ranging points of principle. Thus, in the past 30 years or so, there have been two very well-known and not uncontroversial decisions of the House of Lords concerning property notices, both of which raised fundamental points of law. They were the *United Scientific* case, which concerned the proper approach to contractual time limits, and the *Mannai* case, which involved the proper approach to construction of contracts and notices.

At the other extreme, property notice disputes can also give rise to difficult questions of pure fact, which sometimes cast a shaft of light on an interesting or quirky aspect of life. In *Chapman v Honig*, the landlord famously served notice to quit because he was cross with his tenant for having given evidence against him in another case. In *Kinch v Bullard*, a wife served a notice of severance on her husband because she was dying, but then the husband had a serious heart attack, and it appeared he would pre-decease her; so the wife tore up the notice after it was put through the letter box before the husband saw it.

Most commonly, perhaps, the issues raised in property notice cases are ones which may be characterised as being technical legal questions. Such questions are very often difficult and, even, perhaps surprisingly, rather interesting once one studies the problem. Many, indeed I think most, of the cases referred to in this book bear out that observation. First instance judgments frequently betray the fact that the judge found them difficult, and quite a significant proportion of those judgments were subsequently reversed on appeal.

Over the past few decades the amount of available legal learning on property notices has expanded almost exponentially, as the number of cases concerning notices has increased very substantially. This is no doubt partly due to the rise in the capital and rental values of property, but it is also attributable to successive statutes and rules of court introducing new procedures and rules, and to ingenious lawyers dreaming up new points. The relevant legal principles have been refined and developed, and sometimes confused. In many respects, the law in this area has become even more of a minefield for owners of property interests, and even for the legal and surveying professions, than it had previously been. Of course, the primary concerns of those people actually involved with property, whether lawyers, surveyors, owners, landlords or tenants, are normally practical rather than academic. But the various technical and legal points inevitably have direct and substantial practical consequences.

As a result of the growth in the number and importance of these technical and legal issues, the time is now ripe for a book which concentrates on the topic of property notices. Of course, the subject is covered to some extent in books on property law and the law of landlord and tenant. But it is highly desirable, from the point of view of those with interests in property and the professionals advising them, that there is a book which is devoted to the topic, and which provides a clear and full explanation of the principles and the problems in a way that is systematically structured and easy to find one's way through. Tom Weekes has now written such a book, and he is to be congratulated for having done so. If you have a problem on which you need guidance and to which there is an answer, there are, to my mind, three requirements of a book such as this. First, the answer should be included in the book; secondly, you should be able to find it reasonably easily; and, thirdly, it should be comprehensibly dealt with. This book appears to me to pass all three tests.

Lord Neuberger of Abbotsbury
January 2008

PREFACE

The contents of this book will no doubt disappoint some readers. It contains no prescribed forms or precedents. Nor even does it include any detailed commentary dedicated to any of the particular types of property notice. To find such forms, precedents and commentary, the reader will need to consult the specialist works dealing with the statutory or contractual schemes under which notices are served.

Instead, I have attempted in this book to outline the underlying legal principles relating to the validity of notices; to illustrate how those principles play out in common factual circumstances (eg where a notice contains a fraudulent statement, misidentifies a deadline for service, or misidentifies the server or the recipient); and to explain the general principles relating to service. This approach is, I hope, justified – not least – because, as often as not, the solution to a problem relating to the validity or service of a property notice will not be found in the case law relating to the particular type of notice that has purportedly been served, but rather in authorities, perhaps relating to very different types of notices, which establish or illustrate general principles, or which concern a similar factual situation.

Although much of the law relating to property notices is technical and legalistic in character, my aim has been to provide a concise and practical guide for the busy practitioner.

In writing this book, I have been assisted by colleagues in Chambers and solicitors who have commented on my drafts, especially by Katherine Holland, who read the entire draft at an early stage and provided many helpful comments. I am also grateful to Tony Hawitt and his colleagues at Jordans for their patience and assistance, and to Lord Neuberger – who has delivered many of the most important recent judgments on notices – for taking the time to write the Foreword. Finally, I express my gratitude to Marion Wallace Pannell for her help and support throughout the writing of this book.

I have attempted to state the law as at 15 January 2008.

Tom Weekes
January 2008

TABLE OF CASES

References are to paragraph numbers.

Addis v Burrows [1948] 1 KB 444, [1948] 1 All ER 177, [1948] LJR 1033, 92 Sol Jo 124,
64 TLR 169   3.36, 3.39
Akici v LR Butlin Ltd [2005] EWCA Civ 1296, [2006] 2 All ER 872, [2006] 1 WLR 201,
[2006] 1 P & CR 386, [2006] 07 EG 136, [2006] 1 EGLR 34, [2005] 45 EG 168 (CS),
[2005] All ER (D) 22 (Nov)   2.38
Alford v Vickery (1842) Car & M 280   3.48, 5.11
Allam & Co Ltd v Europa Poster Services Ltd [1968] 1 All ER 826, [1968] 1 WLR 638,
112 Sol Jo 86, 205 Estates Gazette 653   3.19, 3.37, 5.8
Amalgamated Estates Ltd v Joystretch Manufacturing Ltd [1981] 1 EGLR 96, 257 Estates
Gazette 489   3.9
Andrews v Cunningham [2007] EWCA Civ 762, [2007] All ER (D) 343 (Jul)   1.2, 3.1
Aristocrat Property Investments v Harounoff (1982) 43 P & CR 284, 2 HLR 102, 263
Estates Gazette 352   4.14, 4.15
Armherst v James Walker Ltd [1983] 1 Ch 305   3.33
Arundel Corn v Khokher 2003] EWCA Civ 1784, 148 Sol Jo LB 25, [2003] All ER (D)
149 (Dec)   7.19
Australian Blue Metal Ltd v Hughes [1963] AC 74, [1962] 3 All ER 335, [1962] 3 WLR
802, 106 Sol Jo 628   3.35

Barclays Bank plc v Bee Barclays Bank v Bee [2001] EWCA Civ 1126, [2002] 1 WLR 332,
[2002] 1 P & CR 321, 82 P & CR D41, [2001] 34 LS Gaz R 40, [2001] 29 EGCS
121, [2001] 37 EG 153, (2001) The Times, 3 August, 145 Sol Jo LB 206, [2001] All
ER (D) 123 (Jul)   2.23, 2.31, 3.27
Barclays Bank v Ascot [1961] 1 All ER 782, [1961] 1 WLR 717, 105 Sol Jo 323, 178
Estates Gazette 189   1.36
Bathavon Rural District Council v Carlile [1958] 1 QB 461, [1958] 1 All ER 801, [1958] 2
WLR 545, 56 LGR 139, 122 JP 240, 102 Sol Jo 230   3.37
BCCI v Ali [2001] UKHL 8, [2002] 1 AC 251, [2001] 1 All ER 961, [2001] 2 WLR 735,
[2001] ICR 337, [2001] IRLR 292, 151 NLJ 351, (2001) The Times, 6 March, 145
Sol Jo LB 67, [2001] All ER (D) 06 (Mar)   2.33
Beanby Estates Ltd v Egg Stores (Stamford Hill) Ltd [2003] EWHC 1252 (Ch), [2004] 3
All ER 184, [2003] 1 WLR 2064, [2003] 3 EGLR 85, [2003] 26 LS Gaz R 37, [2003]
21 EGCS 190, (2003) The Times, 15 May, [2003] 2 P & CR D44, [2003] All ER (D)
122 (May)   5.11, 7.3, 7.36, 7.45, 7.50, 7.59
Belvedere Court Ltd v Frogmore Ltd [1997] QB 858   1.11
Beresford v Royal Insurance Co [1938] AC 586, [1938] 2 All ER 602, 107 LJKB 464, 82
Sol Jo 431, 158 LT 459, 54 TLR 789   3.12
88 Berkeley Road, NW9, Re [1971] Ch 648, [1971] 1 All ER 254, [1971] 2 WLR 307, 22 P
& CR 188, 115 Sol Jo 34   5.1, 7.15, 7.29, 7.30
Betty's Cafes Ltd v Phillips Furnishing Stores Ltd [1959] AC 20, [1958] 1 All ER 607,
[1958] 2 WLR 513, 102 Sol Jo 228, 171 Estates Gazette 319   3.5
Bird v Defonville (1846) 2 C&K 415   3.2
BL Holdings Ltd v Marcolt Investments Ltd [1979] 1 EGLR 97, 249 Estates Gazette 849   4.10
Blewett v Blewett [1936] 2 All ER 188   3.53

Blunden v Frogmore Investment Ltd [2002] EWCA Civ 573, [2003] 2 P & CR 84, [2002]
    29 EG 153, [2002] 20 EGCS 223, [2002] 2 P & CR D21, [2002] All ER (D) 305
    (Apr)   5.2, 6.2, 7.2, 7.8, 7.22, 7.26, 7.44
Bridges v Stanford (1991) 63 P & CR 18, [1991] 2 EGLR 265, 135 Sol Jo LB 29   3.68
British Rail Pension Trustee Co Ltd v Cardshops Ltd [1987] 1 EGLR 127, 282 Estates
    Gazette 331   3.24
Brown & Root Technology Ltd v Sun Alliance [2001] Ch 733, [2000] 2 WLR 566, 75 P &
    CR 223, [1997] 1 EGLR 39, [1997] 7 LS Gaz R 29, [1997] 18 EG 123, 141 Sol Jo
    LB 38   3.41
Burman v Mount Cook Land Ltd [2001] EWCA Civ 1712, [2002] Ch 256, [2002] 1 All ER
    144, [2002] 2 WLR 1172, [2002] 1 P & CR D31, [2002] HLR 845, [2001] 46 LS Gaz
    R 37, [2001] 48 EGCS 128, [2002] 06 EG 156, 146 Sol Jo LB 12, [2001] All ER (D)
    281 (Nov)   1.2, 1.26, 2.36
Byrnlea Property Investments Ltd v Ramsay [1969] 2 QB 253, [1969] 2 All ER 311, [1969]
    2 WLR 721, 20 P & CR 528, 113 Sol Jo 188, [1969] RVR 183, 209 Estates Gazette
    1439   3.26

Cadogan v Morris (1998) 77 P & CR 336, 31 HLR 732, [1999] 1 EGLR 59, [1999] 04 EG
    155, 143 Sol Jo LB 11, 77 P & CR D13   3.11
Cannon Brewery Co v Signal Press Ltd [1928] All ER Rep 108, 72 Sol Jo 285, 139 LT 384,
    44 TLR 486   7.22, 7.38, 7.57
Capital Land Holdings Ltd v Secretary of State for the Environment 1997 SC 109, 1995
    SLT 1379   6.5
Carradine Properties Ltd v Aslam [1976] 1 All ER 573, [1976] 1 WLR 442, 32 P & CR 12,
    120 Sol Jo 166   2.23
Central Estates Ltd v Secretary of State for the Environment (1995) 72 P & CR 482,
    [1997] 1 EGLR 239, [1995] EGCS 110   3.31
Chapman v Honig [1963] 2 QB 502, [1963] 3 WLR 19, [1963] 2 All ER 513, CA   3.12
Charrington & Co Ltd v Wooder [1914] AC 71, 83 LJKB 220, 58 Sol Jo 152, 110 LT 548,
    30 TLR 176, [1911–13] All ER Rep Ext 1377   2.28
Chez Auguste v Cottat [1951] 1 KB 292, 94 Sol Jo 598, 66 (pt 2) TLR 873   3.39
Chilton Court (Baker Street) Residents Ltd v Wallabrook Property Co Ltd [1989] 2
    EGLR 207, [1989] 43 EG 173   3.28
Chiswell v Griffon Land & Estates Ltd [1975] 2 All ER 665, [1975] 1 WLR 1181, 119 Sol
    Jo 338   5.11, 7.44
City & Country Properties Ltd v Plowden Investments Ltd [2007] L&TR 15   3.18
Collins v Blantern (1767) 2 Wils 341, 95 ER 847, [1558–1774] All ER Rep 33   3.4
Commercial Union Life Assurance Co Ltd v Moustafa [1999] 2 EGLR 44, [1999] 24 EG
    155   7.44, 7.50, 7.59
Commission for the New Towns v Levy [1990] 2 EGLR 121, [1990] 28 EG 119   1.18
Cordon Bleu Freezer Food Centres Ltd v Marbleace Ltd [1987] 2 EGLR 143, 284 Estates
    Gazette 786   4.3
9 Cornwall Crescent London Ltd v Kensington and Chelsea Royal London Borough
    Council [2005] EWCA Civ 324, [2005] 4 All ER 1207, [2006] 1 WLR 1186, [2005]
    HLR 642, [2005] 2 EGLR 131, [2005] 14 EG 128 (CS), (2005) *Times*, 29 March,
    [2005] All ER (D) 374 (Mar)   3.10, 3.11
Crawley BC v Ure [1996] QB 13, [1996] 1 All ER 724, [1995] 3 WLR 95, 71 P & CR 12,
    [1996] 1 FCR 6, [1995] 1 FLR 806, [1995] Fam Law 411, 27 HLR 524   3.50
Cresswell v Duke of Westminster [1985] 2 EGLR 151, 25 RVR 144, 275 Estates Gazette
    461   1.41, 1.42

Daejan Properties Ltd v Mahoney (1995) 28 HLR 498, [1995] NPC 7, [1995] 2 EGLR 75,
    [1995] 45 EG 128   4.15
Datlow v Jones [1985] 2 EGLR 1, 275 Estates Gazette 145   4.2
Davstone (Holdings) Ltd v Al-Rifai (1976) 32 P & CR 18   3.9
Dean and Chapter of Chichester v Lennards Ltd (1977) 35 P & CR 309, 121 Sol Jo 694,
    [1977] 2 EGLR 78, 244 Estates Gazette 807   1.18, 1.19, 3.1
Delta Vale Properties Ltd v Mills [1990] 2 All ER 176, [1990] 1 WLR 445, 134 Sol Jo 316,
    [1990] 9 LS Gaz R 44, [1990] NLJR 290   2.19, 2.23

Derry v Peek (1889) 14 App Cas 337, 54 JP 148, 58 LJ Ch 864, 1 Meg 292, 38 WR 33,
    [1886-90] All ER Rep 1, 61 LT 265, 5 TLR 625   3.3
Divall v Harrison [1992] 2 EGLR 64, [1992] 38 EG 147   3.41, 3.60
Doe d Aslin v Summersett (1830) 1 B & Ad 135, 8 LJOSKB 369   3.48
Doe d Buross v Lucas 1804) 5 Esp 153   5.11
Doe d Cox v Roe (1803) 4 Esp 185   2.9
Doe d Kindersley v Hughes (1840) 7 M&W 139   3.48
Doe d Macartney v Crick (1805) 5 Esp 196   3.2
Doe v Timothy (1847) 2 Car & K 351   3.36
Duchess of Kingston's Case [1775–1802] All ER Rep 623, 20 State Tr 355; 2 Smith, LC,
    12th ed, 754; 1 East, PC 468; 1 Leach, 146   3.4
Dun & Bradstreet Software Services (England) Ltd v Provident Mutual Life Assurance
    Association [1998] 2 EGLR 175   3.41, 4.6
Dymond v Arundel-Times (1990) 23 HLR 397, [1991] 1 EGLR 109, [1991] 21 EG 107   1.42

Earl Cadogan v Straus [2004] EWCA Civ 211, [2004] 2 P & CR 295, [2004] 19 EG 166,
    [2004] 2 EGLR 69, (2004) *Times*, 11 March, [2004] All ER (D) 131 (Feb)   1.42
Egerton v Rutter [1951] 1 KB 472, [1951] 1 TLR 58   3.45
Elsden v Pick [1980] 3 All ER 235, [1980] 1 WLR 898, 40 P & CR 550, 124 Sol Jo 312,
    254 Estates Gazette 503   4.1, 4.12, 4.15
Enfield LBC v Devonish (1996) 74 P & CR 288, 29 HLR 691   3.1, 7.16

Farrow v Orttewell [1933] Ch 480, 102 LJ Ch 133, [1933] All ER Rep 132, 149 LT 101, 49
    TLR 251   4.13
Featherstone v Staples [1986] 2 All ER 461, [1986] 1 WLR 861, 52 P & CR 287, 130 Sol
    Jo 482, [1986] 1 EGLR 6, [1986] LS Gaz R 1226, 278 Estates Gazette 867   3.46
Fernandez v McDonald [2003] EWCA Civ 1219, [2003] 4 All ER 1033, [2004] 1 WLR
    1027, [2004] HLR 189, [2003] 3 EGLR 22, [2003] 42 EG 128, [2003] 34 LS Gaz R
    33, (2003) *The Times*, 9 October, 147 Sol Jo LB 995, [2003] All ER (D) 94 (Aug)   1.29,
                              2.22, 2.37, 3.38
Fifield v W&R Jack Ltd [2001] L&TR 4   4.7
Fox & Widley v Guram [1998] 1 EGLR 91, [1998] 03 EG 142   3.9
Fredco Estates Ltd v Bryant [1961] 1 All ER 34, [1961] 1 WLR 76, 105 Sol Jo 86   3.64

Galinski v McHugh (1988) 57 P & CR 359, 21 HLR 47, [1989] 1 EGLR 109, [1988] NLJR
    303, [1989] 05 EG 89, [1988] EGCS 127, (1988) *The Times*, 13 October   5.10, 5.20, 7.2,
                              7.44, 7.47, 7.48
Garston v Scottish Widows' Fund [1998] All ER (D) 301, [1998] 3 All ER 596, [1998] 1
    WLR 1583, [1998] 2 EGLR 73, [1998] 26 LS Gaz R 32, [1998] 32 EG 88, [1998]
    EGCS 101, 142 Sol Jo LB 199   3.37
Gatwick Investments Ltd v Radviojevic [1978] CLY 1768   3.43
Germax Securities Ltd v Spiegal (1978) 37 P & CR 204, 123 Sol Jo 164, 250 Estates
    Gazette 449   2.20
Glen International Ltd v Triplerose Ltd [2007] EWCA Civ 388, [2007] 26 EG 164, [2007]
    All ER (D) 396 (Mar)   5.18
Goodman v J Eban Ltd [1954] 1 QB 550, [1954] 2 WLR 581, [1954] 1 All ER 763, CA   3.14
Greenwich LBC v McGrady (1982) 81 LGR 288, 46 P & CR 223, 6 HLR 36, 267 Estates
    Gazette 515   3.48

Hallinan (Lady) v Jones [1984] 2 EGLR 20, 272 Estates Gazette 1081   7.58
Hammersmith and Fulham LBC v Monk [1992] 1 AC 478, [1992] 1 All ER 1, [1991] 3
    WLR 1144, 90 LGR 38, 63 P & CR 373, [1992] 2 FCR 129, [1992] 1 FLR 465,
    [1992] Fam Law 292, 24 HLR 206, [1992] 1 EGLR 65, [1992] 3 LS Gaz R 32,
    [1992] 09 EG 135, 136 Sol Jo LB 10   3.46, 3.48
Hankey v Clavering [1942] 2 KB 326, [1942] 2 All ER 311, 111 LJKB 711, 167 LT 193   2.7, 2.13
Harmond Properties Ltd v Gajdzis [1968] 3 All ER 263, [1968] 1 WLR 1858, 19 P & CR
    718, 112 Sol Jo 762   3.60, 3.65
Harris v Black (1983) 46 P & CR 366, 127 Sol Jo 224   3.46
Harrowby v Snelson [1951] 1 All ER 140, 95 Sol Jo 108   3.45
Havant International v Lionsgate (H) Investment [1999] 47 LS Gaz R 34, [1999] EGCS
    144, [1999] All ER (D) 1344   2.28, 3.59

Hawtrey v Beaufront Ltd [1946] KB 280, [1946] 1 All ER 296, 115 LJKB 228, 174 LT 167,
    62 TLR 205   3.68
Henry Smith's Charity Trustees v Kyriakou (1989) 22 HLR 66, [1989] 2 EGLR 110, [1989]
    RVR 106, [1989] 50 EG 42   7.22, 7.38, 7.57
Hirst v Horn (1840) 6 M & W 393   3.39
Hogg v Brooks (1885) 15 QBD 256, 50 JP 118   5.10
Holwell Securities Ltd v Hughes [1974] 1 WLR 155, [1974] 1 All ER 161, CA; affirming
    [1973] 1 WLR 757, [1973] 2 All ER 476, ChD   5.1, 5.18, 7.15
Hounslow LBC v Pilling [1994] 1 All ER 432, [1993] 1 WLR 1242, 91 LGR 573, 66 P &
    CR 22, [1993] 2 FLR 49, [1993] Fam Law 522, 25 HLR 305, [1993] 2 EGLR 59,
    [1993] 15 LS Gaz R 40, [1993] 26 EG 123, 137 Sol Jo LB 87   3.46
Howard v Bodington (1877) 2 PD 203   1.11
Howson v Buxton (1928) 97 LJKB 749, [1928] All ER Rep 434, 139 LT 504   3.48, 3.51, 3.52
Hughes v Metropolitan Railway Co (1877) 2 App Cas 439, 42 JP 421, 46 LJQB 583, 25
    WR 680, [1874–80] All ER Rep 187, 36 LT 932   4.4
Hussein v Mehlman [1992] 2 EGLR 85, [1992] 47 EG 103   5.27

ICS Ltd v West Bromwich BS [1998] 1 All ER 98, [1998] 1 WLR 896, [1998] 1 BCLC 493,
    [1997] NLJR 989, [1997] CLC 1243, [1997] PNLR 541   2.15
Investors Compensation Scheme Ltd v West Bromwich Building Society [1998] 1 All ER
    98, [1998] 1 WLR 896, [1998] 1 BCLC 493, [1997] NLJR 989, [1997] CLC 1243,
    [1997] PNLR 541   2.1
Italica Holdings SA v Bayadea [1985] 1 EGLR 70, 273 Estates Gazette 888, 134 NLJ 311   7.36,
                                                                                        7.44

Jacobs v Chaudhuri [1968] 2 QB 470, [1968] 2 All ER 124, [1968] 2 WLR 1098, 19 P &
    CR 286, 112 Sol Jo 135, 205 Estates Gazette 991   3.52
John v George (1995) 71 P & CR 375, [1996] 1 EGLR 7, [1996] 08 EG 140   4.2
Jones v Lewis (1973) 25 P & CR 375, 117 Sol Jo 373, 226 Estates Gazette 805   3.66
Jones v Phipps (1868) LR 3 QB 567, 33 JP 229, 9 B & S 761, 37 LJQB 198, 16 WR 1044,
    18 LT 813   3.63, 5.5

Kay Green v Twinsectra Ltd [1996] 4 All ER 546, [1996] 1 WLR 1587, 29 HLR 327,
    [1996] 2 EGLR 43, [1996] 38 EG 136   1.12, 1.14, 2.30
Keepers and Governors of the Free Grammar School of John Lyon v Mayhew [1997] 1
    EGLR 88, [1997] 17 EG 163   4.9
Keith Bayley Rogers & Co v Cubes Ltd (1975) 31 P & CR 412   2.30, 3.19, 5.13
Kinch v Bullard [1998] 4 All ER 650, [1999] 1 WLR 423, [1999] 1 FLR 66, [1998] Fam
    Law 738, [1998] 47 EG 140, [1998] EGCS 126, 77 P & CR D1   4.17, 4.18, 5.1, 7.7, 7.12,
                                                            7.15, 7.21, 7.23, 7.39, 7.40, 7.55
Knight and Hubbard's Underlease, Re [1923] 1 Ch 130, 92 LJ Ch 130, 128 LT 503   3.64, 5.5, 5.28

Lafiti v Colherne Court Freehold Ltd [2002] EWHC 2873 (QB), [2003] 1 EGLR 78, [2003]
    12 EG 130, [2002] All ER (D) 240 (Nov)   4.15
Lancecrest Ltd v Asiwaju [2005] EWCA Civ 117, [2005] 1 EGLR 40, [2005] 16 EG 146,
    149 Sol Jo LB 234, [2005] All ER (D) 174 (Feb)   2.27, 3.9, 3.29, 3.32
Land v Sykes [1992] 1 EGLR 1, [1992] 03 EG 115   2.25
Lay v Ackerman [2004] EWCA Civ 184, [2004] HLR 684, [2005] 1 EGLR 139, (2004)
    Times, 24 March, 148 Sol Jo LB 299, [2004] All ER (D) 109 (Mar)   2.26, 2.32, 3.57, 3.61,
                                                                                        5.7
Lazarus Estates Ltd v Beasley [1956] 1 QB 702, [1956] 2 WLR 502, [1956] 1 All ER 341,
    CA   2.25, 3.4, 3.14, 3.68
Leek and Moorelands Building Society v Clarke [1952] 2 QB 788, [1952] 2 All ER 492, 96
    Sol Jo 561, [1952] 2 TLR 401   3.46
Lemmerbell Ltd v Britannia LAS Direct Ltd [1998] 3 EGLR 67, [1998] 48 EG 188, [1998]
    EGCS 138, [1998] All ER (D) 441   3.58
Lemon v Lardeur [1946] KB 613, [1946] 2 All ER 329, 115 LJKB 492, 90 Sol Jo 527, 175
    LT 121, 62 TLR 600   3.37, 3.60
Lex Services plc v Johns (1989) 59 P & CR 427, [1990] 1 EGLR 92, [1990] RVR 51, [1990]
    10 EG 67   7.50, 7.59, 7.61

Liverpool Borough Bank v Turner (1861) 30 LJ Ch 379   1.10
Lloyd v Sadler [1978] QB 774, [1978] 2 WLR 721, [1978] 2 All ER 529, CA   3.51
London & Manchester Assurance Co Ltd v GA Dunn & Co Ltd [1983] 1 EGLR 111, 265
    Estates Gazette 39, 131   3.32
London Borough of Hackney v Hackney African Organisation [1998] EGCS 139, 77 P &
    CR D18, [1998] All ER (D) 455   2.30, 2.32, 3.56
London County Council v Agricultural Food Products Ltd [1955] 2 QB 218, [1955] 2 All
    ER 229, [1955] 2 WLR 925, 53 LGR 350, 99 Sol Jo 305   3.16
Lord Newborough v Jones [1975] 1 Ch 90, [1974] 3 All ER 17   7.22, 7.38, 7.52
Lowenthal v Vanhoute [1947] KB 342, [1947] 1 All ER 116, [1947] LJR 421, 177 LT 180,
    63 TLR 54   4.3
Lower Street Properties Ltd v Jones (1996) 28 HLR 877, [1996] NPC 29, [1996] 48 EG 154   3.38
Lower v Sorrell [1963] 1 QB 959, [1962] 3 All ER 1074, [1963] 2 WLR 1   3.42, 4.16

M&P Enterprises (London) Ltd v Norfolk Square Hotels Ltd [1994] 1 EGLR 129, [1994]
    14 EG 128   2.30, 3.56
MacNiven v Westmoreland Investments Ltd [2001] UKHL 6, [2003] 1 AC 311, [2001] 1
    All ER 865, [2001] 2 WLR 377, [2001] STC 237, 73 TC 1, [2001] NLJR 223, 145
    Sol Jo LB 55, [2001] All ER (D) 93 (Feb)   7.8
Mannai Investment Co Ltd v Eagle Star Life Assurance Co Ltd [1997] AC 749, [1997] 3
    All ER 352, [1997] 2 WLR 945, [1997] CLC 1124, [1997] 1 EGLR 57, [1997] 25 EG
    138, [1997] 24 EG 122, (1997) 16 Tr LR 432, [1997] EGCS 82, (1997) 94(30) LSG
    30, (1997) 147 NLJ 846, (1997) 141 SJLB 130, [1997] NPC 81, (1997) *The Times*,
    May 26, HL; reversing [1996] 1 All ER 55, [1995] 1 WLR 1508, (1996) 71 P & CR
    129, [1996] 1 EGLR 69, [1996] 6 EG 140, [1995] EGCS 124, [1995] NPC 117,
    (1995) 139 SJLB 179, (1995) *The Times*, July 19, CA   1.21, 1.22, 1.25, 2.1, 2.2, 2.4, 2.5, 2.8,
           2.10, 2.11, 2.12, 2.14, 2.15, 2.16, 2.19, 2.20, 2.23, 2.25, 2.28, 2.29, 2.34,
           2.35, 2.38, 3.37, 4.1
Manorlike Ltd v Le Vitas Travel Agency and Consultancy Services Ltd [1986] 1 All ER
    573, [1986] 1 EGLR 79, 278 Estates Gazette 412   3.37
Marks (Morris) v British Waterways Board [1963] 3 All ER 28, [1963] 1 WLR 1008, 107
    Sol Jo 512, 187 Estates Gazette 177   3.5
Master v Miller (1793) 1 Anst 225, 5 Term Rep 367, 2 Hy Bl 141   3.4
Maurice Investments Ltd v Lincoln Insurance Services Ltd [2006] EWHC 376 (Ch), [2007]
    1 P & CR 235, [2006] All ER (D) 402 (Feb)   2.27, 3.22
May v Borup [1915] 1 KB 830, 84 LJKB 823, 113 LT 694   3.36, 4.16
Milne-Berry & Madden v Tower Hamlets LBC (1995) 28 HLR 225, [1995] EGCS 86   4.3
Minay v Sentongo (1982) 45 P & CR 190, 6 HLR 79, 126 Sol Jo 674, 266 Estates Gazette
    433   5.11
Morris v Patel (1987) 281 EG 419   1.39
Morrow v Nadeem [1987] 1 All ER 237, [1986] 1 WLR 1381, 53 P & CR 203, 130 Sol Jo
    822, [1986] 2 EGLR 73, [1986] NLJ Rep 965, 279 Estates Gazette 1083   1.34, 3.56
Munro, Re [1981] 3 All ER 215, [1981] 1 WLR 1358, 125 Sol Jo 512   5.16

National Westminster Bank Ltd v Betchworth Investments Ltd (1975) 234 Estates Gazette
    675   6.3
New Hart Builders v Brindley [1975] Ch 342, [1975] 1 All ER 1007, [1975] 2 WLR 595, 29
    P & CR 476, 119 Sol Jo 256   3.1, 5.11, 5.12
Newborough (Lord) v Jones [1975] 1 Ch 90, [1974] 3 WLR 52, [1974] 3 All ER 17, CA   7.56
Newman v Keedwell (1977) 35 P & CR 393, 244 Estates Gazette 469   3.46
Norfolk County Council v Child [1918] 2 KB 805, 16 LGR 738, 87 LJKB 1122, 119 LT
    639, 34 TLR 592   2.30, 4.16
Norwich Union Life Assurance Society v Sketchley plc [1986] 2 EGLR 126, 280 Estates
    Gazette 773   2.25
Norwich Union Life Insurance Society v Tony Waller Ltd (1984) 128 Sol Jo 300, [1984] 1
    EGLR 126, [1984] LS Gaz R 899, 270 Estates Gazette 42   3.22
Notting Hill Housing Trust v Brackley and Another [2001] EWCA Civ 601, [2001] 35 EG
    106, [2002] HLR 212, CA   3.50
Notting Hill Housing Trust v Roomus [2006] EWCA Civ 407, [2006] 1 WLR 1375, [2006]
    All ER (D) 432 (Mar)   3.38

Old Grovebury Manor Farm Ltd v W Seymour Plant Sales & Hire Ltd, No 2 [1979] 3 All
 ER 504, [1979] 1 WLR 1397, 39 P & CR 99, 123 Sol Jo 719, 252 Estates Gazette
 1103   3.43
Osborn & Co Ltd v Dior [2003] HLR 649, [2003] EWCA Civ 281, [2003] 05 EGCS 144,
 [2003] All ER (D) 185 (Jan)   1.33, 2.25
Osei-Bonsu v Wandsworth LBC [1999] 1 All ER 265, [1999] 1 WLR 1011, [1999] 3 FCR 1,
 [1999] 1 FLR 276, 31 HLR 515, [1999] 1 EGLR 26, [1998] 42 LS Gaz R 34, [1998]
 NLJR 1641, [1999] 11 EG 167, [1998] EGCS 148, 143 Sol Jo LB 12   3.43

Patel v Earlspring Properties Ltd [1991] 2 EGLR 131, [1991] 46 EG 153   1.18
Pearse v Boulton (1860) 2 F&F 133   5.23
Pearson v Alyo (1989) 60 P & CR 56, [1990] 1 EGLR 114, [1990] 25 EG 69   3.56
Peel Developments (South) Ltd v Siemens plc [1992] 2 EGLR 85, [1992] 47 EG 103   5.21
Peer Freeholds Ltd v Clean Wash International Ltd [2005] EWHC 179 (Ch), [2005] 1
 EGLR 47, [2005] 17 EG 124, [2005] All ER (D) 280 (Feb)   3.37
Petch v Gurney (Inspector of Taxes), Gurney (Inspector of Taxes) v Petch [1994] 3 All ER
 731, [1994] STC 689, CA   1.7, 1.8
Phipps and Co (Northampton and Towcester Breweries) Ltd v Rogers [1925] 1 KB 14, 89
 JP 1, 93 LJKB 1009, [1924] All ER Rep 208, 69 Sol Jo 841, 132 LT 240, 40 TLR
 849   2.5, 3.36, 3.39
Prenn v Simmonds [1971] 3 All ER 237, [1971] 1 WLR 1381, 115 Sol Jo 654   2.1
Price v West London Investment Building Society Ltd [1964] 2 All ER 318, [1964] 1 WLR
 616, 108 Sol Jo 276, 190 Estates Gazette 19   7.19, 7.36, 7.37, 7.45, 7.54
Proctor & Gamble Technical Centres Ltd v Brixton plc [2002] EWHC 2835 (Ch), [2003] 2
 EGLR 24, [2003] 32 EG 69, [2002] All ER (D) 305 (Dec)   3.58, 5.4, 5.6
Project Blue Sky Inc v Australian Broadcasting Authority (1998) 194 CLR 355   1.9

R (Morris) v London Rent Assessment Committee [2002] EWCA Civ 276, [2002] EGLR
 149, [2002] 11 EGCS 155, [2002] All ER (D) 75 (Mar)   3.69
R v Cardiff City Council, ex p Cross (1982) 81 LGR 105, 6 HLR 1, [1982] RVR 270,
 [1983] JPL 245   5.28
R v County of London Quarter Sessions Appeal Committee, ex p Rossi [1956] 1 QB 682,
 [1956] 1 All ER 670, [1956] 2 WLR 800, 120 JP 239, 100 Sol Jo 225   7.60
R v Shurmer (1886) 17 QBD 323, 50 JP 743, 55 LJMC 153, 16 Cox CC 94, 34 WR 656,
 55 LT 126, 2 TLR 737   3.1
R v Soneji [2006] EWCA Crim 1125, [2006] All ER (D) 390 (Mar)   1.8, 1.9
Railtrack plc v Gojra [1998] 1 EGLR 63, [1998] 08 EG 158   7.44, 7.45
Raineri v Miles [1981] AC 1050, [1980] 2 All ER 145, [1980] 2 WLR 847, 41 P & CR 71,
 124 Sol Jo 328   3.30
Ravenseft Properties Ltd v Hall [2001] EWCA Civ 2034, [2002] HLR 624, [2002] 11 EG
 156, (2002) *The Times*, 15 January, [2001] All ER (D) 318 (Dec)   1.32, 1.35, 2.22, 2.25
Re Viola's Indenture of Lease, Humphrey v Stenbury [1909] 1 Ch 244, 78 LJ Ch 128,
 [1908-10] All ER Rep 483, 100 LT 33   3.46, 3.48
Reardon Smith Line Ltd v Yngvar Hansen-Tangen [1976] 3 All ER 570, [1976] 1 WLR
 989, [1976] 2 Lloyd's Rep 621, 120 Sol Jo 719   2.1, 2.28
Rees d Mears v Perrot (1830) 4 C&P 230   3.45
Rennie v Westbury Homes (Holdings) Ltd [2007] EWHC 164 (Ch), [2007] 2 P & CR 239,
 [2007] 20 EG 296, [2007] All ER (D) 86 (Feb)   2.24, 2.28
Ridge v Baldwin [1964] AC 40, [1963] 2 All ER 66, [1963] 2 WLR 935, 61 LGR 369, 127
 JP 295, 107 Sol Jo 313   3.12
Right v Cuthell (1804) 5 East 491, 2 Smith KB 33   3.46, 3.47
Riverside Housing Association Ltd v White [2005] EWCA Civ 1385, [2006] 1 EGLR 45,
 [2005] 50 EG 91 (CS), [2005] All ER (D) 79 (Dec)   4.14
Rogan v Woodfield Building Services Ltd (1994) 27 HLR 78, [1995] 1 EGLR 72, [1995] 20
 EG 132, [1994] EGCS 145   3.1
Rostron v Michael Nairn & Co Ltd [1962] EGD 284   7.39
Rous v Mitchell [1991] 1 All ER 676, [1991] 1 WLR 469, 61 P & CR 314, [1991] 1 EGLR
 1, [1990] NLJR 1386, [1991] 03 EG 128, 04 EG 132   3.3, 3.4, 3.5, 3.6
Royal Bank of Canada v Secretary of State for Defence [2003] EWHC 1479 (Ch), [2004] 1
 P & CR 448, [2003] 2 P & CR D50, [2003] All ER (D) 171 (May)   3.20

Royal Life Insurance v Phillips (1990) 61 P & CR 182, [1990] 2 EGLR 135, [1990] 43 EG
    70   2.26, 3.24

Sabella Ltd v Montgomery (1997) 77 P & CR 431, [1998] 1 EGLR 65, [1998] 09 EG 153,
    [1997] EGCS 169, 75 P & CR D41   1.33, 1.37, 1.38
Saffron Walden Second Benefit Society v Rayner (1880) 14 Ch D 406, 49 LJ Ch 465, 28
    WR 681, 43 LT 3   5.17
School Board of London v Peters (1902) 18 TLR 509   5.22
Sharpley v Manby [1942] 1 KB 217, [1942] 1 All ER 66, 111 LJKB 182, 166 LT 44, 58
    TLR 91   7.21, 7.39, 7.55
Shaws (EAL) Ltd v Pennycrook [2004] EWCA Civ 100, [2004] Ch 296, [2004] 2 All ER
    665, [2004] 2 WLR 1331, [2004] 1 P & CR D63, [2004] 2 EGLR 55, [2004] 11 LS
    Gaz R 35, [2004] 18 EG 102, [2004] 08 EGCS 135, (2004) *The Times*, 20 February,
    148 Sol Jo LB 235, [2004] All ER (D) 210 (Feb)   4.17
Sheridan v Blaircourt Investments Ltd [1984] 1 EGLR 139, 270 Estates Gazette 1290   3.22
Shirlcar Properties Ltd v Heintz [1983] 2 EGLR 120, 268 Estates Gazette 362   3.22
Sidebotham v Holland [1895] 1 QB 378, 64 LJQB 200, 14 R 135, 43 WR 228, [1891–4] All
    ER Rep 617, 39 Sol Jo 165, 72 LT 62, 11 TLR 154   3.37
Sidnell v Wilson [1966] 2 QB 67, [1966] 1 All ER 681, [1966] 2 WLR 560, 110 Sol Jo 53,
    197 Estates Gazette 361   4.10
Sidney Bolsom Investment Trust Ltd v Karmios [1956] 1 QB 526, [1956] 1 All ER 536   2.24
Sinclair Gardens Investments (Kensington) Ltd v Poets Chase Freehold Co Ltd [2007]
    EWHC 1776 (Ch), [2007] 49 EG 104, [2007] NLJR 1427, [2007] 32 EG 89 (CS),
    [2007] All ER (D) 425 (Jul)   4.13
Sirius Insurance Co v FAI General Insurance [2004] UKHL 54, [2005] 1 All ER 191,
    [2005] 1 All ER (Comm) 117, [2004] 1 WLR 3251, [2005] 1 Lloyd's Rep 461, [2005]
    Lloyd's Rep IR 294, (2004) *The Times*, 3 December, 148 Sol Jo LB 1435, [2004] All
    ER (D) 24 (Dec)   2.1
Smith v Draper (1990) 60 P & CR 252, [1990] 2 EGLR 69, [1990] 27 EG 69   3.46, 3.56
Speedwell Estates Ltd v Dalziel [2001] EWCA Civ 1277, [2002] 1 P & CR D17, [2002]
    HLR 813, [2001] 32 LS Gaz R 38, [2001] 35 EGCS 104, [2002] 02 EG 104, [2001]
    All ER (D) 454 (Jul)   1.12, 1.34, 1.42
St Ermins Property Co Ltd v Tingay [2002] EWHC 1673 (Ch), [2003] 1 P & CR D20,
    [2002] 3 EGLR 53, [2002] 38 EGCS 205, [2002] 40 EG 174, [2002] All ER (D) 294
    (Jul)   3.16, 3.17
Stait v Fennner [1912] 2 Ch 504, 81 LJ Ch 710, [1911–13] All ER Rep 232, 56 Sol Jo 669,
    107 LT 120   3.41
Starmark Enterprises Ltd v CPL Distribution Ltd [2001] EWCA Civ 1252, [2002] Ch 306,
    [2002] 4 All ER 264, [2002] 2 WLR 1009, [2001] 38 LS Gaz R 37, [2001] NLJR
    1440, [2001] 32 EGCS 89, 145 Sol Jo LB 223, [2001] All ER (D) 472 (Jul)   3.31
Stephenson v Orca Properties Ltd [1989] 2 EGLR 129, [1989] 44 EG 81   7.31
Stidolph v American School in London Education Trust (1969) 20 P & CR 802, 113 Sol
    Jo 689, 211 Estates Gazette 925   3.15
Stile Hall Properties Ltd v Gooch [1979] 3 All ER 848, [1980] 1 WLR 62, 39 P & CR 173,
    207 Estates Gazette 715   4.17
7 Strathray Gardens Ltd v Pointstar Shipping and Finance Ltd [2004] EWCA Civ 1669,
    [2005] 1 P & CR D65, [2005] 07 EG 144, [2005] 1 EGLR 53, [2005] 01 EG 95 (CS),
    (2005) *The Times*, 10 January, 149 Sol Jo LB 58, [2004] All ER (D) 240 (Dec)   1.11, 1.12,
    1.13, 1.16
Stylo Shoes Ltd v Prices Tailors Ltd [1960] Ch 396, [1959] 3 All ER 901, [1960] 2 WLR 8,
    104 Sol Jo 16, 175 Estates Gazette 591   7.21, 7.33, 7.34, 7.36, 7.39, 7.47, 7.55
Sun Alliance and London Assurance Co Ltd v Hayman [1975] 1 All ER 248, [1975] 1
    WLR 177, 29 P & CR 422, 119 Sol Jo 84, 233 Estates Gazette 927   1.38, 1.39, 7.45
Sun Life Assurance plc v Thales Tracs Ltd [2001] EWCA Civ 704, [2002] 1 All ER 64,
    [2001] 1 WLR 1562, [2002] 1 P & CR 151, [2001] 21 LS Gaz R 41, [2001] 2 EGLR
    57, [2001] All ER (D) 141 (May)   3.8
Swanson's Agreement, Hill v Swanson [1946] 2 All ER 628, [1947] LJR 169, 90 Sol Jo 643,
    176 LT 25, 62 TLR 719   4.5, 4.8
Sweeny v Sweeny (1876) IR 10 CL 375   3.45

Tadema Holdings Ltd v Ferguson (1999) 32 HLR 866, [1999] NPC 144, [1999] 47 LS Gaz
   R 32, [1999] EGCS 138, (1999) *The Times*, 25 November   1.39, 5.26
Tanham v Nicholson (1872) LR 5 HL 561   5.15, 5.22, 5.25
Tayleur v Wildin (1868) LR 3 Exch 303, 32 JP 630, 37 LJ Ex 173, 16 WR 1018, 18 LT 655   4.16
Taylor v Crotty [2006] EWCA Civ 1364, [2007] P & CR D22, 150 Sol Jo LB 1330, [2006]
   All ER (D) 32 (Oct)   3.35
Taylor Woodrow Co Ltd v Lonrho Textiles Ltd (1985) 52 P & CR 28   1.18
Tegerdine v Brooks (1978) 36 P & CR 261   1.36, 1.38, 2.25
Tennant v London County Council (1957) 55 LGR 421, 121 JP 428, 169 Estates Gazette
   689   3.16, 4.9
Tennero Ltd v Majorarch Ltd [2003] EWHC 2601 (Ch), [2004] 1 P & CR D30, [2003] All
   ER (D) 115 (Nov)   1.19, 3.1
Thompson v McCullough [1947] KB 447, [1947] 1 All ER 265, [1947] LJR 498, 91 Sol Jo
   147, 176 LT 493, 63 TLR 95   3.41, 5.9
Townsends Carriers Ltd v Pfizer Ltd (1977) 33 P & CR 361, 121 Sol Jo 375, 242 Estates
   Gazette 813   3.65, 3.67, 5.5, 5.21, 5.27
Trafford MBC v Total Fitness (UK) Ltd [2002] EWCA Civ 1513, [2003] 1 P & CR D29,
   [2003] 2 P &CR 8, [2002] 43 LS Gaz R 37, [2002] 44 EGCS 169, [2002] All ER (D)
   462 (Oct)   5.12
Tudor Evans (Swansea) Ltd v Longacre Securities Ltd (31 July 1997, unreported)   3.9, 3.3, 3.6
Tudor v M25 Group Ltd [2003] EWCA Civ 1760, [2004] 2 All ER 80, [2004] 1 WLR 2319,
   [2004] 1 EGLR 23, [2004] 06 EG 146, (2004) *The Times*, 17 February, 147 Sol Jo
   LB 1428, [2003] All ER (D) 73 (Dec), [2004] 1 P & CR D45   1.4, 1.11, 1.12, 1.15

United Scientific v Burnley Council [1978] AC 904, [1977] 2 All ER 62, [1977] 2 WLR
   806, 75 LGR 407, 33 P & CR 220, 121 Sol Jo 223, 243 Estates Gazette 43   3.28, 3.29,
                                                                        3.30, 3.31, 3.33

Van Haarlam v Kasner (1992) 64 P & CR 214, [1992] NPC 11, [1992] 2 EGLR 59, [1992]
   36 EG 135   7.27
Viscount Chelsea v Hirshorn [1998] 2 EGLR 90, [1998] 20 EG 130   3.17
Von Essen Hotels 5 Ltd v Vaughan [2007] EWCA Civ 1349, [2007] All ER (D) 242 (Dec)   5.19

W Davies (Spitalfields) Ltd v Huntley [1947] 1 KB 246, [1947] 2 All ER 371   3.36
Wandsworth LBC v Attwell (1995) 27 HLR 536, [1995] NPC 67, [1996] 1 EGLR 57,
   [1996] 01 EG 100   7.14, 7.17
Warborough Investment Ltd v Central Midlands Ltd [2006] EWHC 2622 (Ch), [2006] All
   ER (D) 146 (Jun)   7.22
Wax v Viscount Chelsea [1996] 2 EGLR 80, [1996] 41 EG 169   3.46
Webber Ltd v Railtrack plc [2003] EWCA Civ 1167, [2004] 3 All ER 202, [2004] 1 WLR
   320, [2004] 1 P & CR 307, [2004] 1 EGLR 49, [2004] 14 EG 142, [2003] 36 LS Gaz
   R 40, (2003) *The Times*, 5 August, 147 Sol Jo LB 902, [2003] All ER (D) 250 (Jul)   7.3,
                                                               7.36, 7.44, 7.45, 7.50, 7.59
Western Bulk Carriers K/S v Li Hai Maritime Inc [2005] EWHC 735 (Comm), [2005] 2
   Lloyd's Rep 389, [2005] All ER (D) 61 (May)   2.25
Westway Homes Ltd v Moores (1991) 63 P & CR 480, [1991] 2 EGLR 193, [1991] 31 EG
   57   3.25, 5.19
White v Riverside Housing Association Ltd [2007] UKHL 20, [2007] 4 All ER 97, [2007]
   HLR 458, (2007) *Times*, 7 May, 151 Sol Jo LB 574, [2007] All ER (D) 205 (Apr)   3.29
Woods v Mackenzie [1975] 2 All ER 170, [1975] 1 WLR 613, 29 P & CR 306, 119 Sol Jo
   187   3.46
Wordsley Brewery Co v Halford (1903) 90 LT 89   3.41
WX Investment Ltd v Begg [2002] EWHC 925 (Ch), [2002] 1 WLR 2849, [2002] 2 P & CR
   D 36, [2002] NPC 69, [2002] 3 EGLR 47, [2002] 24 LS Gaz R 36, [2002] 50 EG
   115, (2002) *The Times*, 6 June, 146 Sol Jo LB 135, [2002] All ER (D) 174 (May)   7.31

Yamaha-Kemble Music (UK) Ltd v ARC Propeties Ltd [1990] 1 EGLR 162   3.56
Yates Building Co Ltd v RJ Pulleyn & Sons (York) Ltd (1975) 119 Sol Jo 370, [1976] 1
   EGLR 157, 237 Estates Gazette 183   6.5

Yenula Properties Ltd v Naidu [2002] EWCA Civ 719, [2003] HLR 229, [2002] 3 EGLR
    28, [2002] 42 EG 162, [2002] 27 LS Gaz R 34, [2002] 23 EGCS 121, (2002) *The
    Times*, 5 June, [2002] All ER (D) 366 (May)   5.10, 5.19
York v Casey (1998) 31 HLR 209, [1998] 2 EGLR 25, [1998] 30 EG 110, [1998] EGCS 26   2.20,
                                                              2.21, 2.22, 2.30

TABLE OF STATUTES

References are to paragraph numbers.

Administration of Estates Act 1925	3.44
s 1(1)	3.44
s 9(1)	3.44
Agricultural Holdings Act 1923	
s 12	3.50, 3.51, 3.52
s 53	7.55
Agricultural Holdings Act 1948	
s 23(1)	4.12
s 24(2)	3.66
Agricultural Holdings Act 1986	3.6, 7.1,
	7.50, 7.51, 7.52, 7.53, 7.54, 7.55,
	7.56, 7.57, 7.58, 7.59, 7.60, 7.61,
	7.62, 7.63, 7.64
s 26(2)	3.6
s 92	7.56
s 93	7.1, 7.50, 7.51, 7.52, 7.53, 7.58, 7.59,
	7.60, 7.63
s 93(1)	7.52
s 93(4)	7.58
Agricultural Tenancies Act 1995	7.1, 7.64,
	7.65, 7.66
s 36	7.1, 7.64, 7.65
s 93	7.66
s 95	7.67
Commonhold and Leasehold Reform	
Act 2002	7.70
s 111(1)	7.70
Companies Act 1929	7.34
Companies Act 1985	3.18, 3.44, 5.12
s 36A	3.18
s 368	5.12
s 654	3.44
Companies Act 2006	7.67, 7.68, 7.69
s 1144	7.68
s 1148(1)	7.68, 7.69
s 1168(2)	7.68
s 1168(4)	7.69
Conveyancing Act 1881	
s 67	7.10
Holdings Act 1948	
s 92	7.22
s 92(1)	7.38
Housing Act 1980	4.3
s 16(6)	4.3
Housing Act 1985	7.70
s 176(2)	7.70

Housing Act 1988	1.29, 1.35, 2.20, 2.30, 2.37,
	3.38, 5.19, 5.26
s 13(2)	5.26
s 20	1.35, 2.20, 2.30, 5.19
s 21(4)	1.29, 2.37, 3.38
Housing Repairs and Rents Act 1954	3.4,
	3.68
s 23	3.4, 3.68
Insolvency Act 1986	3.44
s 283	3.44
s 283(3)(a)	3.44
s 283(A)	3.44
s 306	3.44
Interpretation Act 1978	7.48, 7.49, 7.50, 7.51,
	7.58, 7.59, 7.60, 7.61
s 7	7.48, 7.49, 7.50, 7.51, 7.58, 7.59, 7.60,
	7.61
Land Registration Act 2002	3.44
s 27(1)	3.44
Landlord and Tenant (Covenants) Act	
1995	7.1, 7.33
s 27(5)	7.1, 7.33
Landlord and Tenant Act 1927	7.1, 7.2, 7.3,
	7.21, 7.31, 7.32, 7.33, 7.34, 7.35,
	7.36, 7.37, 7.38, 7.39, 7.40, 7.41,
	7.42, 7.43, 7.44, 7.45, 7.46, 7.47,
	7.48, 7.49, 7.50, 7.54, 7.55, 7.59,
	7.61
s 23	7.3, 7.31, 7.32, 7.33, 7.34, 7.46, 7.47,
	7.48, 7.54, 7.61
s 23(1)	7.1, 7.2, 7.21, 7.36, 7.42, 7.48,
	7.50, 7.54, 7.55, 7.59
s 53	7.21
Landlord and Tenant Act 1954	1.6, 1.34,
	1.36, 1.37, 1.39, 2.24, 2.30, 2.31,
	2.32, 3.5, 3.8, 3.15, 3.27, 3.43, 3.46,
	3.56, 3.68, 3.69, 4.9, 4.17, 5.20, 7.1,
	7.33, 7.36, 7.39, 7.54
s 4	3.69, 5.20
s 25	1.34, 1.36, 1.37, 1.39, 2.30, 2.31, 2.32,
	3.15, 3.27, 3.43, 3.56, 3.68, 4.9,
	7.39
s 25(8)	1.6
s 26	2.24, 3.5, 3.8
s 30	3.5
s 37A	3.5
s 66(4)	7.1, 7.33, 7.36, 7.54

Landlord and Tenant Act 1987   1.11, 1.14,
    1.15, 3.1, 5.18, 7.20, 7.70
  s 11A   1.15
  s 12   1.14
  s 47   7.20
  s 48   5.18, 7.20
  s 48(1)   3.1
  s 49   7.20
  s 54(2)   1.15, 7.70
Law of Property Act 1925   2.38, 3.1, 3.43,
    3.53, 3.67, 4.10, 4.17, 5.24, 5.25,
    5.26, 6.1, 7.1, 7.2, 7.7, 7.8, 7.9,
    7.10, 7.11, 7.12, 7.13, 7.14, 7.15,
    7.16, 7.17, 7.18, 7.19, 7.20, 7.21,
    7.22, 7.23, 7.24, 7.25, 7.26, 7.27,
    7.28, 7.29, 7.30, 7.31, 7.38, 7.39,
    7.40, 7.44, 7.55, 7.57
  s 36(2)   4.17, 7.12
  s 53   7.39
  s 103(i)   7.12
  s 140(2)   7.12
  s 146   2.38, 3.43, 3.53, 4.10
  s 146(1)   7.12
  s 193(3)   7.40, 7.57
  s 196   5.26, 6.1, 7.9, 7.10, 7.11, 7.12, 7.13,
    7.15, 7.16, 7.17, 7.18, 7.23, 7.25,
    7.28, 7.29, 7.31, 7.57
  s 196(1)   3.1
  s 196(2)   3.67, 5.24, 5.25
  s 196(3)   7.1, 7.2, 7.7, 7.8, 7.38, 7.39, 7.55
  s 196(4)   7.44
  s 205(viii)   7.14
Leasehold Property (Repairs) Act 1938   4.10
Leasehold Reform Act 1967   1.1, 1.34, 1.40,
    1.41, 1.42, 3.26, 3.46, 7.1, 7.33
  s 8   1.1, 1.34
  s 8(1)   3.46

Leasehold Reform Act 1967—*continued*
  s 22(5)   7.1
Leasehold Reform, Housing and
    Urban Development Act 1993   1.2,
    1.4, 1.16, 1.26, 1.40, 2.36, 3.10,
    3.11, 3.17, 3.18, 3.61, 4.13, 7.70
  s 13   3.11, 4.13
  s 21   3.10
  s 25   1.6, 1.16
  s 42   3.18
  s 45   1.2, 1.26, 1.28, 2.36, 3.10, 3.61
  s 99(1)   7.70
  s 99(5)(a)   3.17
Leasehold Reform, Housing and
    Urban Development Act 1996
  s 42   5.7

Official Secrets Act 1920   7.27
  s 146   7.27

Party Wall Act 1996
  s 15(1)   7.70
Postal Services Act 2000   7.10, 7.28
Protection from Eviction Act 1977   3.2, 7.17
  s 5   7.17
  s 5(1)   3.2

Recorded Delivery Service Act 1962   7.42
  s 1   7.29, 7.42
Rent Act 1977   4.15
  s 26   4.17

Trusts of Land and Appointment of
    Trustees Act 1996   3.50
  s 11(1)   3.50

Chapter 1

IDENTIFYING THE REQUIREMENTS OF A VALID NOTICE

INTRODUCTION

The 'two-stage approach'

1.1   If an issue arises as to whether or not a notice is valid, invariably the first step involves interpreting the contractual or statutory provision under which the notice has purportedly been served. An attempt should be made to identify the requirements for a valid notice. Having first carried out that exercise, the notice itself should be interpreted in order to establish whether the notice complies with those requirements. In *Speedwell Estates Ltd v Dalziel*,[1] a case relating to an enfranchisement notice served under the Leasehold Reform Act 1967, s 8, Rimer LJ said that:[2]

> 'I consider the better approach is to look at the particular statutory provisions pursuant to which the notice is given and to identify what its requirements are. Having done so, it should then be possible to arrive at a conclusion as to whether or not the notice served under it adequately complies with those requirements ...The key question will always be: is the notice a valid one for the purpose of satisfying the relevant statutory provision.'

1.2   In *Burman v Mount Cook Land Ltd*[3] Chadwick LJ said:[4]

> 'In my view, that passage encapsulates, succinctly and accurately, the correct approach. I may add that I think that that is the approach to be adopted not only in relation to notices served under statute but also to notices served under contractual provisions such as those commonly found in leases.'

In adopting that approach when considering the validity of a landlord's counter-notice served under the Leasehold Reform, Housing and Urban Development Act 1993, s 45 the learned judge said[5] that:

---

[1]   [2001] EWCA Civ 1277, [2002] 1 EGLR 55.
[2]   At p 57.
[3]   [2002] Ch 256. See also *Andrews v Cunningham* [2007] EWCA Civ 762, per Lawrence Collins at para 32.
[4]   At p 270.
[5]   At p 262.

'The task is to construe the words which Parliament has used in the context of the statutory scheme. It is only when the court has informed itself of the true nature of the statutory requirement that it can sensibly address the second question: does the notice in this case meet that requirement?'

The policy of upholding notices that achieve their purpose

1.3   As will be apparent from the remainder of this Chapter, a recurrent theme in the case law relating to the interpretation of the contractual and statutory provisions under which notices are served is a resort to a 'purposive' approach.

1.4   In other words, the courts strive to interpret such contractual and statutory provisions in a manner that will enable notices to be upheld that have achieved their contractual or statutory purpose; thereby preventing recipients of notices that contain supposed 'defects', which – in reality – would cause no misunderstanding or prejudice, from deriving an unmeritorious advantage. In *Tudor v M25 Group Ltd*,[6] which concerned a leasehold enfranchisement notice served under the Leasehold Reform, Housing and Urban Development Act 1993, Carnwath LJ[7] quoted with approval the following passage of the judgment of HHJ Cooke at first instance:

'One ought to remember that these sort of statutory provisions are aimed at providing a commercially fair result so that recipients of notices are told what they have to be told but that the object of the exercise is the giving of information and the defining of issues, not the prescription of steps in a ritual dance or complex game, one false step in which is intended to produce disaster.'

'MANDATORY REQUIREMENTS' AND 'DIRECTORY REQUIREMENTS'

Statutory notices

1.5   A failure to comply with a 'requirement' of a statutory notice, which has been prescribed by the statutory provision under which a notice has been served, does not necessarily mean that the notice is invalid. For example, although statutory provisions frequently provide that a notice 'shall' or 'must' contain a particular statement or contain specified information, that does not necessary have the consequence that the omission of the prescribed statement or information will render a notice invalid.

---

6   [2003] EWCA Civ 1760, [2004] 1 WLR 2319.
7   At p 2327.

1.6   Some statutory provisions make clear that non-compliance with a 'requirement' invalidates a notice. For example, the Landlord and Tenant Act 1954, s 25(8) provides that a 'section 25 notice', being a notice served by a landlord to terminate a business tenancy, 'shall not have effect', in the event that it states that the landlord is not opposed to the grant of a new tenancy, unless it sets out the landlord's proposals relating to the new tenancy. However, much more often, statutory provisions prescribing the requirements for a notice do not identify the *consequences* of non-compliance with those requirements. In such cases, whether or not non-compliance with a statutory requirement will invalidate a notice is an issue of statutory interpretation: the question being whether, given the statutory context, an intention should be imputed[8] to Parliament that non-compliance with the requirement will invalidate a notice.

1.7   This *type* of issue arises, not only in the context of statutory provisions under which notices are served, but also in other statutory contexts. In *Petch v Gurney*,[9] a case about time limits for challenging income tax assessments, Millett LJ[10] said that:

> 'The question whether strict compliance with a statutory requirement is necessary has arisen again and again in the cases. The question is not whether the requirement should be complied with; of course it should: the question is what consequences should attend a failure to comply. The difficulty arises from the common practice of the legislature of stating that something 'shall' be done (which means that it 'must' be done) without stating what are to be the consequences if it is not done.'

1.8   Traditionally, this type of issue has been analysed by distinguishing between those requirements that are 'mandatory' (or 'imperative' or 'obligatory'), non-compliance with which will be fatal to the attempted exercise of a statutory right or power; and those requirements which are merely 'directory', non-compliance with which will either not fatal or, in the case of some types of directory requirement, will only fatal if there has been less than *substantial* compliance.[11]

1.9   However, in recent years, analyzing this type of issue by reference to a 'rigid characterisation' of statutory requirements as either 'mandatory' or 'directory' has been criticised, albeit not in the authorities relating to property notices. It has been said that focusing too intently on those labels risks losing sight of the real issue. The courts

---

8   An intention will typically need to be imputed, rather than inferred, because usually it will be reasonable to suppose that Parliament did not, in fact, have any intention one way or the other.

9   [1994] 3 All ER 731.

10   At p 736.

11   *Petch v Gurney* [1994] 3 All ER 731, per Millett LJ at p 738, and *R v Soneji* [2005] UKHL 49, [2005] 3 WLR 303, per Lord Steyn at p 311.

should instead adopt a flexible approach 'focusing intensely on the consequences of non-compliance, and posing the question, taking into account those consequences, whether Parliament intended the outcome to be total invalidity'.[12] In *London & Clydeside Ltd v Aberdeen District Council*,[13] Lord Hailsham said that:[14]

> 'It may be that what the courts are faced with is not so much a stark choice of alternatives but a spectrum of possibilities in which one compartment or description fades gradually into another.'

Notwithstanding this criticism of the rigid mandatory/directory distinction, the recent authorities concerning property notices have continued to adopt the terminology of mandatory and directory requirements.

How to determine whether a statutory requirement relating to a notice is a mandatory requirement or a directory requirement

1.10 No universal rule can be laid down for determining whether an intention should be attributed to Parliament that non-compliance with a statutory requirement for a notice will result in the invalidity of a notice that fails to comply with the requirement.[15]

1.11 It is always necessary to consider 'the substance of the statutory requirement and the reasons for it',[16] with a view to establishing the importance of the requirement given the purpose that the notice plays in the statutory scheme.[17] In *Belvedere Court Ltd v Frogmore Ltd*[18] Hobhouse LJ said that:[19]

> 'I am strongly attracted to the view that legislation of the present kind [being the *Landlord and Tenant Act 1987*] should be evaluated and construed on an analytical basis. It should be considered which of the provisions are substantive and which are secondary, that is, simply part of the machinery of the legislation. Further, the provisions which fall into the latter category should be examined to assess whether they are essential parts of the mechanics or are merely supportive of the other provisions so that they need not be insisted on regardless of the circumstances.'

---

[12] *R v Soneji* [2005] UKHL 49, [1995] 3 WLR 303, per Lord Steyn at p 312, and *Project Blue Sky Inc v Australian Broadcasting Authority* (1998) 194 CLR 355.

[13] [1980] 1 WLR 182.

[14] At p 189.

[15] *Liverpool Borough Bank v Turner* (1861) 30 LJ Ch 379, per Lord Campbell LC at p 380.

[16] *7 Strathray Gardens Ltd v Pointstar Shipping and Finance Ltd* [2004] EWCA Civ 1669, [2005] 1 EGLR 53, per Arden LJ at p 58.

[17] *Tudor v M25 Group Ltd* [2003] EWCA Civ 1760, [2004] 1 WLR 2319, per Carnwath LJ at p 2327, and *Howard v Bodington* (1877) 2 PD 203, per Lord Penzance at p 211.

[18] [1997] QB 858.

[19] At p 886.

1.12   Often non-compliance with a statutory requirement will relate to a failure in a notice to provide prescribed information. In such cases, it will be necessary to consider the importance of the omitted information to the recipient and whether, if not included in the notice, the information would, in any event, be 'readily and indisputably ascertainable'[20] (albeit that the position of the actual recipient is irrelevant[21]). The consequences to the server if the notice is held to be invalid might also be relevant: if the consequences of an invalid notice would be disastrous, it might be less easy to impute to Parliament an intention that non-compliance with a statutory requirement should invalidate a notice.[22]

1.13   A holding by a court that non-compliance with a statutory requirement has not invalidated a notice might appear to have the result, in effect, of 'interpreting' the requirement out of existence (ie of converting a requirement into something that is merely optional). Accordingly, part of the process of determining whether a requirement is mandatory or directory might also involve attempting to identify the function of a statutory requirement if it is not a pre-condition to the validity of a notice.[23]

Examples of requirements of notices that have been held to be directory (ie where non-compliance with the requirement has been held not to invalidate a notice)

1.14   In *Kay Green v Twinsectra Ltd*[24] residential tenants served a 'purchase notice' under the Landlord and Tenant Act 1987, s 12 to exercise an entitlement to acquire the landlord's interest from a purchaser after the original landlord had failed to offer the tenants a right of first refusal. Subsection (3) of that provision provided that such a notice,

> 'shall, where the estate or interest that was the subject matter of the original disposal related to any property in addition to the premises to

---

[20]   See *Tudor v M25 Group Ltd* [2003] EWCA Civ 1760, [2004] 1 WLR 2319, per Carnwath LJ at p 2328 and *Kay Green v Twinsectra Ltd* [1996] 1 WLR 1587, per Staughton LJ at p 1604, although see *7 Strathray Gardens Ltd v Pointstar Shipping & Finance Ltd* [2004] EWCA Civ 1669, [2005] 1 EGLR 53, per Arden LJ at p 58.

[21]   *Tudor v M25 Group Ltd* [2003] EWCA Civ 1760, [2004] 1 WLR 2319, per Carnwath LJ at p 2328, and *Speedwell Estates Ltd v Dalziel* [2001] EWCA Civ 1277, [2002] 1 EGLR 55, per Rimer LJ at p 58.

[22]   *7 Strathray Gardens Ltd v Pointstar Shipping & Finance Ltd* [2004] EWCA Civ 1669, [2005] 1 EGLR 53, per Arden LJ at p 58.

[23]   In *7 Strathray Gardens Ltd v Pointstar Shipping & Finance Ltd* [2004] EWCA Civ 1669, [2005] 1 EGLR 53, Jacob LJ speculated at p 59 that non-compliance with the statutory requirement under consideration might result in liability for breach of statutory duty or negligence.

[24]   [1996] 1 WLR 1587.

which this Part applied at the time of the disposal ... require the new
landlord to dispose of that estate or interest only so far as relating to those
premises.'

In fact, the purchase notice required the purchaser to dispose, not only
of premises to which the Act applied, but also other premises.
Nevertheless, the Court of Appeal held that the notice was valid. One
factor identified by Staughton LJ[25] was that 'it must have been perfectly
obvious to the new landlord which parts of [the estate] could, and which
could not, qualify under Part I of the Act'.

1.15 *Tudor v M25 Group Ltd*[26] was another case relating to the service
of a notice under the Landlord and Tenant Act 1987. Tenants had
served a notice under LTA 1987, s 11A requesting information about a
disposal of the landlord's interest after the landlord had failed to offer
his interest to the tenants. LTA 1987, s 54(2) imposed a requirement that
such a notice should specify the address of the flats of which the persons
who served the notice were qualifying tenants. The notice served by the
tenants had not complied with that requirement. It was held that the
requirement to include those addresses was merely directory, with the
result that the tenants' notice was valid. The Court of Appeal adopted
the reasoning of His Honour Judge Cooke at first instance, who had
observed[27] that requirements to provide statements that,

> 'are common ground or readily and indisputably ascertainable are likely to
> be regarded as directory only. It will be helpful to have them but the
> purpose of the notice is achieved without them.'

1.16 Finally, in *7 Strathray Gardens Ltd v Pointstar Shipping &
Finance Ltd*[28] a landlord served a counter-notice under the Leasehold
Reform, Housing and Urban Development Act 1993, s 25 in response to
a notice exercising leaseholders' rights of collective enfranchisement.
That notice failed, in breach of the Leasehold Reform (Collective
Enfranchisement) (Counter-notices) (England) Regulations 2002, para 4
to contain a statement as to whether or not the specified premises were
within the area of a scheme approved as an estate management scheme.
The counter-notice should have contained a statement that the premises
were not subject to such a scheme. The Court of Appeal held that the
failure to provide that information did not invalidate the notice. A mere
negative statement cannot have been intended to be mandatory because
there could be no possible prejudice to the leaseholders if that
information was not provided. However, it would have been different if

---

[25] At p 1604.
[26] [2003] EWCA Civ 1760, [2004] 1 WLR 2319.
[27] See p 2327.
[28] [2004] EWCA Civ 1669, [2005] 1 EGLR 53.

the notice had failed to contain the required statement in circumstances in which the property was, in fact, subject to an Estate Management Scheme. Arden LJ said[29] that:

> 'I leave aside the case where the premises are in fact subject to an EMS scheme. That is not the case. I have no difficulty, in principle, that a statutory requirement can be in part directory and in part mandatory. Accordingly, it is not part of my reasoning that, if the requirements of part 43 are mandatory where the premises are subject to an EMS, those requirements must necessarily be mandatory where the premises are not subject to an EMS. [A] single provision [can] be in part directory and in part mandatory. The contrary conclusion would be a triumph for form over substance in a context where substance has to be examined.'

Contractual notices

1.17   The same issue can arise in the context of a contractual notice. Whether or not a notice will be invalidated by virtue of a failure to comply with a requirement prescribed by the contractual provision under which the notice has been served will depend upon the proper interpretation of the contract.

1.18   For example, in *Dean and Chapter of Chichester v Lennards Ltd*[30] a lease permitted the landlord to trigger a rent review by serving '[a notice] stating the suggested rent to be reserved'. Nevertheless, a landlord's notice triggering a rent review was held to be valid even though it had failed to specify the proposed rent. The requirement that a notice should specify the proposed rent was held to be merely directory. Lord Denning MR said[31] that: '[The notice] ought not to be held invalid because of the omission of that little bit of machinery'.[32] Equally, in *Patel v Earlspring Properties Ltd*[33] a requirement that a tenant's counter-notice should specify the rent that the tenant was willing to pay was held to be directory. Whilst in *Taylor Woodrow Co Ltd v Lonrho Textiles Ltd*,[34] a requirement that a notice triggering a rent review must

---

[29]   At p 59.
[30]   (1977) 35 P & CR 309.
[31]   At p 314.
[32]   However, in *Commission for the New Towns v Levy* [1990] 2 EGLR 121, it was held that a requirement that a notice triggering a rent review should specify the proposed rent was held to be mandatory. That decision turned on the wording of the material terms of the lease and the fact that time was of the essence in respect of the deadline for the service of such a notice (albeit, in *Patel v Earlspring Properties Ltd* [1991] 2 EGLR 131, Woolf LJ said at p 133 that 'I do not regard it as appropriate to make any comment either one way or the other as to the correctness of the decision in that case'). In *Warborough Investments Ltd v Central Midlands Estates Ltd* [2007] L&TR 10, Michael Briggs QC, sitting as a deputy judge of the High Court, expressed the view that a requirement to state the rent would be a mandatory requirement where the rent identified in a rent notice 'can be determinative of the party's rights'.
[33]   [1991] 2 EGLR 131.
[34]   (1985) 52 P & CR 28.

refer the tenant to the terms of the rent review was also held to be only directory. BA Hytner QC (sitting as a deputy judge) said that:[35]

> 'If the requirement to state the proposed rent in a notice is regarded as a "little bit of machinery", the requirement to refer in the most formal manner to some of the terms of the document already held and signed by the tenants would, in my view, merely constitute a minor cog in that machinery.'

1.19   However, a requirement in a contract that a notice must be given in writing will usually be a mandatory, with the result that any oral notification will be invalid.[36]

'FORMAL REQUIREMENTS'

1.20   There is an important distinction to be drawn between two different *types* of requirement relating to notices. That distinction is between: (i) a requirement, imposed by the contractual or statutory provision under which a notice has been served, that the notice be capable of communicating a particular *meaning* to the recipient (without it being prescribed *how* the notice should do so); and (ii) a 'formal requirement' for a notice to be in a particular prescribed form, to contain specified information, or to include a particular statement.

Requirements merely to convey a particular meaning

1.21   The leading modern case on notices, *Mannai Investment Co Ltd v Eagle Star Assurance Co Ltd*,[37] which is considered in detail in Chapter 2, provides an example of a requirement that a notice be capable of conveying a particular meaning; without it being prescribed how the notice should achieve that task.

1.22   In *Mannai Investment* the issue before the House of Lords was whether break notices served by a tenant were valid. Those break notices were stated 'to determine [the leases] on 12 January 1995'. The landlord challenged the validity of the notices on the ground that, under the break clause pursuant to which the notices had been served, the leases could only be brought to an end on the third anniversary of the term, which was on 13 January 1995 rather than on 12 January 1995. So the break notices had mis-identified the date on which the leases would determine if the right to break the leases was exercised.

---

[35]   At p 33.

[36]   *Tennero Ltd v Majorarch Ltd* [2003] EWHC 2601 (Ch), (2003) 47 EG 154 (CS), per Neuberger J at para 32 of the transcript (agreeing with the obiter observations of Lord Russell in *Dean and Chapter of Chichester v Lennards Ltd* (1977) 33 P&CR 309, at p 314).

[37]   [1997] AC 749.

1.23   The validity of the notices fell 'to be tested against the terms of the power under which they were served'.[38] The break clauses provided that: 'The tenant may by serving not less than six months' notice in writing on the landlord or its solicitors such notice to expire on the third anniversary of the term commencement date determine this lease ...'. The majority of the House of Lords[39] held that the break clause did not 'prescribe as an indispensable condition for its effective exercise that the notice must contain specific information'[40] or 'require the tenant to use any particular form of words'.[41] Instead, the break clause merely required that a break notice unambiguously communicate to the 'reasonable recipient' that tenant was exercising its right to break the lease under the break clause.

1.24   Accordingly, there was, on the proper interpretation of the break clause, no requirement that a break notice should identify the date on which the lease would expire; with the result that the misidentification of that date related to information that the notice was not, in fact, required to contain. Moreover, the misidentification of the date of the expiry of the leases did not prevent those notices from communicating the *meaning* that the notices *were* required to communicate. Lord Steyn said[42] that:

> 'Crediting a reasonable recipient with knowledge of the terms of the lease and the third anniversary date (13 January), I venture to suggest that it is obvious that a reasonable recipient would have appreciated that the tenant wished to determine the leases on the third anniversary date of the leases but wrongly described it as the 12th instead of the 13th.'

'Formal requirements'

1.25   In *Mannai Investment* Lord Hoffmann said[43] that: 'If the [break] clause had said that the notice had to be on blue paper it would have been no good serving a notice on pink paper, however clear it might have been that the tenant wanted to terminate the lease.' A requirement that a notice must be on blue paper would be an example of a 'formal requirement'. Whilst it might be improbable that a contractual or statutory provision relating to a property notice would ever specify the colour of the paper on which a notice was required to be served, other types of 'formal requirement' are commonplace.

---

[38]   Per Lord Clyde at p 780.
[39]   Lord Steyn, Lord Hoffmann and Lord Clyde (Lord Goff and Lord Jauncey dissented).
[40]   Lord Steyn at p 767.
[41]   Lord Hoffmann at p 774.
[42]   At pp 768–769.
[43]   At p 776.

1.26 An example of a 'formal requirement' of a notice is provided by *Burman v Mount Cook Land Ltd*[44]. That case concerned a landlord's counter-notice served in response to a tenant's notice under the Leasehold Reform, Housing and Urban Development Act 1993 to exercise a right to a new long lease of a flat. The tenant alleged that the counter-notice was invalid on the ground that it had failed to comply with LRHUDA 1993, s 45, which provided that:

> 'The counter-notice must comply with one of the following requirements –
> (a) state that the landlord admits that the tenant had on the relevant date
> the right to acquire a new lease of his flat; (b) state that, for such reasons as
> are specified in the counter-notice, the landlord does not admit that the
> tenant had such a right on that date ....'

1.27 The counter-notice served by the landlord had not expressly *stated* whether or not the landlord admitted that the tenant had on the relevant date the right to acquire a new lease of his flat. However, the counter-notice did state that the landlord did not accept the premium proposed by the tenant and it made a counter-proposal in relation to the premium. At first instance, the notice was held to be valid on the ground that the reasonable recipient of the notice would have realised, from the fact that the counter-notice stated that the landlord did not accept the premium, that the landlord admitted that the tenant had the right to acquire the new lease of his flat.

1.28 The Court of Appeal allowed the tenant's appeal. The judge at first instance was wrong to hold that LRHUDA 1993, s 45 merely required that a counter-notice communicate a particular *meaning* to the tenant as to whether or not the tenant's right to a new lease was admitted by the landlord. Instead, s 45 imposed a formal requirement, being a pre-condition for the validity of a counter-notice, by providing that a counter-notice shall *state* whether or not the landlord admitted the tenant's right to a new lease. There were good reasons for that requirement: the proper working of the statutory scheme required that the tenant be left in no doubt as to whether the landlord made such an admission. Given that the counter-notice had not contained a *statement* as to whether the landlord admitted the tenant's right to a new lease, the counter-notice was invalid.

1.29 Another example of a formal requirement for the validity of a notice is provided by the Housing Act 1988, s 21(4), which provides that a court shall make an order for possession of a dwelling-house let on an assured shorthold tenancy which is a periodic tenancy if the court is satisfied,

> 'that the landlord ... has given to the tenant a notice in writing stating that,
> after a date specified in the notice, being the last day of a period of the

---

[44]   [2002] 1 All ER 144.

tenancy and not earlier than two months after the date the notice was given, possession of the dwelling-house is required by virtue of this section.'

In *Fernandez v McDonald*[45] a landlord had served a section 21 notice specifying a date that – mistakenly – was the day after the last day of a period of the tenancy. The landlord argued that the notice was valid because the reasonable recipient of the notice would not have been misled by the inaccuracy. The Court of Appeal rejected that submission. The Housing Act 1988, s 21(4) required, as an indispensable requirement of a valid notice, that the notice *specify a date which is the last day of a period of the tenancy*. The notice had failed to comply with that formal requirement and so the notice was invalid.

The significance of the distinction between requirements to convey a particular meaning and 'formal requirements'

1.30 If the validity of a notice is challenged on the ground that it contains an inaccuracy or an omission, the approach of the Court will vary depending on whether the inaccuracy or omission relates to a requirement merely to convey a particular meaning or whether it relates to a 'formal requirement'.

1.31 If the inaccuracy or omission relates to a requirement to convey a particular *meaning*, the validity of the notice is likely to depend whether, notwithstanding the inaccuracy or omission, the notice would convey the required meaning to the 'reasonable recipient' (ie a reasonable person in the circumstances of the parties). Thus the focus of the court's enquiry is likely to be on the interpretation of the notice itself when read in light of the circumstances in which the notice has been served. However, if an inaccuracy or omission has resulted in a failure to comply with a 'formal requirement' (such as a failure to include a prescribed statement in a notice or a failure to adopt a prescribed form), the notice is likely to be invalid unless it can be established that, on the proper interpretation of the provision under which the notice has been served, non-compliance with the 'formal requirement' does not invalidate the notice (ie on the ground that the requirement is merely a 'directory' rather than a 'mandatory'(see above)).

PRESCRIBED FORMS

1.32 Statutory provisions requiring a notice to be in a prescribed form usually also expressly provide that a notice can be in a form 'substantially to the like effect' or 'substantially to the same effect'. In

---

45   [2003] EWCA Civ 1219, [2003] 4 All ER 1033.

Ravenseft Properties Ltd v Hall,[46] Mummery LJ said that[47], whether or not a departure from the prescribed form will prevent a notice from complying with such a requirement,

> 'is a question of fact and degree in each case, turning on a comparison between the prescribed form ... and the particular form of notice given. The resolution of that question is not a decision on a point of law that is binding on later courts. The value of the authorities is in illustrating the general approach of the court to the issue of the validity of a notice under attack for its errors or omissions.'

The general approach of the court: does the inaccuracy or omission go to the substance of the notice?

1.33 The general approach that emerges from the authorities is that, in order to determine whether a notice that departs from a prescribed form is nevertheless 'substantially to the like effect' or 'substantially to the same effect' as the prescribed form, it is necessary to identify the statutory *purpose* of the notice and then to ask whether, notwithstanding any inaccuracy or omission, the notice nevertheless achieves that purpose. In *Osborn & Co Ltd v Dior*,[48] Arden LJ said[49] that 'the court has to reach a conclusion as to whether what was omitted or misstated was of importance or valuable, such as to go to the substance of the form'. In *Sabella Ltd v Montgomery*[50] Aldous LJ said[51] that:

> 'Once the differences have been ascertained, then the decision as to the whether [the notice is] to substantially to like effect will depend upon the importance of the differences rather than their number or amount.'

1.34 In *Morrow v Nadeem*[52] it was held that the misidentification of the landlord in a notice served under the Landlord and Tenant Act 1954, s 25 to terminate a business tenancy meant that the notice was not in the prescribed form 'or one substantially to the like effect'.[53] The accurate identification of the landlord in a section 25 notice was held to be important because the tenant has an entitlement to serve a counter-notice on the landlord, and so the tenant needs to know the person on whom such a notice should be served. *Speedwell Estates Ltd v Dalziel*[54] concerned a notice served by a tenant of a house under the

---

46 [2001] EWCA Civ 2034, [2002] 1 EGLR 9.
47 At pp 10–11.
48 [2003] EWCA Civ 281, [2003] HLR 45.
49 At p 663.
50 [1998] 1 EGLR 65.
51 At p 67.
52 [1986] 1 WLR 1381.
53 Albeit that Nicholls LJ said at p 1387 that: 'There might perhaps be an exceptional case in which, notwithstanding the inadvertent mis-statement or omission of the name of the landlord, any reasonable tenant would have known that that was a mistake and known clearly what was intended.'
54 [2001] EWCA Civ 1277, [2002] 1 EGLR 55.

Leasehold Reform Act 1967, s 8 to exercise a right to acquire the freehold. It was held that a failure to provide particulars of the periods during which the tenant has been in occupation was 'an omission of information of crucial importance'[55] because it related to whether the tenant had the right to enfranchise, and it was information that might not be known to the landlord. So, when combined with other defects, that omission meant that the tenant had failed to serve a notice in the prescribed form or 'a form substantially to the same effect'.

1.35 On the other hand, notices that were once required to be served under the Housing Act 1988, s 20 in order to create an assured shorthold tenancy, which had be served in a prescribed form or a form 'substantially to the same effect', have been held not to be invalidated if they misidentified the commencement date or the end date of the tenancy; misstated the law relating to assured tenancies and assured shorthold tenancies; or failed to identify or misidentified the name of the landlord.[56] The purpose of a 'section 20 notice' was merely to inform the tenant that the proposed tenancy would be an assured shorthold tenancy, and to provide the tenant with information about certain special features of that type of tenancy, rather than to provide the tenant with particulars or details of the proposed tenancy.

The omission of material that would have been irrelevant to the actual recipient

1.36 Where a notice can be served in a form 'substantially to the same effect' or 'substantially to like effect' as a prescribed form, a failure to include material appearing on the prescribed form will not invalidate a notice if that material would have been irrelevant to the rights and obligations of the recipient. In *Tegerdine v Brooks*[57] a landlord served a notice under the Landlord and Tenant Act 1954, s 25 to terminate a business tenancy. The notice, which was required to be in a prescribed form or a form 'substantially to the like effect', stated that the landlord would not oppose an application by the tenant for a new tenancy. Accordingly, the notice was not invalidated on the ground that it omitted notes providing information about circumstances in which a landlord *did* oppose such an application. Cairns LJ said that:[58]

> 'I think that what this court has to consider is whether in the circumstances of this case it could properly be said that the form was substantially to the like effect as the form set out by the regulations. In my view, it was, because there could be no purpose in setting out in that notice notes which were irrelevant.'[59]

---

[55] Per Rimer LJ at p 60.
[56] *Ravenseft Properties Ltd v Hall* [2001] EWCA Civ 2034, [2001] 1 EGLR 9.
[57] (1978) 36 P & CR 261.
[58] At p 264.
[59] See also *Barclays Bank v Ascot* [1961] 1 WLR 717, in which the omission of notes

1.37 For the purpose of identifying the material that would be irrelevant to the actual recipient, the recipient's circumstances should be considered as at the date of the service of the notice. In *Sabella Ltd v Montgomery*[60] a notice served under the Landlord and Tenant Act 1954, s 25 was held to be invalid because it had failed to include information relating to a statutory ground which the notice stated would be relied upon for opposing any application by the tenant for a new tenancy even though the landlord subsequently disclaimed any reliance upon that ground.

It is irrelevant whether the actual recipient was, in fact, prejudiced

1.38 Although a notice will not be prevented from being 'substantially to the like effect' or 'substantially to the same effect' as a prescribed form if it omits material that would have been irrelevant to the recipient's circumstances (see above), it is immaterial whether the actual recipient has, in fact, been prejudiced by any departure from a prescribed form. In *Sabella Ltd v Montgomery*[61] it was held that, for the purpose of establishing whether a 'section 25 notice' was 'substantially to the like effect' as a prescribed form given that it had omitted an 'Act Quick' warning notice, it was irrelevant that the actual recipient had access to, or had consulted, solicitors and so might not have benefited from the warning notice. Aldous LJ said that:[62]

> '[T]he comparison to be made is between the notices served and the form, and it is immaterial that any addition or omission had no material effect upon the actual recipient.'

The adoption of a version of a prescribed form that has been superseded

1.39 A form may well be held to be 'substantially to the like effect' or 'substantially to the same effect' as a prescribed form even if the version of the form that has been adopted has, by the date of the service of the notice, been superseded. In *Morris v Patel*[63] and *Sun Alliance & London Assurance Co Ltd v Hayman*[64] it was held that notices served under the Landlord and Tenant Act 1954, s 25 to terminate business tenancies, which had adopted versions of a prescribed form that had been

---

from the prescribed form of a section 25 notice did not invalidate the notice because those notes were irrelevant to the particular recipient's rights and obligations.

[60]   [1998] 1 EGLR 65.
[61]   [1998] 1 EGLR 65. See also *Sun Alliance and London Assurance Co Ltd v Hayman* [1975] 1 WLR 177, per Stephenson LJ at p 182 and Lord Salmon at p 185, and *Tegerdine v Brooks* (1977) 36 P&CR 261, per Cairns LJ at p 266.
[62]   At p 67.
[63]   (1987) 281 EG 419.
[64]   [1975] 1 WLR 177.

replaced, were nevertheless 'substantially to the like effect' as the current prescribed form. In *Tadema Holdings v Ferguson*[65] the Court of Appeal rejected a submission that a notice to increase the rent payable by a tenant under an assured tenancy, which had adopted a superseded version of the prescribed form, was not substantially to the same effect as the current prescribed form. Gibson LJ said[66] that:

> 'I do not doubt that the draftsman of a new form would, if possible, deliberately be careful not to introduce a radically different from because of the common experience that old forms continue to be used inadvertently after they have ceased to be in the prescribed form. It would be unfortunate if the prescribing of a new form always had the effect of invalidating a notice on a previously prescribed form.'

INACCURACIES IN 'PARTICULARS'

1.40 A notice served by a tenant of a house under the Leasehold Reform Act 1967, and a notice served by a tenant of a flat (or by tenants of flats) under the Leasehold Reform Housing and Urban Development Act 1993, exercising rights to enfranchise are required to contain specified particulars. However, such notices served under the 1967 Act 'shall not be invalidated by any inaccuracy in the particulars'[67] and similar (but, note, not identical) provisions in the 1993 Act provide that such notices 'shall not be invalidated by any inaccuracy in *any of* the particulars ...'.[68]

1.41 For the purpose of the provisions in the Leasehold Reform Act 1967, 'any inaccuracy in the particulars' refers to the particulars when viewed as a whole. So a partial *omission* of information that should have been included in the particulars, such as a failure to reveal that the tenant had lived in Paris for a period of six months, is capable of constituting an 'inaccuracy'.[69]

1.42 The case law establishes that a point may be reached where a deviation from the full truth will cease to be regarded as an 'inaccuracy' and will constitute a failure to provide the requisite particulars. In *Cresswell v Duke of Westminster*[70] Sir John Donaldson MR said that:[71]

> 'In the end I suspect that a court has to ask itself: "Looking at the facts as they were and what was stated in the notice, can this fairly be said to be an

---

[65] (2000) HLR 866.
[66] At p 871.
[67] Leasehold Reform Act 1967, Sch 3, para 6(3).
[68] See the Leasehold Reform, Housing and Urban Development Act 1993, Sch 3, para 6 and Sch 12, para 9(1).
[69] *Cresswell v Duke of Westminster* [1985] 2 EGLR 151.
[70] [1985] 2 EGLR 151.
[71] At p 152.

inaccuracy, or is it simply a notice which does not on a fair view relate to the facts?" Where we draw the line I do not know, and I doubt whether it is in anybody's interests that I should attempt to draw that line. Many cases will answer the question themselves on their own facts.'

In *Speedwell Estates Ltd v Dalziel*[72] notices served under the Leasehold Reform Act 1967 were held to be invalid because, in relation to required particulars relating to occupancy and residence, tenants – by simply stating 'not applicable' in their notices – had failed to provide 'the main substance of the information ... required of them, and so failed to provide particulars crucial to their claim to enfranchise'.[73] An omission or other inaccuracy deliberately calculated to mislead the landlord cannot qualify as an 'inaccuracy' for these purposes.[74]

---

[72] [2001] EWCA Civ 177, [2002] 1 EGLR 55.
[73] Per Rimer LJ at p 60. Compare *Earl Cadogan v Straus* [2004] EWCA Civ 21, [2004] 2 EGLR 69.
[74] *Dymond v Arundel-Times* [1991] 1 EGLR 109, per Slade LJ at p 113.

Chapter 2

THE INTERPRETATION OF NOTICES

INTRODUCTION

2.1   In recent years, there has been a reappraisal, led by a series of decisions in the House of Lords, of the principles relating to the interpretation of documents, including contracts[1] and also unilateral documents such as notices. The tendency is against literalism[2] and in favour of an approach that is 'commercial' and which favours 'business common sense'. In the most important modern authority on the interpretation of notices, *Mannai Investment Co Ltd v Eagle Star Life Assurance Co Ltd*,[3] the House of Lords, reflecting that approach, held that the interpretation of a contractual notice should accord with the way in which the 'reasonable recipient', being the reasonable person situated in the circumstances of the server and the recipient, would have understood the notice.

THE DECISION IN MANNAI INVESTMENT V EAGLE STAR

The facts of Mannai Investment

2.2   In *Mannai Investment* a lease[4] of office premises and car parking space in Jermyn Street, London contained a tenant break clause. The lease was for a term of 10 years 'from and including 13 January 1992'. The break clause provided that: 'The tenant may by serving not less than six months' notice in writing on the landlord or its solicitors *such notice to expire on the third anniversary of the term commencement date*

---

[1]   *Prenn v Simmonds* [1971] 1 WLR 1381, *Reardon Smith Line Ltd v Yngvar Hansen-Tangen* [1976] 1 WLR 989, and *Investors Compensation Scheme Ltd v West Bromwich Building Society* [1998] 1 WLR 896 being the leading authorities on the interpretation of contracts.

[2]   In *Sirius Insurance Co v FAI General Insurance* [2004] UKHL 54, [2004] 1 WLR 3251, Lord Steyn said at p 3258: 'What is literalism? It will depend on the context. But an example is given in *The Works of William Paley* (1938 edn), vol III, p 60. The moral philosophy of Paley influenced thinking on contract in the 19th century. The example is as follows: the tyrant Temures promised the garrison of Sebastia that no blood would be shed if they surrendered to him. They surrendered. He shed no blood. He buried them all alive. That is literalism. If possible it should be resisted in the interpretative process.'

[3]   [1997] AC 749.

[4]   In fact, there were two identical leases (and two identical break notices).

determine this lease and upon expiry of such notice the lease shall cease and determine and have no further effect ...'. The tenant attempted to exercise its entitlement to determine the lease by serving a break notice under that provision.

2.3   However, the contents of the tenant's break notice contained an error. Whilst the break clause provided that a break notice was 'to expire on the third anniversary of the term commencement date' (ie on 13 January 1995), the break notice served by the tenant stated that: 'Pursuant to Clause 7(13) of the lease we as tenant hereby give notice to you to determine the lease on 12 January 1995'.[5] So the break notice misidentified the date on which the lease could be brought to an end by the exercise of the tenant's right to break the term. The issue before the House of Lords was whether that error invalidated the notice.

The law before Mannai Investment

2.4   The decision in *Mannai Investment* can be properly understood only by reference to the law that preceded it. In particular, it is necessary to understand:

- a pre-*Mannai Investment* rule about the interpretation of break clauses;

- the traditional approach to the interpretation of notices.

The pre-Mannai Investment rule about the interpretation of break clauses

2.5   Before *Mannai Investment* break clauses in leases were interpreted, not merely as requiring that any break notice must communicate to the recipient an intention to exercise the right to determine the lease conferred by the break clause, but also as requiring that the wording of a break notice be expressed in a particular way. Break clauses were interpreted as requiring, as an indispensable condition for their successful exercise, that any break notice should be worded so as to be expressed to expire on the date upon which the break clause permitted the lease to be brought to an end.[6] That could be done either by naming the date of expiry or, alternatively, by adopting an appropriate description of that date (eg 'the [X] anniversary of the term').

---

[5]   The Court of Appeal, and all of their Lordships in the House of Lords, rejected the trial judge's holding that *either* 12 January 1995 *or* 13 January 1995 could constitute 'the third anniversary of the term'

[6]   See *Phipps and Co (Northampton and Towcester Breweries) Ltd v Rogers* [1925] 1 KB 12, per Atkin LJ at p 27, and the dissenting speeches of Lord Goff (at p 755) and Lord Jauncey (at p 762) in *Mannai Investment*.

The traditional approach to the interpretation of notices

2.6   Traditionally, there was an inflexible, 'literal' approach to the interpretation of the contents of notices and, save under very limited circumstances, extrinsic evidence about the factual context in which a notice had been served was inadmissible as an aid to interpretation.

2.7   This approach is illustrated by *Hankey v Clavering*,[7] concerning a lease for a term of 21 years from 25 December 1934, in which a break clause gave either the landlord or the tenant the right, by giving six calendar months' notice, to determine the lease at the expiration of the first seven years. The pre-*Mannai Investment* rule about the interpretation of break clauses (see above) meant that the break clause was interpreted as requiring the break notice to be *expressed* to expire on 25 December 1941 (being the seventh anniversary of the term). In the event, the landlord served the tenant with a break notice that was stated to expire on 21 December 1941. The Court of Appeal held that the break notice was invalid. Interpreting the notice 'strictly' and literally prevented the Court *interpreting* '21 December 1941' as being a reference to '25 December 1941', even though it would have been obvious to a reasonable recipient of the notice that the landlord had intended to refer to '25 December 1941' and had stated '21 December 1941' as a result of a slip.

2.8   In *Mannai Investment*, Lord Hoffmann[8] explained that this 'strict' approach to the interpretation of notices was associated with 'an old rule about the admissibility of extrinsic evidence to construe legal documents', namely:

> '[I]n its pure form, the rule …that if the words of the document were capable of referring unambiguously to a person or thing, no extrinsic evidence was admissible to show that the author was using them to refer to something or someone else …On the other hand, if there was no one to whom the description accurately applied, there was said to be a 'latent ambiguity' and evidence of background facts which showed what the [author of the document] must have meant, notwithstanding that he had used the wrong words, was admitted.'

2.9   An illustration of the type of 'latent ambiguity' which permitted extrinsic evidence to be admitted as an aid to the interpretation of a notice is provided by *Doe d Cox v Roe*,[9] in which a landlord of a public house in Limehouse served on his tenant a notice to quit 'the premises which you hold of me …commonly called or known by the name of The Waterman's Arms'. The only property let by the landlord to the tenant was a public house called *The Bricklayer's Arms* and there was no public house in Limehouse called *The Waterman's Arms*. The 'latent ambiguity'

---

[7]   [1942] 2 KB 326.
[8]   At pp 776–7.
[9]   (1803) 4 Esp 185.

enabled the notice to be upheld on the ground that it should be interpreted as referring to *The Bricklayer's Arms*.

The decision in Mannai Investment

2.10 In *Mannai Investment* the majority[10] rejected both the way in which break clauses had previously been interpreted and they also rejected the traditional, literalistic approach to the interpretation of notices.

The interpretation of break clauses

2.11 The majority in *Mannai Investment*, overturning the traditional rule that had previously governed the interpretation of break clauses, held that the fact that the break clause under consideration provided, in respect of any break notice served by the tenant, 'such notice to expire on the third anniversary of the term commencement date' did *not* require a break notice to be worded so as to be *expressed* to expire on the third anniversary of the term commencement date. Lord Clyde, in a passage that will be applicable to the vast majority of break clauses, said that:[11]

> 'The sub-clause ... states that the notice is to expire on the third anniversary to the term commencement date. The significance of that statement is that the period of six months is to terminate on that date. This regulates the time for the giving of the notice. The third anniversary marks the end of the period prior to which a notice under clause 7(13) must be given. But it is not required that the notice should include mention of the date of the intended determination of the lease.'

2.12 Accordingly, the break clause in *Mannai Investment* was interpreted simply as requiring that any break notice served by the tenant should communicate the tenant's intention to determine the lease by exercising the right reserved in the break clause. Lord Hoffmann said that:[12]

> 'The clause does not require the tenant to use any particular form of words. He must use words which unambiguously convey a particular meaning, namely an intention to terminate the lease on 13 January.'

---

[10]   Lord Steyn, Lord Hoffmann and Lord Clyde (Lord Goff and Lord Jauncey dissenting).

[11]   At p 781.

[12]   At p 774.

The interpretation of notices

2.13 Lord Hoffmann said,[13] in holding that *Hankey v Clavering* was no longer good law,[14] that the traditional approach to the interpretation of notices was 'highly artificial and capable of producing results which offend against common sense'.

2.14 The approach propounded by the majority of their Lordships in *Mannai Investment* involves asking how the 'reasonable recipient', being the reasonable person in the circumstances of the server and the recipient, would have understood the contents of the notice. Lord Steyn said that:[15] 'The issue is how a reasonable recipient would have understood the notices. And in considering this question the notices must be construed taking into account the relevant objective contextual scene.' The importance of that approach to the interpretation of notices is that, in circumstances in which there is no 'latent ambiguity' in a notice, the 'reasonable recipient' might nevertheless recognise an 'error' in the contents of notice, arising from a slip or some other mistake, and might *interpret* the mistaken wording as a reference to whatever it was that the server of the notice must have intended to refer.

2.15 In *ICS Ltd v West Bromwich BS*,[16] Lord Hoffmann said[17] (in the context of a discussion of the principles relating to the interpretation of contracts, but in a passage equally applicable to the interpretation of notices):

> 'The background may not merely enable the reasonable man to choose between the possible meanings of words which are ambiguous but even (as occasionally happens in ordinary life) to conclude that the parties must, for whatever reason, have used the wrong words or syntax ....'

In *Mannai Investment*, Lord Hoffmann said[18] that:

> 'It is a matter of constant experience that people can convey their meaning unambiguously although they have used the wrong words. We start with an assumption that people will use words and grammar in a conventional way but quite often it becomes obvious that, for one reason or another, they are not doing so and we adjust our interpretation of what they are saying accordingly. We do so in order to make sense of their utterance: so that the different parts of the sentence fit together in a coherent way and also to enable the sentence to fit the background of facts which plays an indispensable part in the way we interpret what anyone is saying. No one, for example, has any difficulty in understanding Mrs Malaprop when she says "She is as obstinate as an allegory on the banks of the Nile", we reject

---

[13] At p 778.
[14] See also Lord Steyn (at p 772) and Lord Clyde (at p 782).
[15] At p 767.
[16] [1998] 1 WLR 896.
[17] At p 913.
[18] At p 774.

the conventional or literal meaning of allegory as making a nonsense of the sentence and substitute "alligator" by using our background knowledge of the things likely to be found on the banks of the Nile and choosing one which sounds rather like "allegory".

Mrs Malaprop's problem was an imperfect understanding of the conventional meanings of English words. But the reason for the mistake does not really matter. We use the same process of adjustment when people have made mistakes about names or descriptions or days or times because they have forgotten or become mixed up. If one meets an acquaintance and he says "And how is Mary?" it may be obvious that he is referring to one's wife, even if she is in fact called Jane. One may even, to avoid embarrassment, answer "Very well, thank you" without drawing attention to the mistake. The message has been unambiguously received and understood.'

2.16   Indeed, if – as will often be the case – a provision under which a notice has been served merely requires the notice to convey a particular *meaning*, perhaps that a particular right is being exercised (without, for example, requiring that a notice contain a particular statement or be in a particular form), errors or inaccuracies in the contents of a notice, very often, would not prevent that meaning from being conveyed to the reasonable recipient. In *Mannai Investment*, Lord Steyn said[19] that such notices will be valid, even if they contain errors, if they are 'sufficiently clear and unambiguous to leave a reasonable recipient in no reasonable doubt as to how and when they are intended to operate'.

The application of the 'reasonable recipient test' to the facts

2.17   Their Lordships held that the fact that the tenant's break notice had wrongly identified the date on which the lease would end if the right to terminate the lease was successfully exercised (ie contained a mistake in a statement that the notice was not, in fact, required to contain) would not have prevented the 'reasonable recipient' from understanding that the tenant wanted to determine the lease in accordance with the right contained in the break clause. The break notice was valid because it conveyed the meaning that it was required to convey. Lord Steyn said that:[20]

'Crediting a reasonable recipient with knowledge of the terms of the lease and the third anniversary date (13 January), I venture to suggest that it is obvious that a reasonable recipient would have appreciated that the tenant wished to determine the leases on the third anniversary date of the leases but wrongly described it as the 12th instead of the 13th. The reasonable recipient would not have been perplexed in any way by the minor error in the notices. The notices would have achieved their intended purpose.'

---

[19]   At p 768.
[20]   At p 768.

2.18   Lord Hoffmann said:[21]

> '[The reasonable recipient] will reject as too improbable the possibility that the tenant meant unless he could terminate on 12 January, he did not want to terminate at all. He will therefore understand the notice to mean that the tenant wants to terminate on the date on which, in accordance with clause 7(13), he may do so, ie 13 January.'

Indeed, the reference in the break notice to '12 January 1995' could be *interpreted* as a reference to '13 January 1995'. Lord Steyn said that:[22]

> 'Counsel also argued that as a matter of legal logic a process of interpretation can never permit one to substitute 13 January for 12 January. Why should that be so? If a contract contains a termination date linked to an intended three-year period, which is variously expressed in the contract as 12 January and 13 January, why should the court not as a matter of interpretation be able to select the date which best matches the contractual intent? The same reasoning must apply to unilateral documents such as contractual notices. It is surely permissible in all cases satisfying the test that no reasonable recipient of the notice could be misled. Counsel's argument is based on too formulistic a formulation of the question to be decided. The question is not whether 12 January can *mean* 13 January: it self-evidently cannot. The real question is a different one: does the notice construed against its contextual setting unambiguously inform a reasonable recipient how and when the notice is to operate *under the right reserved?* As Lord Hoffmann has observed we no longer confuse the meaning of words with the question of what meaning in a particular setting the use of the words was intended to convey.'[23]

CONTRACTUAL AND STATUTORY NOTICES FALL TO BE INTERPRETED IN THE SAME WAY

2.19   In *Mannai Investment* their Lordships made clear that they were propounding a test that applied to all types of *contractual* notice. Lord Steyn said that:[24]

> 'There is no justification for placing notices under a break clause in leases in a unique category. Making due allowance for contextual differences, such notices belong to the general class of unilateral notices served under contractual rights reserved, e g notices to quit, notices to determine licences and notices to complete: *Delta Vale Properties Ltd v Mills* [1990] 1 WLR 445, 454E–G. To those examples may be added notices under charter parties, contracts of affreightment and so forth.'

---

[21]   At p 774.

[22]   At p 772.

[23]   Lord Clyde said at p 767 that: 'The landlord would in my view recognise that in each case the reference to 12 January was to be read as a reference to 13 January and I would so construe the notices.'

[24]   At p 768.

2.20 In *York v Casey*,[25] which concerned a notice served under the Housing Act 1988, s 20, it was held by the Court of Appeal that the principles of interpretation established in *Mannai Investment* apply, not only to contractual notices, but also to statutory notices. Peter Gibson LJ – after noting that Lord Hoffmann's judgment in *Mannai Investment* had referred to an authority about a statutory notice (namely *Germax Securities Ltd v Spiegal*[26]) – said that:[27]

> 'For my part, I see no material distinction between the approach in a case such as the present and the approach which the House of Lords has said should be adopted in the case of a notice in a contractual setting.'

Since then, there have been numerous cases in which the approach to interpretation adopted in *Mannai Investment* has been applied to the interpretation of statutory notices.

THE SIGNIFICANCE OF AN OBVIOUS MISTAKE

2.21 In *York v Casey*[28] Peter Gibson LJ said[29] that,

> 'what the court must do is to see whether the error in the notice was obvious or evident and, secondly, whether notwithstanding that error the notice read in its context is sufficiently clear to leave a reasonable recipient in no reasonable doubt as to the terms of the notice.'

2.22 However, in *Ravenseft Properties Ltd v Hall*[30] Mummery LJ (perhaps due to a concern that the two-stage test in *York v Casey* risked reintroducing something akin to the 'latent ambiguity rule') said that:[31]

> 'There is no statutory or common law doctrine of "obvious mistake", or any requirement to apply a two-stage test. In some authorities, such as *York*, this court has found it helpful, on the particular facts before it, to analyse the case in that way, but without putting into a legalistic straitjacket what is, and should remain, predominantly a question of fact and degree in each case.'

In *Fernandez v McDonald*[32] Hale LJ added that:[33]

> 'In my view, the obviousness or otherwise of an error is simply a factor in deciding what the reasonable recipient would understand by the notice.

---

[25] [1998] 2 EGLR 25.
[26] (1978) 37 P & CR 204.
[27] At p 27.
[28] [1998] 2 EGLR 25.
[29] At p 27.
[30] [2001] EWCA Civ 2034, [2002] 1 EGLR 9.
[31] At pages 12 to 13.
[32] [2003] EWCA Civ 1219, [2003] 4 All ER 1033.
[33] At p 1039.

The more obvious it is that a slip has been made, the less likely is the reasonable recipient to be in any doubt as to what was meant.'

THE 'REASONABLE RECIPIENT' WOULD HAVE TO BE IN NO DOUBT

2.23   In *Mannai Investment*, Lord Steyn said that:[34]

'Even if such notices under contractual rights reserved contain errors they may be valid if they are "sufficiently clear and unambiguous to leave a reasonable recipient in no reasonable doubt as to how and when they are intended to operate": the *Delta* case, at p 454E–G, per Slade LJ and adopted by Stoker and Bingham LJJ; see also *Carradine Properties Ltd v Aslam* [1976] 1 WLR 442, 444. That test can only be satisfied where the reasonable recipient could be left in no doubt whatever.'

However, Lord Clyde[35] took Slade LJ's reference in *Carradine Properties* to *reasonable* doubt to mean that: 'It is not an absolute clarity or an absolute absence of any possible ambiguity which is desiderated'. However, in *Barclays Bank v Bee*[36] Lord Steyn's insistence of absolute certainty was preferred. Aldous LJ said[37] that:

'[Counsel for the Claimants] went on to suggest that the fact that there was doubt would not in certain circumstances settle the matter. I listened to that submission, but I believe it to be misguided. Every statement in the *Mannai* is to the contrary ....'

THE TEST IS OBJECTIVE: IT IS IRRELEVANT HOW THE RECIPIENT OR THE SERVER INTERPRETED A NOTICE

The server's subjective interpretation of a notice is irrelevant

2.24   A notice falls to be interpreted to accord with how it would have been understood by the 'reasonable recipient'. Accordingly, it is irrelevant, for the purposes of interpreting a notice, what the person who served the notice subjectively intended to convey. In *Sidney Bolsom Investment Trust Ltd v Karmios*[38] Harman J said (in relation to a notice served under the Landlord and Tenant Act 1954, s 26 requesting a new tenancy):

---

34   At p 773.
35   At p 782.
36   [2001] EWCA Civ 1126, [2002] 1 WLR 332.
37   At p 340.
38   [1956] 1 QB 526.

'I cannot think that it could be right to go behind a document of this sort and say: Well, as in the inmost heart of the writer he intended something else, he must not be taken to have meant what he wrote. If that were accepted, a state of chaos in regard to all documents would soon be produced.'

Indeed, in *Rennie v Westbury Homes (Holdings) Ltd*,[39] Henderson J said[40] that,

'it is inherent in the objective nature of the *Mannai* test that a document that was never intended by its sender to be a valid notice may nevertheless operate as one, and vice versa.'

The actual recipient's subjective interpretation of a notice is irrelevant

2.25 The actual recipient's response to, or his subjective understanding of, a notice is immaterial to the proper interpretation of the notice. In *Mannai Investment*, Lord Steyn said that:[41]

'The question is not how the landlord [being the recipient of the notice in that case] understood the notices. The construction of the notices must be approached objectively. The issue is how a reasonable recipient would have understood the notices.'

Accordingly, for the purpose of determining whether an omission or an inaccuracy has invalidated a notice, it is irrelevant that recipient of the notice may not, in fact, been misled or prejudiced. The recipient's understanding of a notice cannot turn what would otherwise have been an invalid notice into a valid notice.[42]

2.26 In at least two cases it has been held that the actual recipient's response to a notice can, at the least, provide *evidence* about how *the*

---

[39] [2007] EWHC 164 (Ch), [2007] 20 EG 296.

[40] At pp 300–301.

[41] At p 767.

[42] *Tegerdine v Brooks* (1978) 36 P&CR 261, per Roskill LJ at p 266, *Ravenseft Properties Ltd v Hall* [2001] EWCA Civ 2034, [2002] 1 EGLR 9, per Mummery LJ at p 12, *Osborn & Co Ltd v Dior* [2003] EWCA Civ 281, [2003] HLR 45, per Arden LJ at p 664, and *Western Bulk Carriers K/S v Li Hai Maritime Inc* [2005] EWHC 735, [2005] 2 Lloyds Rep 389, per Jonathan Hirst QC at p 406. Compare *Land v Sykes* [1992] 1 EGLR 1, in which Scott LJ said that: '[I]f a notice to quit in fact communicates the correct information to the recipient tenant, I do not think that it is any business of the courts, or that there is any requirement of the law of landlord and tenant that operates, to deprive the notice of validity by reference to what some hypothetical reasonable tenant might have thought the notice meant. I agree that, if objectively construed in the light of the facts known to both landlord and tenant the meaning of the notice is clear, that is an end of the matter. But if, in fact, the tenant was not confused, I for my part think that that would suffice' (see also *Lazarus Estates Ltd v Beasley* [1956] 1 QB 707, per Denning LJ at p 710, and *Norwich Union Life Assurance Society v Sketchley plc* [1986] 2 EGLR 126, per Scott J at p 228).

reasonable recipient would have interpreted the notice. In *Royal Life Insurance v Phillips*[43] Nolan J held[44] that the fact that a tenant, who was articulate and intelligent, had treated a letter from her landlord as a notice triggering a rent review was evidence that the reasonable recipient would have interpreted that letter in the same way. Similarly, in *Lay v Ackerman*,[45] in which a leasehold enfranchisement counter-notice had mis-identified the landlord who had served that notice, Arden LJ said[46] that:

> 'It is plain that the [leaseholders] were not in fact misled into thinking that the notice came from the landlord. That supports the conclusion that I have reached, that, applying the standard of reference of a reasonable recipient in the context of the circumstances of this case ...the error would not have misled a reasonable recipient.'

2.27 However, in *Lancecrest Ltd v Asiwaju*[47] a majority[48] of the Court of Appeal held that, for the purposes of determining how the 'reasonable recipient' would understand a notice, 'to rely in any way upon the reaction of the actual recipient is unsound in principle, and could well lead to inconsistency and unfairness'.[49] The following justification was given for that rule:

- Subsequent conduct of the parties is inadmissible for the purposes of interpreting a contract and the proper approach to the interpretation of notices is the same as that of contracts.

- If the reaction of the actual recipient was admissible it would lead to inconsistency in the interpretation of cases relating to similar or identical 'errors' and therefore additional uncertainty in an area bedevilled by uncertainty.

- It would be unfair to the server if the fact that the recipient regarded a notice as invalid support a contention that the notice was invalid.

---

[43] [1990] 2 EGLR 135.

[44] At p 139.

[45] [2004] EWCA Civ 184, [2005] 1 EGLR 146.

[46] At p 146.

[47] [2005] EWCA Civ 117, [2005] 1 EGLR 40. See also *Maurice Investments Ltd v Lincoln Insurance Services Ltd* [2006] EWHC 376 (Ch), per HHJ Weeks at paragraph 44 of his judgment.

[48] Neuberger and Brooke LJJ, Clarke LJ dissenting.

[49] Per Neuberger LJ at p 44.

THE 'OBJECTIVE CONTEXTUAL SCENE' AGAINST WHICH NOTICES FALL TO BE INTERPRETED

2.28   The approach to the interpretation of notices propounded in *Mannai Investment* requires asking how a 'reasonable recipient' would have interpreted a notice. For that purpose, the 'reasonable recipient' is a reasonable person 'circumstanced as the actual parties were':[50] in other words, the perspective is that of a person who is aware of the background reasonably available to both[51] the server and the recipient as at the date of the service of the notice. That does not necessarily involve identifying the surrounding circumstances that, as a matter of fact, were in the minds of the server and the recipient. In *Reardon Smith Line v Hansen-Tangen*,[52] in a passage about the interpretation of contracts that is equally applicable to the interpretation of notices, Lord Wilberforce said that:[53]

> '[All of the speeches of their Lordships in *Charrington & Co Ltd v Wooder* [1914] AC 71] seem to me implicitly to recognise that, in the search for the relevant background, there may be facts, which from part of the circumstances in which the parties contract, in which one or both may take no particular interest, their minds being addressed to or concentrated on other facts, so that if asked they would assert that they did not have these facts in the forefront of their mind, but that will not prevent those facts from forming part of an objective setting in which the contract is to be construed.'[54]

2.29   In *Mannai Investment* Lord Hoffmann said that in relation to the interpretation of notices served under leases:[55]

> 'In practice, the only relevant background will be ... the terms of the lease itself, which may show beyond any reasonable doubt what was the intention of the person who gave the notice There will be no question of the parties not being privy to the same background – both of them will have the lease – and no room for dispute over what the relevant background is.'

In fact, the case law demonstrates that the 'relevant background' against which notices fall to be interpreted frequently includes matters going well beyond the contractual or statutory provision under which the notice has been served.

---

[50]   See *Mannai Investment*, per Lord Steyn at p 768.
[51]   *Rennie v Westbury Homes (Holdings) Ltd* [2007] EWHC 164 (Ch), [2007] 20 EG 296.
[52]   [1976] 3 All ER 570.
[53]   At p 575.
[54]   See *Havant International v Lionsgate (H) Investment* [2000] 2 L&TR 297, in which Hart J said at p 303 that: 'I am unable to read the words *circumstanced as the actual parties were* as admitting evidence the sole purpose of which is to demonstrate what the parties would have thought.'
[55]   At p 779.

Covering letters

2.30 A letter under cover of which a notice has been served may affect how the 'reasonable recipient' would interpret a notice. In *M&P Enterprises (London) Ltd v Norfolk Square Hotels Ltd*,[56] Judge Rich QC, sitting as a judge of the High Court, said[57] (in relation to whether four notices served under the Landlord and Tenant Act 1954, s 25 should be interpreted as comprising a single notice):

> 'In order to discover whether that is the way in which these particular notices should be construed, I think, I am entitled to look at the letter under cover of which they were in fact served upon the tenant.'

In *York v Casey*[58] the fact that a letter enclosing a notice served under the Housing Act 1988, s 20 stated the landlord was offering a tenancy 'for six months from the 28th September 1996' supported a finding that the 'reasonable recipient' would recognise, and correct, an error in the notice relating the date of the expiry of the term of the proposed tenancy.[59] And, in *London Borough of Hackney v Hackney African Organisation*[60] a counter-notice served in response to a landlord's notice served under the Landlord and Tenant Act 1954, s 25 was held to be valid, notwithstanding that it named only one of the four joint tenants as 'the tenant', in part on the ground that a covering letter had used the expression 'our counter-notice'.

Other notices

2.31 In *Barclays Bank v Bee*[61] a landlord served a notice under the Landlord and Tenant Act 1954, s 25 to terminate a business tenancy which stated that the landlord would not oppose an application by the tenant for a new tenancy. The notice would have been valid had it been served on its own. But the landlord simultaneously served another incomplete notice (which, had it been served on its own, would have been invalid) stating that the landlord would oppose an application for a new tenancy. The former notice was held to be invalid because the inclusion of the latter notice had meant that 'the central message to the tenant was hopelessly and instantaneously confused'.[62]

---

[56] [1994] 1 EGLR 129.
[57] At p 130.
[58] [1998] 2 EGLR 25.
[59] See also *Keith Bayley Rogers & Co v Cubes Ltd* (1976) 31 P & CR 412, *Kay Green v Twinsectra Ltd* [1996] 1 WLR 1587, per Aldous at p 1601, and *Norfolk County Council v Child* [1918] 2 KB 805.
[60] (1998) 77 P&CR D18.
[61] [2001] EWCA Civ 1126, [2002] 1 WLR 332.
[62] Per Wilson J at p 344.

Rent demands and litigation

2.32 In *Lay v Ackerman*[63] the Court of Appeal interpreted a leasehold enfranchisement counter-notice served by a landlord by reference to knowledge that the recipient would, or reasonably could, have derived, amongst other things, from rent demands and previous litigation.[64]

The non-factual background

2.33 The background against which notices fall to be interpreted is not confined to the *factual* background. In *BCCI v Ali*[65] Lord Hoffmann said,[66] in relation to the interpretation of contracts but in a passage equally applicable to the interpretation of notices, that the relevant background,

> 'can include the state of the law (as in cases in which one takes into account that the parties are unlikely to have intended to agree to something unlawful or legally ineffective) or proved common assumptions which were in fact quite mistaken.'

TYPES OF 'DEFECT' AMENABLE TO THE REASONING IN *MANNAI INVESTMENT*

2.34 If the contractual or statutory provision under which a notice has been served is interpreted, as will often will the case, merely as requiring that a notice *convey a particular meaning* the reasoning in *Mannai Investment* will frequently justify a finding that a mistake or omission in the contents of the notice has not invalidated the notice. For example, an inaccuracy in a notice may well not prevent the notice from conveying to the recipient an intention on the part of the server to exercise a particular contractual or statutory right.

2.35 On the other hand, if the relevant contractual or statutory provision is properly interpreted as requiring, as an indispensable condition for the validity of a notice, that the notice *contain a particular statement* or *include prescribed information* or to be in a *prescribed form*

---

63 [2004] EWCA Civ 184, [2005] 1 EGLR 139.

64 See also *London Borough of Hackney v Hackney African Organisation* (1998) 77 P&CR D18 in which a counter-notice served in response to a landlord's notice served under the Landlord and Tenant Act 1954, s 25 was held to be valid even though it described only one of the four joint tenants as "the tenant". That was partly on the ground that the notice had been served against the background of forfeiture proceedings in which the person described as the tenant in the notice had acted as the representative of all of the tenants with the result that "it might accordingly be thought somewhat bizarre to suppose that with regard to the related 1954 Act notices he was acting on a frolic of his own" (per Simon Brown LJ).

65 [2002] 1 AC 251.

66 At p 269.

there will be little or no scope for contending that the 'reasonable recipient' would, notwithstanding the error, have understood the notice as complying with such a requirement. In *Mannai Investment*, Lord Hoffmann said that:[67]

> 'If the clause had said that the notice had to be on blue paper, it would have been no good serving a notice on pink paper, however clear it might have been that the tenant wanted to determine the lease.'

2.36 *Burman v Mount Cook Land Ltd*[68] concerned a counter-notice served by a landlord under the Leasehold Reform, Housing and Urban Development Act 1993, s 45 in response to a notice served by a tenant exercising a right to a new lease. Subsection (2) of s 45 provides that such a counter-notice must 'state that the landlord admits that the tenant had on the relevant date the right to acquire a new lease of his flat'. Alternatively, the counter-notice had to 'state that ... the landlord does not admit that the tenant had such a right on that date'. The trial judge held that, even though the counter-notice contained neither of those statements, the notice was valid because it would have brought home to the 'reasonable recipient' that the landlord did not dispute the tenant's entitlement to a new lease. The Court of Appeal held that to be the wrong test. Section 45 was properly interpreted as imposing, as an indispensable condition for the validity of a counter-notice, that a counter-notice contain a *statement* of whether or not the landlord admitted that the tenant had on the relevant date the right to acquire a new lease. Nothing less than such a statement would do.

2.37 Equally, the Housing Act 1988, s 21(4) provides that a court shall make an order for possession of a dwelling-house let on an assured shorthold tenancy that is a periodic tenancy only if the landlord has,

> 'given to the tenant a notice in writing *stating that, after a date specified in the notice, being the last day of a period of the tenancy* and not earlier than two months after the date the notice was given, possession of the dwelling-house is required by virtue of this section.'

In *Fernandez v McDonald*[69] a landlord served a section 21 notice which stated that it would expire on a date that was not, in fact, the last day of a period of the tenancy. The Court of Appeal rejected the landlord's submission that it was sufficient that the 'reasonable recipient' would interpret the notice *as if* it had accurately specified the last day of a period of the tenancy. Section 21(4) of the Housing Act 1988 was properly interpreted as requiring, as an indispensable condition for the validity of a 'section 21 notice', that a notice *correctly* identify a date that was the last day of a period of the tenancy.

---

[67] At p 776.
[68] [2002] 1 EGLR 61.
[69] [2003] EWCA Civ 1219, [2003] 4 All ER 1033.

2.38   Finally, in *Akici v LR Butlin Ltd*[70] the Court of Appeal held that a notice served under the Law of Property Act 1925, s 146 was ineffective for the purposes of a purported forfeiture on the ground of an unlawful parting with possession of the demised premises because the notice failed to comply with the requirement that a notice under s 146 is a notice 'specifying the particular breach complained of'. Neuberger LJ said[71] that:

> 'Even applying *Mannai*, the notice has to comply with the requirements of s 146(1) of the 1925 Act, and if, as appears pretty plainly to be the case, it does not specify the right breach, then nothing in *Mannai* can save it.'

---

[70]   [2005] EWCA Civ 1296, [2006] L&TR 1.
[71]   At p 13.

Chapter 3

COMMON ISSUES

IS A WRITTEN NOTICE REQUIRED?

3.1   The Law of Property Act 1925, s 196(1) and (5) provide that, unless a contrary intention appears, any notice 'required'[1] to be served by any instrument affecting property executed or coming into operation after the commencement of that Act shall be in writing.[2] Where those provisions do not apply, and if the contractual or statutory provision under which a notice is to be provided does not *expressly* require a notice to be in writing, it may nevertheless be held that a requirement for a written notice is *implicit*. A reference to the 'service' of a notice will establish that a written notice is required.[3] In *Rogan v Woodfield Building Services Ltd*[4] it was held that the Landlord and Tenant Act 1987, s 48(1), which provides that a landlord of certain types of residential premises 'shall by notice furnish the tenant with an address in England and Wales at which notices ... may be served on him ...', is referring to a written notice. Moreover, a requirement to provide notice in writing should be interpreted as a 'mandatory requirement', with the result that an oral notification will be invalid.[5]

3.2   A notice to quit served under the common law to determine a periodic tenancy can be given orally;[6] albeit that the Protection from Eviction Act 1977, s 5(1) requires notices to quit served by landlords or tenants in respect of premises let as a dwelling to be in writing and in a prescribed form.

---

[1]   Notwithstanding the reference in subsection (5) to notices 'required' to be served, that provision probably applies to provisions affording a *choice* over whether or not to serve a notice (see *Enfield LBC v Devonish* (1996) 74 P & CR 288, in which Kennedy LJ said at p 294 that he inclined to the view that sub-s (5) applied to a provision in a tenancy agreement enabling the tenancy to be brought to an end on four weeks' notice).

[2]   *New Hart Builders v Brindley* [1975] 1 Ch 342, applying those provisions, held that a notice to renew an option was required to be in writing.

[3]   See *Andrews v Cunningham* [2007] EWCA Civ 762, per Lawrence Collins LJ at para 51, and *R v Shurmer* (1886) 17 QBD 323.

[4]   [1995] 1 EGLR 72.

[5]   *Tennero Ltd v Majorarch Ltd* [2003] EWHC 2601 (Ch), (2003) 47 EG 154 (CS), per Neuberger J at paragraph 32 of the transcript (agreeing with the obiter observations of Lord Russell in *Dean and Chapter of Chichester v Lennards Ltd* (1977) 33 P&CR 309, at p 314).

[6]   *Doe d Macartney v Crick* (1805) 5 Esp 196, and *Bird v Defonville* (1846) 2 C&K 415.

FRAUDULENT STATEMENTS

3.3　Fraud unravels everything. So a notice is likely to be held to be invalid if it contains a statement of fact and if that statement is found to have been, not only untrue, but made fraudulently,[7] even in the absence of any express provision in the contractual or statutory provision under which the notice has been served providing that a notice will be invalidated on that ground. It will be irrelevant whether the recipient has, in fact, been deceived by a fraudulent statement,[8] and a fraudulent statement can invalidate a notice even if the notice was not required to contain that statement.[9]

3.4　In *Lazarus Estates Ltd v Beasley*[10] a landlord served a notice on a statutory tenant under the Housing Repairs and Rents Act 1954, s 23 to increase the rent. The notice was required to contain a declaration by the landlord that work of repair to a value specified in the Act had been carried out during a specified period. The Act provided that the tenant had 28 days in which to apply to the county court to determine whether such repair work had been carried out and it provided that, subject to that right to apply to the court, the validity of the landlord's declaration in the notice 'shall not be questioned'. The tenant failed to make an application to the county court and the landlord contended that its notice had been effective to increase the rent. Nevertheless, it was held that the tenant was entitled, in subsequent proceedings seeking to recover rent arrears that were alleged to have accrued by virtue of the notice, to contend that the notice to increase the rent was invalid on the ground that the statement about the supposed repair works had been made dishonestly. Denning LJ said that:[11]

> 'No court in this land will allow a person to keep an advantage which he has obtained by fraud. No judgment of a court, no order of a Minister, can be allowed to stand if it has been obtained by fraud. Fraud unravels everything. The court is careful not to find fraud unless it is distinctly pleaded and proved; but once it is proved, it vitiates judgments, contracts and all transactions whatsoever: see as to deeds, *Collins v Blantern*; as to judgments, *Duchess of Kingston's* case; and as to contracts, *Master v*

---

[7]　In *Derry v Peek* (1889) 14 App Cas 337, Lord Hershall said at p 374 that: '[F]raud is proved when it is shown that a false representation has been made (1) knowingly, or (2) without belief in its truth, or (3) recklessly, careless whether it be true or false. Although I have treated the second and third as distinct cases, I think the third is but an instance of the second, for one who makes a statement under such circumstances can have no real belief in the truth of what he states. To prevent a false statement being fraudulent, there must, I think, always be an honest belief in its truth. And this probably covers the whole ground, for one who knowingly alleges that which is false, has obviously no such honest belief.'

[8]　*Rous v Mitchell* [1991] 1 WLR 469, per Glidewell LJ at p 485 and Nourse LJ at pp 496–7.

[9]　*Tudor Evans (Swansea) Ltd v Longacre Securities Ltd* (31 July 1997, unreported).

[10]　[1956] 1 QB 702.

[11]　At p 712.

Miller. So here I am of opinion that if this declaration is proved to have been false and fraudulent, it is a nullity and void and the landlords cannot recover any increase of rent by virtue of it.'[12]

3.5   A landlord under a business tenancy can, in response to a notice served by a tenant under the Landlord and Tenant Act 1954, s 26 seeking a new tenancy, serve a counter-notice under sub-s (6) of that provision stating that he will oppose any application for a new tenancy. Such a counter-notice is required to 'state on which of the grounds mentioned in section 30 of [the 1954 Act] the landlord will oppose the application'. Even though there is nothing in the 1954 Act expressly vitiating counter-notices if they contain fraudulent statements, a counter-notice will be invalid unless the statement of the landlord's intention is honestly made.[13]

3.6   In *Rous v Mitchell*[14] a notice served under the Agricultural Holdings Act 1986, s 26(2) to terminate an agricultural tenancy, which stated that the landlord's reason for recovering possession was a breach by the tenant of a covenant against assigning or letting the demised premises, was held to be invalid on the ground that that statement was made fraudulently. Finally, in *Tudor Evans (Swansea) Ltd v Longacre Securities Ltd*[15] it was held that a rent review notice was invalidated on the ground that it contained the following (fraudulently made) statement on the part of the landlord's surveyors:

'Please be advised now that, having considered carefully the size and corner location of the subject property, and the terms of your tenancy ... that we determine the market rental value as at [the relevant date] to be in the [specified sum].'

PROPOSALS AND REQUESTS

3.7   Where a notice is required to make a request (eg a request for a new tenancy) or contain a proposal (eg a proposal relating the terms of a new tenancy or a rent or a premium) it will be a question of the

---

[12]   In *Rous v Mitchell* [1991] 1 WLR 469, Nourse LJ said at p 496 that: 'The principle is that fraud cancels the advantage which would otherwise have been obtained from the transaction by avoiding the transaction altogether.'

[13]   See *Betty's Cafes Ltd v Phillips Furnishing Stores Ltd* [1959] AC 20, per Lord Denning at pp 50–51 ('It would be deplorable if a landlord could be allowed to get an advantage by misrepresenting his state of mind or any other fact'); *Marks (Morris) v British Waterways Board* [1963] 1 WLR 1008, per Lord Denning MR at p 1015, Harman LJ at p 1018, and Pearson LJ at p 1020; and *Rous v Mitchell* [1991] 1 WLR 469, per Glidewell LJ at p 487. See also the Landlord and Tenant Act 1954, s 37A which provides the tenant with a right to compensation if the landlord has obtained an order for possession, or caused the tenant to vacate the building, as a result of misrepresentations or the concealment of material facts.

[14]   [1991] 1 WLR 469.

[15]   31 July 1997, unreported.

interpretation of the contractual or statutory provision under which the notice has been served whether the requirement for the request or the proposal implies something about the server's subjective state of mind; with the result that an issue might arise whether a notice will be invalidated on the ground that the server did not genuinely *want* what he had 'requested', or did not (or reasonably could not) have *believed* that his 'proposal' was realistic or likely to be adopted.

3.8   In most statutory and contractual contexts, a requirement for a notice to contain a 'request' or a 'proposal' will imply nothing about the server's state of mind. For example, *Sun Life Assurance plc v Thales Tracs Ltd*[16] concerned the service by a tenant of a notice under the Landlord and Tenant Act 1954, s 26 requesting a new tenancy. In an attempt to avoid paying compensation when the tenant – in the event – vacated the demised premises, the landlord contended that the section 26 notice was invalid on the ground that the tenant, when it served the notice requesting the tenancy, had not, in fact, intended to take up a new tenancy. It was held that the notice was nevertheless valid. Dyson LJ said[17] that:

> 'The words "request" and "proposal" are ordinary English words. A request is an act of asking for something. A proposal is something that is put forward for consideration ...Both "request" and "proposal" are what [counsel for the tenant] called "performance utterances". They describe an act. They *do* something. It is not meaningful to ask whether a request or a proposal say anything about the state of mind of the person who makes the request or puts forward the proposal. The meaning of a request and a proposal is judged objectively. The state of mind of the person who makes the request and the proposal is irrelevant to their meaning. Nor is it meaningful to consider whether they are true. On the other hand, there are different kinds of words that *do* say something about the *state of mind* of the person using them. Thus, for example, if a person says that he believes or intends something, he is undoubtedly saying something about his state of mind. It is meaningful, and may be relevant, to consider the truth of a statement of belief or intention.
>
> I would therefore hold, as a matter or ordinary language, that the fact that a request is made or a proposal is put forward says nothing about the state of mind of the person making the request or proposal. A may make a proposal to B which he believes, and possibly even hopes, B will refuse. A may do this solely in order to show himself in a good light in the eyes of C, where he would be deeply unhappy if B were to accept the proposal. He does not wish or intend B to accept the proposal but, as a matter of ordinary language, it is nevertheless a proposal. Take another example: suppose that A makes a proposal which he believes means X, but in fact it means Y, and, if he had understood that it meant Y, he would not have been willing to make it. Again, as a matter of ordinary language, what A puts forward is a "proposal", notwithstanding his mistake. This is because

---

[16]   [2001] EWCA Civ 704, [2001] 1 WLR 1562.
[17]   At p 1568.

whether something is a proposal is to be judged objectively and without regard to the state of mind of the proposer.

This ordinary meaning of the word "proposal" is reflected in the law. It is trite law that in the contractual context the existence and meaning of an offer has to be determined objectively. The law is not concerned with the subjective intention of the offer has to be determined objectively. The law is not concerned with the subjective intention of the offeror.'

3.9   Equally, it has been held that a proposal for a new rent contained in a landlord's notice triggering a rent review is not required to be 'a rent capable of qualifying as the [reviewed rent]', or a bona fide and genuine pre-estimate of the market rent (see *Davstone (Holdings) Ltd v Al-Rifai*,[18] *Amalgamated Estates Ltd v Joystretch Manufacturing Ltd*[19] and *Fox & Widley v Guram*[20]). In *Lancecrest Ltd v Asiwaju*,[21] Neuberger LJ said[22] that:

'In light of the wording of the rent review clause in the instance case, I am prepared to accept that it might well be right that the landlord could specify a rent that was substantially in excess even of its honest view of the market rent.'

However, a rent review trigger notice might be invalidated if it, not only specifies a proposed rent that is not a genuine pre-estimate of the market rent, but also contains a statement, which is made fraudulently, relating to how the landlord has identified that proposed rent. In *Tudor Evans (Swansea) Ltd v Longacre Securities Ltd*[23] a rent review trigger notice was held to be invalid because it contained the following fraudulent-made statement by the landlord's surveyor:

'Please be advised now that, having considered carefully the size and corner location of the subject property, and the terms of your tenancy ... that we determine the market rental value as at [the relevant date] to be in the [specified sum].'[24]

3.10 In *9 Cornwall Crescent London Ltd v Kensington and Chelsea Royal London Borough Council*[25] it was held that, in counter-notices served by landlords in response to initiating notices served by leaseholders under the Leasehold Reform, Housing and Urban Development Act 1993, ss 21 and 45 exercising a right to collective enfranchisement or a new lease, there is no requirement that the landlord should have a bona fide belief that any counter-proposal relating to the

---

[18]   (1976) 32 P & CR 18.
[19]   [1981] 1 EGLR 96.
[20]   [1998] 1 EGLR 91.
[21]   [2005] EWCA Civ 117, [2005] 1 EGLR 40.
[22]   At p 42.
[23]   31 July 1997, unreported.
[24]   See paras **3.3–3.6** above.
[25]   [2005] EWCA Civ 324, [2005] 2 EGLR 131.

premium payable for his interest was 'realistic'. Nevertheless, Arden LJ, in recognising that the word 'propose' can sometimes imply a subjective state of mind, said that:[26]

> 'Confusion may arise in the present case from parliament's use of the word "propose" and cognate expressions in section 21 and related provisions. This is because the word "propose" has more than one meaning. The *Shorter Oxford English Dictionary*, 2002, gives as the primary meaning of "propose":
>
> (i)   verb trans Put forward as a scheme or plan, suggest (a thing), (foll by *to do, that, doing*). Also, intend, resolve (on), purpose, (to do, doing). ME ...
>
> Thus, the cognate expression "proposal" means:
>
> (i)   The action or an act of stating or propounding something.
> (ii)   An act proposing something; a course of action etc proposed; a scheme, a plan, motion; or suggestion, an idea ...
>
> Accordingly, in some contexts, "propose" means a state of mind similar to intention, as in the phrase "I propose to make an agreement"...
>
> In my example, "propose" is followed by the infinitive, connoting action by the proposer. Indeed, it is difficult to see how "propose" followed by the infinitive could ever be a suggestion that someone other than the maker of the suggestion should do anything, or how it could ever be more than a statement of the maker's intention as opposed to a suggested plan of action. If it were a suggested plan of action, the word "propose" would more naturally be followed by "that" as in "I propose that I should make an agreement". In some contexts, "to propose" means "to put forward for consideration" as in "I propose this resolution". Sometimes, the word "propose" could have either meaning, as in the phrase "I propose that this term should be included in the agreement". This could connote either a state of mind or the putting forward of a term for consideration, or, possibly, both. It all depends upon the context: to whom and upon what occasion it was said, and so on ...
>
> Thus, although I have set out the dictionary meanings of "propose" and "proposal" above, I have done so to illustrate the range of meanings that these words have. The dictionary is a good place to start to find such a range of meaning, but it is not essential that a particular meaning to be applied in a statute should be shown in the dictionary.'

3.11 In *Cadogan v Morris*[27], which was held in *9 Cornwall Crescent London Ltd v Kensington and Chelsea Royal London Borough Council*[28] to have been correctly decided, it was held that initiating notices served

---

[26]   At p 137.
[27]   [1999] 1 EGLR 60.
[28]   [2005] EWCA Civ 324, [2005] 2 EGLR 131.

by a tenant or tenants under the Leasehold Reform, Housing and Urban Development Act 1993, s 13 or 42 exercising a right to collective enfranchisement or a new lease, when 'specify[ing] the premium which the tenant[s] propose[s] to pay', do have to contain genuine proposals made in good faith. That interpretation was influenced by the fact that recipients of such initiating notices required a safeguard against proposals for unrealistically high premiums: if the landlord failed to serve a counter-notice the premium paid by the tenant or tenants would be determined by the premium specified in the initiating notice and the premium proposed in the initiating notice would determine the amount of the deposit that could be demanded.

THE SERVER'S MOTIVATION

3.12 For the purpose of determining whether a notice is valid, the server's motivation for serving a notice will usually be irrelevant. Indeed, the motivation of the server will typically be immaterial even if that motivation is improper to the extent of constituting a serious criminal offence. In *Chapman v Honig*[29] a landlord served a notice to quit in order to punish the tenant for having given evidence against him in a case relating to another tenant. The Court of Appeal[30] held that the notice was valid. Pearson LJ said that:[31]

> 'Common experience is that, when the validity of an act done in purported exercise of a right under a contract or other instrument is disputed, the inquiry is limited to ascertaining whether the act has been done in accordance with the provisions of the contract or other instrument. I cannot think of any case in which such an act might be invalidated by proof that it was prompted by some vindictive or other wrong motive. Motive is disregarded as irrelevant. A person who has a right under a contract or other instrument is entitled to exercise it and can effectively exercise it for a good reason or a bad reason or no reason at all. If the rule were different, if the exercise of such a right were liable to be otherthrown, in an action brought at any time within the limitation period, by proof that the act was done with a wrong motive, there would be a great unsettlement of property titles and commercial transactions and relationships.'

---

[29] [1963] 2 QB 502.
[30] Denning LJ delivered a forceful dissenting judgment. At p 512, the learned judge said: 'Just as no criminal can enforce rights resulting from his own crime (see *Beresford v Royal Insurance Co*), so also no contemnor can enforce rights resulting from his own contempt. Just as the dismissal of a police officer is invalid if he has not been heard in his defence (see *Ridge v Baldwin*), so also a notice to quit is invalid if it is given in contempt of court. This seems so obvious as not to need demonstration.'
[31] At pp 520–1.

SIGNATURES

3.13 Some types of notice – usually statutory notices – are required to be authenticated by being signed by, or sometimes on behalf of, the server or servers of the notice.

What is a signature?

3.14 A natural person can 'sign' a document using a rubber stamp with his own signature upon it.[32] However, in *Lazurus Estates Ltd v Beasley*,[33] Morris LJ said,[34] in respect of a notice served by a company to increase the rent paid by a statutory tenant that was required to be signed by the landlord, that: 'It may be that the sufficiency as a signature of having the mere name of a limited company imposed by a rubber stamp might have been challenged in the action ...'.[35]

Signatures in covering letters

3.15 In *Stidolph v American School in London Education Trust*[36] it was held that a requirement for a signature on a notice served under the Landlord and Tenant Act 1954, s 25 to terminate a business tenancy could be satisfied by a signature in a letter under cover of which the notice was served. Denning LJ said[37] that:

> 'Any defect in the prescribed form can be made good by the covering letter or the stamped, addressed envelope. They can and should be read together. So long as the envelope contains the information which the Act requires, and is sufficiently authenticated, the notice is a good notice.'

Signatures of agents

3.16 As a general proposition, things that can be done by an individual may be done either personally or by a duly authorised agent.[38] So the common law rule is that a person sufficiently 'signs' a document if it is signed by himself; or by his duly authorised agent in the agent's name; or if the server's name is affixed to the document by someone with due authority *per procurationem*.[39] That common law rule was not displaced

---

[32] *Goodman v J Eban Ltd* [1954] 1 QB 550.
[33] [1956] 1 QB 702.
[34] At p 717.
[35] See also Denning LJ at p 710.
[36] (1969) 20 P&CR 802.
[37] At p 805.
[38] *St Ermins Property Co Ltd v Tingay* [2002] EWHC 1673, [2002] L&TR 6.
[39] In *London County Council v Agricultural Food Products Ltd* [1955] 2 QB 218 a clause in a tenancy agreement provided that, if the landlords wanted to terminate the tenancy, it must be by 'a written notice signed by the valuer of the council'. It was held

by a statutory provision requiring notices to be in a prescribed form on which the word 'landlord' appeared alongside a space for a signature.[40]

3.17 Nevertheless, the proper interpretation of a contractual or statutory provision under which a notice is served may sometimes require a departure from that common law rule with the result that the server of a notice must personally sign the notice. For example, in *Viscount Chelsea v Hirshorn*[41] and *St Ermins Property Co Ltd v Tingay*[42] it was held that the Leasehold Reform, Housing and Urban Development Act 1993, s 99(5)(a), which requires notices given under ss 13 or 42 of that Act to be 'signed by each of the tenants or (as the case may be) by the tenant by whom it is given', imposed a requirement that notices be signed by leaseholders personally. That was because other types of notice to be served under that Act were required to 'be signed by *or on behalf of* each of the tenants'.

3.18 In *City & Country Properties Ltd v Plowden Investments Ltd*[43] it was held that, where a company served a notice under the Leasehold Reform, Housing and Urban Development Act 1993, s 42, the notice had, in accordance with the Companies Act 1985, s 36A, to be under seal or signed by two directors of the company or a director and a secretary of the company, with the consequence that a notice signed only by a director of a company was invalid.

NOTICES SERVED 'WITHOUT PREJUDICE' TO AN EARLIER NOTICE

3.19 It is well established that a notice can be served without prejudice to a contention that an earlier notice is valid. In *Keith Bayler Rogers & Co v Cubes Ltd*[44] a break notice was served by a landlord under cover of a letter which stated that it was served 'without prejudice [to] our contentions that [an] earlier [break] notice is not invalid'. Templeman J said[45] that:

> '[Counsel] attacks that second notice and says that the landlord cannot have two notices and contend that they are both valid or that one of them is valid: he must make up his mind between them; but in my judgment the landlord may contend that the first notice is good, but if it is not, he may rely on the second notice.'

---

that a signature made by an agent, albeit in the name of the valuer, would satisfy that requirement, even if the letters 'p.p.' were not added to show that the signature was by proxy.

[40] *Tennant v London County Council* (1957) 55 LGR 421, per Jenkins LJ at p 431.
[41] [1998] 2 EGLR 90.
[42] [2002] EWHC 1673, [2002] L&TR 6.
[43] [2007] L&TR 15.
[44] (1976) 31 P&CR 412.
[45] At p 416.

In *Allam & Co v Europa Poster Services*,[46] which concerned a notice to quit that had been served without prejudice to an earlier notice to quit, Buckley J said that:[47]

> 'It is well established that where a landlord, having given notice to quit, feels it desirable to give a second notice, perhaps because of some doubt as to the validity of the first notice, and gives a second notice, that that notice does not amount to a waiver of the earlier notice, and to put into a second notice of that kind words which expressly state that the second notice is without prejudice to the validity of the earlier notice is merely to state a fact.'

3.20 In *Royal Bank of Canada v Secretary of State for Defence*[48] Lewison J said[49] that the meaning of a letter under cover of which a break notice was served with stated that the notice was 'without prejudice to our previous notice' was 'that the giver of the notice was not to be taken to have withdrawn the earlier notice and was to remain free to argue that it had validly terminated the lease ...'.

NOTICES SERVED 'SUBJECT TO CONTRACT' OR 'WITHOUT PREJUDICE'

3.21 The expression 'subject to contract' signifies that a document is not intended to have any legally binding result; whilst the expression 'without prejudice' signifies that a document is intended to communicate privileged negotiations and cannot be referred to in proceedings between the parties. The use of either expression in a letter or other document which might otherwise have constituted a notice might invalidate the document as a notice on the ground that it would have created doubt on the part of the reasonable recipient as to whether the document was intended to operate as a notice.

3.22 In *Shirlcar Properties Ltd v Heintz*[50] a landlord contended that it had increased the rent payable under a lease by serving a 'trigger notice' under rent review provisions by serving a letter which stated that: 'The rent required as from the review date is [X] per annum exclusive, and we look forward to receiving your agreement'. At the foot of the letter, were the words: 'SUBJECT TO CONTRACT'. It was held that the letter was not a valid 'trigger notice' because it had not make it clear to the recipient that it was intended to operate as such. By stating that the landlord looked forward to reaching an agreement with the tenant, and by using the words 'subject to contract', the recipient might reasonably

---

[46]   [1968] 1 All ER 826.
[47]   At p 839.
[48]   [2004] EWCA Civ 7982, [2004] 1 P&CR 28.
[49]   At para46 of the judgment.
[50]   [1983] 1 EGLR 125.

have understood the letter simply as an invitation to enter into negotiations over the amount of the rent. In *Norwich Union Life Insurance Society*[51] a letter headed 'without prejudice' was held to be incapable of constituting a valid notice triggering a rent review, and, in *Maurice Investments Ltd v Lincoln Insurance Services Ltd*,[52] a letter described as being 'subject to contract' and 'without prejudice' was held incapable of constituting a valid trigger notice. In *Sheridan v Blaircourt Investments Ltd*[53] it was held that a letter headed 'without prejudice and subject to contract' could not operate as a valid counter-notice by a tenant so as to require the reviewed rent to be determined by an arbitrator.

3.23 However, the expressions 'subject to contract' and 'without prejudice' are often misused, especially by surveyors, and the context may be such as would make clear to the reasonable recipient that, notwithstanding the use of either or both of those expressions, a document *was* intended to operate as a notice.

3.24 For example, in *Royal Life Insurance v Phillips*[54] a landlord contended that its surveyors had triggered a rent review by a letter, which was headed 'subject to contract' and 'without prejudice', which stated that:

> 'We are writing to inform you that your rent is to be reviewed as at December 25 1986. In accordance with the terms of the lease we hereby notify you that the rent from the review date will be £39,000 per annum exclusive. This notice is served by us as agents for and on behalf of the landlords ...'.

It was held that reasonable recipient would have regarded the words 'subject to contract' and 'without prejudice' as meaningless estate agents' verbiage and that the letter was a valid trigger notice. That conclusion was supported by the fact that the letter described itself as a notice and it was sent by recorded delivery (as the lease required) only just before the expiry of the time for serving a trigger notice. Equally, in *British Rail Pension Trustee Co Ltd v Cardshops Ltd*[55] a letter was held to have operated as a valid tenant's counternotice containing the tenant's proposal for the reviewed rent, even though it was headed 'subject to contract'. Vinelott J held that it would be unreal to regard the letter as containing an offer to which the tenant expected a rely before determining whether to serve a counternotice as part of the mandatory negotiations under the rent review.

---

[51]   [1984] 1 EGLR 126.
[52]   [2006] EWHC 376.
[53]   [1984] 1 EGLR 139.
[54]   [1990] 2 EGLR 135.
[55]   [1987] 1 EGLR 127.

3.25 Finally, in *Westway Homes Ltd v Moores*[56] – in which a notice exercising an option to purchase land was headed 'subject to contract' – those words were again held to be mere surplusage with no legal significance. Russell LJ said[57] that the notice was,

> 'a clear and unambiguous document written in formal terms, and the words "subject to contract" at the head of the [notice] simply cannot sensibly exist so as to give those three words any meaning.'

INCONSISTENCIES

3.26 A notice may be rendered invalid if an internal inconsistency in the contents of the notice prevents the notice from complying with a requirement in the contractual or statutory provision under which it has been served. For example, a notice served by a leaseholder under the Leasehold Reform Act 1967 was required to state whether the leaseholder was exercising a right to acquire the freehold or a right to a long lease. In *Byrnlea Property Investments Ltd v Ramsay*[58] the notice stated that the leaseholder claimed 'the freehold or a long lease'. The failure to specify one or other of those alternatives meant that the notice was invalid.

3.27 Indeed, a notice that would otherwise have been valid may be rendered invalid as a result between an inconsistency between the contents of the notice and something else in the factual background against which the notice must be interpreted. In *Barclays Bank plc v Bee*[59] a landlord, in an attempt to terminate a business tenancy, inadvertently served his tenant with two notices under the Landlord and Tenant Act 1954, s 25. One of those notices, which was incomplete and so could not have constituted a valid notice, stated that the landlord would oppose an application by the tenant for a new tenancy. The other notice, which would have been valid had it been served on its own, stated that the landlord would not oppose such an application. It was held that the latter notice was invalid because the inclusion of the former notice meant that the 'central message to the tenant was hopelessly and instantaneously confused'.[60]

---

[56]   [1991] 2 EGLR 193.
[57]   At p 197.
[58]   [1969] 2 QB 253.
[59]   [2002] 1 WLR 332.
[60]   Per Wilson J at p.344.

DEADLINES FOR THE SERVICE OF NOTICES

The usual rule

3.28 Generally speaking, if a contractual or statutory provision stipulates a deadline by which a notice shall be served, a notice served after that deadline will be invalid. For example, a notice to exercise an option (eg an option purchase land or to extend a lease) or a break notice[61] will be invalid if it is served after the expiry of a deadline specified in the lease or other contract under which the notice is served. In *Chilton Court (Baker Street) Residents Ltd v Wallabrook Property Co Ltd*,[62] a notice served by a vendor of parts of a block of flats to exercise a contractual right to exclude from the sale some leases of certain of those flats was held to be invalid on the ground that it had been served after the expiry of a deadline for the service of the notice.

Rent review notices

3.29 In contrast to this usual rule, in *United Scientific Holdings Ltd v Burnley BC*[63] the House of Lords, controversially,[64] held that, for the most part, notices served under rent review provisions (eg a landlord's notice triggering a rent review or a tenant's counter-notice taking issue with the proposed new rent) will not be invalidated by virtue of being served after a stipulated deadline for service.

3.30 Their Lordships reached that conclusion by applying the rule of equity that time is generally 'not of the essence' in respect of a time stipulation in a contract. That expression is usually taken to indicate that a breach of a time stipulation will generally not 'be treated as a breach of a condition precedent to the contract, that is as a breach which would entitle the innocent party to treat the contract as terminated or which would prevent the defaulting party from suing for specific performance'.[65] However, in *United Scientific*, the House of Lords treated the fact that deadlines contained in a timetable in rent review machinery should not usually be regarded as being of the essence as meaning that late serve of a notice was not a condition precedent *to exercising rights under the rent review machinery*; with the consequence that a rent review notice is generally not invalidated by virtue of being served after a stipulated deadline.[66]

---

[61]   See *United Scientific v Burnley Council* [1978] AC 904, per Lord Diplock at p 936.
[62]   [1989] 2 EGLR 207.
[63]   [1978] AC 904.
[64]   *White v Riverside Housing Association Ltd* [2007] UKHL 20, [2007] L&TR 22, per Lord Neuberger at p 352, and *Lancecrest Ltd v Asiwaju* [2005] EWCA Civ 117, [2005] 1 EGLR 40, per Neuberger LJ at p 40.
[65]   *Raineri v Miles* [1981] AC 1050, per Lord Fraser at p 1093.
[66]   *Raineri v Miles* [1981] AC 1050, per Lord Fraser at p 1092.

3.31 In that sense, time *will* be 'of the essence' in respect of a deadline for the service of a rent review notice[67] – with the result that late service will invalidate a notice – only if the parties to a lease have expressly made time of the essence in respect of that deadline,[68] or if there are sufficient 'contra-indications' *implying* that time was intended to be of the essence. Such 'contra-indications' can be found in:[69]

- the express words of the lease (e g time will be of the essence in respect of the deadline for the service of a tenant's counter-notice if there is a 'deeming provision' stating that, if a counter-notice is not served by that deadline, the rent shall be the rent proposed in the landlord's notice triggering the rent review);[70]

- the interrelation of the rent review clause itself and other clauses in the lease (e g time will be of the essence where the same timetable is set for a rent review and also for a tenant's right to determine the tenancy by serving a break notice, in respect of which time will be of the essence);[71]

- the surrounding circumstances.

3.32 The presumption that time is not of the essence in respect of rent review deadlines, including deadlines for the service of rent review notices, is a strong one capable of being rebutted only by a compelling counter-indication.[72] It is especially difficult to rebut the presumption that time is not of the essence in respect of a particular deadline if time is expressly made of the essence in respect of one or more other deadlines.[73]

3.33 If time is not of the essence for the service of a landlord's notice triggering a rent review, mere delay on the part of the landlord in serving such a notice will not result in the 'abandonment' of the right to serve a notice. Indeed, prolonged delay by a landlord in serving a 'trigger notice', even if combined with hardship on the part of the tenant, will not disentitle the landlord from serving such a notice unless the combination of delay and hardship give rise to an estoppel.[74] For those purposes, it will be difficult to establish hardship on the part of the tenant arising from the late service of a notice by a landlord triggering a rent review because, pending the service of the notice, the tenant can

[67]   Or in respect of any other deadline in rent review machinery.

[68]   *United Scientific*, per Lord Diplock at p 923.

[69]   *United Scientific*, per Lord Diplock at p 930.

[70]   *Starmark Enterprises Ltd v CPL Distribution Ltd* [2002] Ch 306.

[71]   *Central Estates Ltd v Secretary of State for the Environment* (1995) 72 P & CR 482.

[72]   *Phipps-Faire Ltd v Malbern Construction Ltd* [1987] 1 EGLR 129.

[73]   *London & Manchester Assurance Co Ltd v GA Dunn & Co Ltd* [1983] 1 EGLR 111, per Slade LJ at p 116, and *Lancecrest v Asiwaju* [2005] EWCA Civ 117, [2005] 1 EGLR 40, per Neuberger LJ at p 42.

[74]   *Armherst v James Walker Ltd* [1983] 1 Ch 305, per Oliver LJ at p 316.

estimate the increased rent that would be payable on a rent review and – until required to pay that increased rent – he can retain the difference between the passing rent and the reviewed rent. Moreover, a tenant can *make* time of the essence in respect of the deadline for the service of the landlord's 'trigger notice' by serving a notice specifying a reasonable period within which he requires a trigger notice to be served.[75]

SPECIFICATION OF THE DATE OF THE EXPIRY OF A NOTICE

3.34 Many types of property notice expire on a particular date. In the absence of a mandatory requirement that such notices accurately specify the date on which they will expire, notices will typically be valid so long as they unambiguously inform the reasonable recipient how, and when, they are intended to operate – even if they fail to specify, or inaccurately specify, the date of expiry.

3.35 A term will not be implied into a licence that can be determined on reasonable notice that a notice terminating the licence must name the date on which it will expire.[76] In *Taylor v Crotty*[77] it was held that an option contained in a lease entitling the tenant to purchase the freehold on three months' written notice had been exercised by a letter that did not mention the notice period and simply stated:

> 'Pursuant to [the clause containing the option], please take this letter as notice on behalf of our clients that they wish to exercise the option in that clause ....'

3.36 In *W Davies (Spitalfields) Ltd v Huntley*,[78] which concerned a tenancy that could be determined on three months' notice, a notice to quit was held to be valid which stated that 'we regret that we must give you 3 months' notice to terminate the lease'. The tenant unsuccessfully submitted that the notice was invalid on the ground that it had failed to identify the *date* on which it would expire. Henn Collins J said that:[79] 'Does not the tenant know perfectly well when the notice expires, namely, in three months from the moment it meets his eye?' Equally, notices to quit have been held to be valid which were expressed to expire 'at the expiration of the present year's tenancy',[80] 'at the earliest possible moment',[81] and 'at the expiration of your tenancy which will expire next

---

[75] *United Scientific*, per Lord Diplock at pages 933 to 934. Time can be made of the essence in respect of other deadlines in the same way.

[76] *Australian Blue Metal Ltd v Hughes* [1963] AC 802.

[77] [2006] EWCA Civ 1364.

[78] [1947] 1 KB 246.

[79] At p 247.

[80] *Doe v Timothy* (1847) 2 Car & K 351.

[81] *May v Borup* [1915] 1 KB 830.

after the end of one half year from the service of this notice'.[82] However, in *Phipps and Co (Northampton and Towcester Breweries) Ltd v Rogers*[83] a tenancy which could be brought to an end by three months' notice to quit to expire 'on any one of the days appointed as special transfer sessions by the justices for the district in which the premises are situate' was held not to have been determined by a notice to quit 'on the earliest day on which your tenancy can be brought to an end' on the ground that 'it requires a degree of knowledge on the part of the tenant to make it clear and unambiguous which the Court will not impute to him'.[84]

3.37 Break notices have been held to be valid which were expressed to expire 'at the earliest date after the service of this notice that [the licence] can lawfully be terminated',[85] and which required the tenant to give up possession 'within a period of three months' (in respect of a break clause that required the landlord to give 'not less than three months notice').[86] In *Mannai Investment Co Ltd v Eagle Star Life Assurance Co Ltd*[87] the House of Lords held that a break notice had validly exercised an entitlement to determine a lease on the third anniversary of the term, even though it was stated to expire on the day preceding the third anniversary.[88] In light of *Mannai Investment*, the line of authorities[89] holding that a notice to quit will be invalid if it specifies a date other than a date on which the tenancy can be brought to an end should no longer be regarded as being good law; albeit that, or order to be valid, the reasonable recipient would need to be in no doubt as to date – being the last date of a period of the tenancy – on which the tenancy must have been intended to expire.

3.38 However, sometimes a contractual or statutory provision under which a notice can be served will properly be interpreted as imposing, as a mandatory requirement for the validity of a notice, that the notice accurately specify the date on which it will expire. For example, the

---

[82] *Addis v Burrows* [1948] 1 All ER 177.

[83] [1925] 1 KB 14.

[84] However, Scrutton LJ delivered a dissenting judgment and, in *Addis v Burrows* [1948] 1 All ER 177, Lord Greene MR said at pp 183–184 that: 'Some reasons given by the Lord Justices are difficult to reconcile with other reasons given in the course of the judgments. That it is a decision binding in all cases of similar facts, I cannot, of course, question, but it is to be observed that it was a case where there was a combination of difficulties presented to the tenant, (i) a difficulty of construction, and (ii) a difficulty of fact. I am not prepared to extend the operation of that authority beyond a comparable case.'

[85] *Allam & Co Ltd v Europa Poster Services Ltd* [1968] 1 All ER 826.

[86] *Manorlike Ltd v Le Vitas Travel Agency and Consultancy Services Ltd* [1986] 1 All ER 573.

[87] [1997] AC 749.

[88] See the detailed commentary on *Mannai Investment* in Chapter 2, and also *Garston v Scottish Widows' Fund* [1998] 1 WLR 1583, and *Peer Freeholds Ltd v Clean Wash International Ltd* [2005] EWCA 179, [2005] 1 EGLR 47.

[89] *Sidebotham v Holland* [1895] 1 QB 378, *Lemon v Lardeur* [1946] KB 613, and *Bathavon Rural District Council v Carlile* [1958] 1 QB 461.

Housing Act 1988, s 21(4) provides that a court shall make an order for possession of a dwelling-house let on an assured shorthold tenancy only if the landlord has given to the tenant a notice 'stating that, after a date specified in the notice, being the last day of a period of the tenancy ..., possession of the dwelling-house is required ...'. In *Fernandez v McDonald*[90] the Court of Appeal held that a failure in a section 21 notice to identify a date that was the last day of a period of the tenancy would be fatal to the validity of the notice because s 21(4) was properly interpreted as requiring the notice to identify the correct date.[91]

3.39 It is well established that notices can specify, in the alternative, two or more dates on which the notice will expire. Often this is achieved by naming a particular date and also, in the alternative, by referring to a formula from which the correct date can be ascertained.[92]

THE IDENTITY OF THE CORRECT SERVER AND RECIPIENT

Legal proprietors

3.40 Generally speaking, property notices are required to be served by a server in his capacity as the proprietor of an interest in land, and on a recipient in his capacity as the proprietor of another interest in land.

3.41 Accordingly, it is usually the case that a property notice will be invalid unless it is served *by*, or on behalf of, the person in whom, as at the date of the service of the notice, the *legal estate* was vested of the interest in land to which the notice relates.[93] For example, a tenant's break notice will be invalid if it is served by the person in whom only the

---

[90]   [2003] EWCA Civ 1219, [2003] 4 All ER 1033.
[91]   Albeit that the correct date can be identified by reciting the statutory language – ie stating that possession is required 'after the last day of a period of the tenancy that is not earlier than two months after the date the notice was given' – or by stating that possession is required '*at* the end of the period of your tenancy which will end after expiry of two months from the service upon you of this notice' (see *Lower Street Properties Ltd v Jones* (1996) 28 HLR 877, and *Notting Hill Housing Trust v Roomus* [2006] EWCA Civ 407, [2006] 1 WLR 1375).
[92]   *Hirst v Horn* (1840) 6 M&W 393, *Addis v Burrows* [1948] 1 All ER 177, per Evershed LJ at pp 180–181, and *Phipps and Co (Northampton and Towcester Breweries) Ltd v Rogers* [1925] 1 KB 14. However, in *Chez Auguste v Cottat* [1951] 1 KB 292 it was held that a notice served on 20 September 1949 to 'quit and deliver up possession of the ... premises ... on Monday, October 3, 1949 or at the expiration of the current period of your tenancy, which shall expire next after the service upon you of this notice' had not brought to an end (what was) a yearly tenancy because the notice presupposed that the tenancy was a weekly tenancy.
[93]   This is separate to the issue of whether a notice is invalid on the ground that, although it *has* been served by the person entitled to serve the notice, the notice *misidentifies* the server of the notice (being an issue discussed in paras **3.54–3.65** below).

equitable interest of the tenancy is vested[94] and, in the 'registration gap' between the completion of the assignment of a lease and the registration at HM Land Registry of the assignee as the lessee, a tenant's break notice should be served by the assignor as the legal proprietor.[95] Equally, a notice to quit served by an assignee of the landlord's interest will be invalid if it is served before the vesting of the legal estate in the assignee;[96] a notice to quit will be invalid if served after the grant by the landlord of a concurrent lease (which operates as an assignment of the reversion for the duration of the concurrent term);[97] and, following the death of a landlord and the grant of probate, a notice to quit will be invalid if it is served, not by the executors, but by the beneficiary of the landlord's estate.[98]

3.42 In *Lower v Sorrell*[99] Donovan LJ suggested that this principle prevented the service of a notice to quit prior to the creation of a tenancy. The learned judge said that:[100]

> 'In my opinion …a notice to quit given by an existing landlord to an existing tenant, and, if that view be right, it follows that a person cannot give a valid notice to quit before he has become a landlord and the recipient of the notice his tenant, or before legal relations exist between them which otherwise permit such a notice.'

3.43 Similarly, a notice required to be served *on* a person in his capacity as the owner of an interest in land must be served on the person in whom, as at the date of the service of the notice, the legal estate of that interest is vested.[101] A notice served under the Law of Property Act 1925, s 146 as a condition for the forfeiture of a lease will be invalid if it is served on the original tenant rather than the current tenant who has taken an assignment of the lease[102] and, following the bankruptcy of a tenant, a notice served under the Landlord and Tenant Act 1954, s 25 to terminate a business tenancy must be served on the trustee in bankruptcy.[103] In *Osei-Bonsu v Wandsworth LBC*[104] it was held that a notice to quit was valid even though it was served, not on the person in

---

[94] See *Stait v Fennner* [1912] 2 Ch 504, and *Dun & Bradstreet Software Services (England) Ltd v Provident Mutual Life Assurance* [1998] 2 EGLR 175.

[95] *Brown & Root Technology Ltd v Sun Alliance* [2001] Ch 733.

[96] *Thompson v McCullough* [1947] 1 KB 447.

[97] *Wordsley Brewery Co v Halford* (1903) 90 LT 89.

[98] *Divall v Harrison* [1992] 2 EGLR 64.

[99] [1963] 1 QB 959.

[100] At p 975.

[101] This is separate to the issue of whether a notice will be invalid on the ground that, although it has been served on the correct recipient, it misidentifies the recipient of the notice (being an issue discussed in paras **3.66–3.69** below).

[102] *Old Grovebury Manor Farm Ltd v W Seymour Plant Sales & Hire Ltd (No 2)* [1979] 3 All ER 504.

[103] *Gatwick Investments Ltd v Radviojevic* [1978] CLY 1768.

[104] [1999] 1 WLR 1011.

whom the reversion immediately expectant on the lease was vested (being a tenant under a concurrent lease), but on the freeholder and original landlord.

3.44   For the purpose of establishing the identity of the necessary server or the recipient of a notice, it should be noted that:

- dispositions of estates in land registered at HM Land Registry which are required to be completed by registration do not operate at law until the relevant registration requirements are met;[105]

- subject to certain exceptions,[106] the property of a bankrupt vests in the trustee in bankruptcy immediately upon his appointment taking effect or, in the case of the official receiver, on his becoming trustee;[107]

- on the dissolution of a company, property and rights, save for property held by the company on trust for any other person, will vest in the Crown (or the Duchy of Lancaster or the Duchy of Cornwall) *bona vacantia*;[108]

- on the death of a legal proprietor, real estate will vest in the deceased's personal representatives,[109] save that, on an intestacy or where there are no executors to administer a will, the deceased's real estate vests initially in the Public Trustee pending the grant of representation.[110]

An apparent exception to the general rule: service of a notice to quit following the death of the tenant

3.45   In *Egerton v Rutter*,[111] Lord Goddard said that:[112]

> 'A landlord cannot know, on the death of a tenant, whether he or she died intestate, or when letters of administration are granted, except perhaps by making a search which might take a great deal of time during which he might lose the opportunity of serving the necessary notice.'

Accordingly, a rule has developed that, if a tenant under a periodic tenancy dies and before personal representatives are appointed, the landlord is entitled to serve a notice to quit to determine the tenancy on

---

[105]   See the Land Registration Act 2002, s 27(1).
[106]   Including property held on trust and certain types of residential tenancy (see the Insolvency Act 1986, ss 283(3)(a) and 283(A)).
[107]   Insolvency Act 1986, ss 283 and 306.
[108]   Companies Act 1985, s 654.
[109]   Administration of Estates Act 1925, s 1(1).
[110]   Administration of Estates Act 1925, s 9(1) and (2).
[111]   [1951] 1 KB 472.
[112]   At p 476.

any person (such as a widow, a child or a friend of the tenant) who remains in possession of the demised premises.[113] This rule is, however, possibly founded upon a presumed agency on the basis that: 'When the tenant is dead the landlord should be entitled to treat the persons he finds in possession as the representative of the estate, and deal with it accordingly'.[114]

JOINT OWNERS

The correct server of a notice where a legal estate is jointly owned

The general rule: notices must be served by, or on behalf of, all of any joint owners

3.46　If a legal estate is vested in two or more persons then, as against the outside world, those joint proprietors are in the position of a single owner.[115] So, where a notice is to be served in respect of an interest vested in two or more persons, then, generally speaking, a notice will be valid only if it has been served by, or at least with the authority of, all of the joint owners.[116] Accordingly, a notice to complete a contract for the sale of land will be invalid if it is served by, or on behalf of, only two out of three vendors.[117] If land is let to two or more tenants, all of the tenants must join in serving a tenant's break notice;[118] a tenant's notice exercising an option to renew the tenancy;[119] a counter-notice served under the Agricultural Holdings (Notices to Quit) Act 1977, s 2 in response to a landlord's notice to quit;[120] a notice served under the Leasehold Reform Act 1967, s 8(1) to exercise a right to acquire the

---

[113]　*Rees d Mears v Perrot* (1830) 4 C&P 230, *Sweeny v Sweeny* (1867) IR 10 CL 375, and *Harrowby v Snelson* [1951] 1 All ER 140.

[114]　*Sweeny v Sweeny* (1876) IR 10 CL 375, per Dowse B at p 382, *Egerton v Rutter* [1951] 1 KB 472, per Lord Goddard CJ at p 477, and *Harrowby v Snelson* [1951] 1 All ER 140, per Cassels J at p 145.

[115]　*Hammersmith LBC v Monk* [1992] 1 AC 478, per Lord Browne-Wilkinson at p 492.

[116]　This is a separate question to whether a notice is invalid on the ground that, although it *has* been served by – or with the authority of – all co-owners, the notice has failed to *state* that the notice is served by all of the co-owners (perhaps stating that it is 'from' only one of the co-owners). That issue, which relates to the contents of the notice, is considered in paras **3.54–3.65** below.

[117]　*Woods v Mackenzie* [1975] 1 WLR 613, per Megarry J at p 615.

[118]　*Re Viola's Indenture of Lease, Humphrey v Stenbury* [1909] 1 Ch 244, *Newman v Keedwell* (1977) 35 P&CR 393, per Fox J at p 398, *Hammersmith LBC v Monk* [1992] 1 AC 478, per Lord Bridge at p 489, and *Hounslow LBC v Pilling* [1993] 1 WLR 1242.

[119]　*Newman v Keedwell* (1977) 35 P&CR 393, per Fox J at p 398, and *Leek and Moorelands Building Society v Clarke* [1952] 2 QB 788, per Somervell LJ at pp 792–3.

[120]　See *Newman v Keedwell* (1977) 35 P&CR 393, and *Featherstone v Staples* [1986] 2 All ER 461 (albeit that, in the latter case, the Court of Appeal left open the question whether, where the landlord was also a joint tenant, a counter-notice could be served by all of the tenants other than the landlord himself).

freehold of a house;[121] or a counter-notice served under the Landlord and Tenant Act 1954 in response to a section 25 notice.[122] Equally, if there are two or more landlords, all of the landlords must join in serving a break notice[123] or a section 25 notice.[124]

3.47 If a notice is invalid on the ground that it has not been served by all of the joint owners, it cannot be made good by being subsequently 'ratified' by the owners who did not join in serving the notice. In *Right v Cuthell*,[125] in which a landlord's break notice was held to be invalid on the ground that it had not been served by all the joint landlords, Lawrence J said that:[126]

> 'I think that ... for the notice to be good it ought to be binding on all the parties concerned at the time when it was given, and not to depend for its validity, in part, upon any subsequent recognition of one of them: because the tenant is to act upon the notice at the time, and therefore it should be such as he may act upon it with security.'

An exception to the general rule: notices to quit

3.48 Notices to quit provide an exception to the generally rule that, where a notice is to be served in respect of an interest vested in joint owners, the notice must be served by, or on behalf of, all of the joint owners. In *Hammersmith and Fulham LBC v Monk*[127] the House of Lords upheld a long line of authority[128] to the effect that, unless the terms of the tenancy agreement provide otherwise,[129] one only of several joint landlords or tenants can serve a notice to quit to determine a periodic tenancy. Lord Bridge, explaining the justification for the exception to the general rule, said that:[130]

> 'As a matter of principle I see no reason why this question should receive any different answer in the context of the contractual relationship of landlord and tenant than that which it would receive in any other contractual context. If A and B contract with C on terms which are to

---

[121] *Wax v Viscount Chelsea* [1996] 2 EGLR 80.
[122] *Harris v Black* (1983) 46 P&CR 366. See also *London Borough of Hackney v Hackney African Organisation* (1998) 77 P&CR D18 in which, although a counter-notice was *stated* to have been served by only one of the joint tenants, it was held to have been validly served with the authorization of all of the tenants.
[123] *Right v Cuthell* (1804) 5 East 491.
[124] *Smith v Draper* [1990] 2 EGLR 69.
[125] (1804) 5 East 491.
[126] At p 500.
[127] [1992] 1 AC 478.
[128] *Doe d Aslin v Summersett* (1830) 1 B&Ad 135, *Doe d Kindersley v Hughes* (1840) 7 M&W 139, *Alford v Vickery* (1842) Car & M 280, and *Greenwich LBC v McGrady* (1982) 81 LGR 288. See the contrary view in *Howson v Buxton* (1928) 97 LJKB 749, per Scrutton LJ at p 752.
[129] Lord Bridge at p 491, and *Re Viola's Indenture of Lease, Humphrey v Stenbury* [1909] 1 Ch 245.
[130] At pp 483–4.

continue in operation for one year in the first place and thereafter from year to year unless determined by notice at the end of the first or any subsequent year, neither A nor B has bound himself contractually for longer than one year. To hold that A could not determine the contract at the end of any year without the concurrence of B and vice versa would presuppose that each had assumed a potentially irrevocable contractual obligation for the duration of their joint lives, which, whatever the nature of the contractual obligations undertaken, would be such an improbable intention to impute to the parties that nothing less than the clearest express contractual language would suffice to manifest it. Hence in any ordinary agreement for an initial term which is to continue for successive terms unless determined by notice, the obvious inference is that the agreement is intended to continue beyond the initial term only if and so long as all parties to the agreement are willing that it should do so ...

Thus the application of ordinary contractual principles leads me to expect that a periodic tenancy granted to two or more joint tenants must be terminable at common law by an appropriate notice to quit given by any one of them whether or not the others are prepared to concur ...

[Moreover, the authorities relating to joint tenancies established that] from the earliest times a yearly tenancy has been an estate which continued only so long as it was the will of both parties that it should continue, albeit that either party could only signify his unwillingness that the tenancy should continue beyond the end of any year by giving the appropriate advance notice to that effect. Applying this principle to the case of a yearly tenancy where either the lessor's or the lessee's interest is held jointly by two or more parties, logic seems to me to dictate the conclusion that the will of all the joint parties is necessary to the continuance of the interest.'

3.49   Nevertheless, Lord Browne-Wilkinson added[131] that: 'It may be that, as between the lessees, the giving of the notice to quit was a breach of trust, theoretically giving rise to a claim ...for breach of trust'.

3.50   However, in *Crawley BC v Ure*[132] and *Notting Hill Housing Trust v Brackley*,[133] the Court of Appeal held that the determination of a tenancy by one of two or more joint tenants by the service of a notice to quit did not constitute a breach of trust. In the latter case, the Court considered the scope of the Trusts of Land and Appointment of Trustees Act 1996, s 11(1), which provides that trustees of land,

'shall in the exercise of any function relating to land subject to the trust ...so far as practical, consult the beneficiaries ...and ...so far as consistent with the general interest of the trust, give effect to the wishes of those beneficiaries, or (in case of dispute) of the majority (according to the value of their combined interests).'

---

[131]   At p 493.
[132]   [1996] 1 All ER 724.
[133]   [2001] EWCA Civ 601, [2001] 3 EGLR 11.

Peter Gibson LJ said[134] that the service of a notice to quit by one co-owner,

> 'is not the exercise by the trustee, as trustee of a power or duty of the trustees. It is no more than the exercise by the joint tenant of his or her right to withhold his or her consent to the continuation of the tenancy into a further period.'

Another exception to the general rule: Agricultural Holdings Act 1923, s 12

3.51 The Agricultural Holdings Act 1923, s 12 provides another exception to the general rule that, where a notice is required to be served by 'the tenant' and where there are two or more joint tenants, 'the tenant' will be interpreted as a reference to all of the joint tenants. In *Howson v Buxton*[135] it was held that a notice served by 'the tenant' under that provision, which would exercise an entitlement to compensation for losses in connection with the sale or removal of chattels arising from the service by the landlord of a notice to quit, could be served by only one of two or more joint tenants. In *Lloyd v Sadler*,[136] Megaw LJ said:[137]

> 'In my opinion, the judgment of Scrutton LJ in *Howson v Buxton* (1928) 97 LJKB 749, [1928] All ER 434 shows that, where the strict application of the doctrine of joint tenancy would lead to unreasonable results, or results which the legislature is unlikely to have intended, it is permissible for the court to conclude that the legislature did not so intend; that that, instead, in such a case, the phrase "the tenant", where there is a joint tenancy, is to be read as meaning "the joint tenants or any one or more of them". There is thus authority that the doctrine of joint participation by joint tenants is not a sacrosanct or immutable doctrine of statutory interpretation, where such phrases as "the tenant" and "the tenancy" are used.'

3.52 The justification for the departure in *Howson v Buxton* from 'strict application of the doctrine of joint tenancy' was that, under the Agricultural Holdings Act 1923, s 12, compensation was payable to the tenant, *qua* owner of chattels, rather than *qua* owner of the tenancy, and the chattels might be owned by only one of the joint tenants.[138]

The identity of the recipient of a notice where an estate in land is vested in joint owners

3.53 Where a notice is required to be served on a person in his capacity as the owner of an interest in land and where that interest is vested in joint owners, a notice will typically be invalid unless it is served on all of

---

[134] At p 13.
[135] (1928) 97 LJKB 749.
[136] [1978] QB 774.
[137] At pp 786–7.
[138] *Jacobs v Chaudhuri* [1968] 2 QB 470, per Winn LJ at p 596.

the joint owners.[139] For example, a notice served under the Law of Property Act 1925, s 146 as a condition for forfeiting a lease will, where the tenancy is vested in joint owners, be invalid unless the notice is served on all of the tenants.[140]

MISIDENTIFICATION OF THE SERVER

3.54 A notice will be valid only if it has been served by, or on behalf of, the person with the contractual or statutory entitlement to serve the notice (see above). However, sometimes a notice, although served by the correct person, inaccurately states that it has been served by someone else. The question will then arise whether the inaccuracy in the contents of the notice has invalidated the notice.

3.55 The first step, as always, is to interpret the contractual or statutory provision under which the notice has been served. Does that provision require, as an indispensable condition of a notice's validity, that the notice accurately identify the person who has served the notice? Or, perhaps (and this is more likely), does the provision under which a notice has been served merely require that the notice convey the meaning to the recipient that the notice has been served by the person enjoying the entitlement to serve the notice? In the latter case, in which a misidentification of the person who has served the notice might not be fatal, it may or may not be necessary that the notice be sufficient to enable the reasonable recipient to identify the server by name.

3.56 In *Morrow v Nadeem*[141] and *Yamaha-Kemble Music (UK) Ltd v ARC Propeties Ltd*[142] notices served by landlords under the Landlord and Tenant Act 1954, s 25 to terminate business tenancies were held to be invalid on the ground that the notices, which adopted a prescribed form, had misidentified the landlord.[143] However, in the former case, Nicholls LJ said[144] that:

---

[139] A notice may, of course, be served on all of the owners, even if the notice does not identify all of the joint owners as recipients of the notice. The circumstances in which a notice will be invalidated on the ground that it fails accurately to identify the recipients of the notice is considered in paras **3.66–3.69** below.

[140] *Blewett v Blewett* [1936] 2 All ER 188. See also *Rostram v Michael Nairn & Co Ltd* [1962] EGD 284.

[141] [1986] 1 WLR 1381.

[142] [1990] 1 EGLR 162.

[143] Section 25 notices have also been held to be invalid on the ground that they failed to name *all* of the landlords (see *Smith v Draper* [1990] 2 EGLR 69, and *Pearson v Alyo* [1990] 1 EGLR 114).

[144] At p 1387.

'There might perhaps be an exceptional case in which, notwithstanding the inadvertent mis-statement or omission of the name of the landlord, any reasonable tenant would have known that that was a mistake and known clearly what was intended.'

An example of such circumstances are illustrated by *M&P Enterprises (London) Ltd v Norfolk Square Hotels Ltd*[145] in which it was held that a section 25 notice, served by 'Norfolk Square Hotels No 2 Ltd', was valid even though it identified the landlord as 'Norfolk Square No 2 Ltd'. Equally, in *Hackney LBC v Hackney African Organisation*[146] a counter-notice served by four joint tenants in response to a section 25 notice was held to be valid even though the notice described only one of the tenants as 'the tenant'. That was on the ground that it would have been apparent from the context in which the notice was served that it was being served on behalf of all of the tenants. That context included a covering-letter which used the expression 'our counter-notice' and other court proceedings in which the person described in the notice as the tenant was acting as the representative of all of the tenants.

3.57 Break clauses in leases are not interpreted as requiring, as an indispensable condition of validity of a break notice, that a break notice correctly name the person serving the notice. However, a break notice must convey to the recipient that it has been served by the person entitled to determine the lease (ie either the landlord or the tenant). In *Lay v Ackerman*,[147] Neuberger LJ said[148] that:

'After all, the purpose [of a tenant's break clause is] not to identify the tenant to the landlord, but to communicate to the landlord an unequivocal desire to determine the lease in accordance with its terms. Once a person other than the actual tenant has been identified in the notice as the person on whose behalf the notice was served, the notice could be valid only if it could be shown that, despite the misidentification, a reasonable person in the position of the landlord could have been in no doubt that the notice was served on behalf of the person who was the tenant.'

3.58 Whether a mis-identification of the person who has served a break notice *will* prevent a break notice from achieving that purpose depends upon the factual circumstances in which it has been served. In *Lemmerbell Ltd v Britannia LAS Direct Ltd*[149] and *Proctor & Gamble Technical Centres Ltd v Brixton plc*[150] break notices served by tenants inaccurately stated that they had been served, not by the tenant, but by companies in the same group as the tenant. The break notices were held to be invalid on the ground that, in the particular circumstances in which

---

[145] [1994] 1 EGLR 129.
[146] (1998) 77 P&CR D18.
[147] [2004] EWCA Civ 184, [2005] 1 EGLR 139.
[148] At p 144.
[149] [1998] 3 EGLR 67.
[150] [2003] 2 EGLR 24.

the notices had been served, the 'reasonable recipient' would not have known whether the notices had been served by:

- the tenant (in which case the break notices would have been valid);

- the company identified in the notices as the tenant following an unlawful assignment of the lease (in which case the notices, again, would have been valid); or

- the company identified as the tenant even though that company was not, in fact, the tenant and had no right to serve a break notice (in which case the notices would have been invalid).

3.59 However, in *Havant International v Lionsgate (H) Investment*,[151] another case in which a tenant's break notice inaccuracy stated that it had been served by a company in the same group as the tenant, it was held that, given the circumstances in which the notice had been served, the reasonable recipient would have been in no doubt that the notice had been served by the tenant and that a mistake had been made when naming the server. The primary reason supporting that finding was that the entitlement to determine the lease was personal to the original tenant. Hart J said that:[152]

> 'The question therefore resolves to this. Would the reasonable recipient assume that there had been a mistake in the description of the company giving the notice? Or would he entertain, as a matter giving rise at least to a reasonable doubt, the possibility that [the subsidiary company] had taken an unlawful assignment and had done so in the mistaken belief that it had thereby become entitled to the benefit of [the original tenant's] personal right?... The personal nature of HIHL's right ...makes [the former possibility] the only explanation of the notice which carries conviction.'

3.60 Equally, it is not an indispensable condition of a valid notice to quit that it should accurately name the person serving the notice (ie the landlord or the tenant).[153] A notice to quit will be valid, even if it has misidentified the server, so long as the 'reasonable recipient' would have been in no doubt that it was served on behalf of the person entitled to serve the notice.[154]

---

[151] [2000] 2 L&TR 297.

[152] At p 306.

[153] *Harmond Properties Ltd v Gajdzis* [1968] 1 WLR 1858.

[154] *Lemon v Lardeur* [1946] 1 KB 613 and *Divall v Harrison* [1992] 2 EGLR 64 suggest that, save in the case of a notice to quit served by a general agent, a notice to quit will be invalid if it was stated to be served by, or on behalf of, anyone other than the landlord. Such a blanket proposition no longer reflects the law.

3.61 In *Lay v Ackerman*[155] it was held that a counter-notice served by a landlord under the Leasehold Reform, Housing and Urban Development Act 1993, s 45 in response to a notice served by leaseholders exercising a right of collective enfranchisement was valid even though it had mis-identified the landlord by naming the trustees of a non-existent trust. Section 45 did not require a counter-notice to name the landlord, but, by implication, it did require that a counter-notice be in terms that would enable the reasonable recipient to appreciate that it had been given by the landlord. In the particular circumstances of the case, the counter-notice had achieved that purpose. The leaseholders would have been in no doubt that the counter-notice had been served by and with the authority of the landlord because: (i) the counter-notice had been served in response to a notice served on the landlord; (ii) the counter-notice correctly identified the landlord's address; (iii) the counter-notice was stated to have been served by the landlord's agent; and (iv) of the history of previous litigation between the parties. Neuberger LJ explained[156] that the misidentification of the server was more likely to invalidate an originating notice than a counter-notice because:

'An originating notice normally has no documentary source other than the statutory or contractual provision pursuant to which it was served. On the other hand, a notice in reply must be judged not merely in its statutory or contractual context but also by reference to the originating notice in answer to which it is served. Where an originating notice has been served on a landlord in the context of a statutory or contractual provision under which the recipient can be expected to protect its position by serving a notice in rely, such a notice is obviously very likely to come from the landlord. First, like the originating notice, it is only the landlord that can validly serve the notice. Secondly, and unlike an originating notice, it is inherently improbable that anyone other than the landlord will serve the notice in reply. If the originating notice was served on the wrong person, the question of a notice in reply is academic. If the originating notice was served on the right person, it would seem little short of absurd that a counternotice would have been served by the wrong person, although it is far from absurd, or even unlikely, that the right person's agent might identify the wrong person as the landlord.'

Notices identifying an agent as the server

3.62 A line of authorities establishes that, in some circumstances, an agent can serve a valid notice in his own name (ie a notice that does not purport to be given by, or on behalf of, the principal). Subject to a mandatory requirement that a notice accurately identify the server himself, that will be the case where the reasonable recipient of the notice

---

[155] [2004] EWCA Civ 184, [2005] 1 EGLR 139.
[156] At p 145.

would have had no reason to doubt that the notice had been served by the person entitled to serve the notice.[157]

3.63 In *Jones v Phipps*[158] a landlord had, for many years, permitted the equitable owner of the reversion to assume entire control over the management of the demised premises, and, as a result, the tenant had assumed that the equitable owner was indeed his landlord. The equitable owner served a notice to quit in his own name that made no mention of the landlord. That notice was held to be valid. However, Lush J said:[159]

> 'It is clear that the notice [in order to be valid] must be such as the tenant may act upon with safety, that is, one which is in fact, and which the tenant has reason to believe to be, binding on the landlord. The notice in this case does fulfil these conditions.'

3.64 In *Re Knight and Hubbard's Underlease*[160] the trustees of a friendly society were the lessors under a lease that contained a break clause. A break notice was served by the society itself – being the equitable owner – in its own name. Nevertheless, the notice was held to be valid because the trustees had entrusted the management of the demised premises to the society. Sargant J said that:[161]

> '[I]t is abundantly clear that the trustees, as the legal owners of the property, allowed the society, as the absolute beneficial owners, to have full management of it, and to deal directly with the [tenant]; and that any notice to terminate given by the society ... was one given with the full authority of the trustees so far as was necessary ... The case is not one in which the [tenant] was misled, or ran the slightest chance of being misled.'

In *Fredco Estates Ltd v Bryant*[162] a notice to increase the rent payable by a residential tenant, which was signed by a firm of surveyors in their own name, was held to be valid on the ground that it was well known to the tenants that the surveyors were the agents of the landlord.

3.65 In *Townsends Carriers Ltd v Pfizer Ltd*[163] a break notice was held to be valid even though it purported to have been served, not by the tenant, but by a company clothed with full authority by the tenant to act on the tenant's behalf. Finally, in *Harmond Properties Ltd v Gajdzis*[164] a notice to quit was held to be valid even though it was served on behalf of

---

[157] The emphasis placed in some of these authorities upon whether the agent was a 'general agent' (ie a person with authority to do anything in relation to the subject-matter of the agency without reference to the principal), rather than a special agent, seems misplaced.

[158] (1868) LR 3 QB 567.

[159] At p 573.

[160] [1923] 1 Ch 130.

[161] At p 142.

[162] [1961] 1 All ER 34.

[163] (1977) 33 P&CR 361.

[164] [1968] 1 WLR 1858.

a director of the landlord. The director had managed the property, he had acted as if he was the landlord, and the tenant had always thought of him as the landlord.

MISIDENTIFICATION OF THE RECIPIENT

3.66 Sometimes a notice, although served on the correct recipient, misidentifies the person on whom the notice has been – and was required to be – served. The starting point when considering this type of error is to ascertain whether the contractual or statutory provision under which the notice has been served requires, as an indispensable condition of the validity of the notice, that the notice accurately identify the recipient or recipients. If there is such a mandatory requirement, the notice will be invalid. For example, in *Jones v Lewis*[165] a notice served under the Agricultural Holdings Act 1948, s 24(2) giving notice of disrepair which was stated to be addressed to only one of the two tenants was held to be invalid on the ground that the notice had to be served in a prescribed from which required all of any joint tenants to be named.

3.67 If the notice is not required – as an indispensable condition for its validity – to accurately identity the recipient (as will usually be the case[166]) the validity of the notice will depend upon whether the mis-identification of the recipient prevents the notice from conveying the *meaning* that, as a matter of interpretation of the relevant statutory or contractual provision, the notice was required to convey. In *Townsends Carriers Ltd v Pfizer Ltd*[167] Megarry V-C said,[168] in relation to a break notice, that:

> 'If the notice was addressed to the wrong person but was nevertheless delivered to the right person, the question would be whether the mis-addressing prevented the notice from being 'given' to the right person.

---

[165] (1973) 25 P&CR 375.

[166] Many types of property notice are not required to *name* the recipient at all. Section 196(2) of the Law of Property Act 1925 provides that: 'Any notice required or authorised by this Act to be served on a lessee or mortgagor shall be sufficient, although only addressed to the lessee or mortgagor by that designation, without his name, or generally to the persons interested, without any name ...' (and, by virtue of subsection (5), that provision applies 'to notices required to be served by any instrument affecting property executed or coming into operation after the commencement of this Act ...'). Moreover, in *Townsends Carriers Ltd v Pfizer Ltd* (1977) 33 P&CR 361, which concerned a break notice, Megarry J said at p 366 that: '[The break clause] says nothing about addressing a notice. The requirement is merely that the party concerned 'shall give to the other party 12 months previous notice in writing of such its desire ...'. If one party were to deliver to the other a notice which was not addressed to any named person, but simply stated 'I hereby give you notice ...,' and so on, I do not see why that should not suffice to comply with the lease.'

[167] (1977) 33 P&CR 361.

[168] At p 366.

The purpose of the notice is, of course, to convey information; and if the notice, despite its being mis-addressed, suffices to convey the requisite information to the right person, I would have thought that it would satisfy the terms of the lease.'

3.68 For example, in *Hawtrey v Beaufront Ltd*[169] a notice to quit addressed to the directors of the tenant was held to be valid on the ground that,

'any solicitor looking at this document would see that, while it is addressed to the directors, it is addressed to them, not in their capacity as tenants or as parties to the [lease], but as being the persons acting on behalf of the limited company.'[170]

In *Lazurus Estates Ltd v Beasley*[171] a notice served by a landlord under the Housing Repairs and Rents Act 1954, s 23 to increase the rent payable by a statutory tenant was addressed to 'Mr E G Beasley, tenant of 13, The Palatinate, SE1', whereas, in fact, the tenant was Mrs Violet Beasley, who had become the statutory tenant on the death of her husband – Mr E C Beasley – two years previously. It was held that: 'This misnomer was an obvious mistake which does not affect the validity of the [notice]'.[172] In *Bridges v Stanford*[173] a notice served by a landlord under the Landlord and Tenant Act 1954, s 25 to terminate a business tenancy, instead of naming the tenant (Bridges), was addressed to a company in the same group of companies as the tenant and which ran the tenant's business from the premises. The Court of Appeal upheld the trial judge's holding[174] that:

'This is not a case of a notice being given to the wrong company or tenant. There was never any doubt as to the identity of the intended recipient of the notice but merely as to the name under which they chose to be known at the date of service of the notice. I do not therefore regard the use of the name Hamptons and not Bridges as directing the notice to the wrong recipient ....'

3.69 There was a contrary outcome in *R (Morris) v London Rent Assessment Committee*,[175] in which it was held that a misidentification of the recipient had invalidated a notice because the error might well have misled the reasonable recipient. The landlord under a long residential tenancy had sent a notice to the demised premises under the Landlord

---

[169]   [1946] 1 KB 280.

[170]   Per Croom-Johnson J at p 289.

[171]   [1956] 1 QB 702.

[172]   See Denning LJ at p 710. Note that the decision appears to have been based on the fact that the tenant 'was not misled in any way', whereas it is now clear that, in principle, the subjective interpretation of a notice by the recipient is a matter that should be totally ignored (see paras **2.26–2.27** above).

[173]   [1991] 2 EGLR 265.

[174]   See the judgment of Lloyd J at p 268.

[175]   [2002] EWCA Civ 276, [2002] 2 EGLR 13.

and Tenant Act 1954, s 4 proposing a statutory tenancy upon the expiry of the term. That notice was (incorrectly) addressed to the original tenant of the long lease (Mr Barnby), rather than to the current tenant (Mr Fry). Mummery LJ said that:[176]

'The notice was not addressed to the tenant, Mr Fry, either expressly by name or implicitly by status as tenant. It was expressly and unambiguously addressed by name to an altogether different person, Mr HG Barnby. That was not a minor error or slip. Mr Barnby was not Mr Fry, and he was not, and had long since ceased to be, tenant of the flat. The reaction of the reasonable tenant receiving the notice addressed to Mr HG Barnby (or receiving an envelope so addressed) would be to think that the notice or the envelope and its contents were meant for Mr Barnby. The notice cannot be construed as a notice given to Mr Fry ....'

---

[176] At p 15.

Chapter 4

WAIVER, ESTOPPEL AND THE WITHDRAWAL OF NOTICES

INTRODUCTION: WAIVER AND ESTOPPEL

4.1   Generally speaking, a contractual or statutory right enuring for the benefit of a person can be waived by that person.[1] So, in many instances, it will be possible for a person to waive an entitlement to serve – or to rely upon – a notice, or to waive a right to dispute the validity of a notice on the ground that it is – in some respect – deficient. A right will be waived if, with knowledge of the right, the person entitled to the right clearly communicates an intention that he will not rely upon that right.[2] Equally, an estoppel can deprive a person of an entitlement to serve or to rely upon a notice, or a right to dispute the validity of a notice. The three types of estoppel that are most likely to achieve that result are:

- *an estoppel by representation* (requiring a representation of fact intended to be acted upon and detrimental reliance upon that representation);

- *a promissory estoppel* (requiring a promise intended to affect a legal relationship and detrimental reliance upon that promise);

- *an estoppel by convention*[3] (where the parties have proceeded on the basis of a shared underlying assumption, of either of fact or law that was communicated between the parties, and it would be unfair or unjust to allow the parties to go back on the assumption).[4]

---

[1]   *Elsden v Pick* [1980] 1 WLR 898, per Shaw LJ at p 906.

[2]   For a detailed account of the law on waiver see Wilken and Villiers *The Law of Waiver, Variation and Estoppel* (2002), chs 3–5.

[3]   In *Mannai Investment Co Ltd v Eagle Star Life Assurance Co Ltd* [1997] AC 749, Lord Steyn said at p 768 that: 'Depending on the circumstances a party may be precluded by an estoppel by convention from raising a contention contrary to a common assumption of fact or law (which could include the validity of a notice) upon which they have acted.'

[4]   For a detailed account of those types of estoppel see Wilken and Villiers *The Law of Waiver, Variation and Estoppel* (2002), chs 8, 9 and 10.

LOSS OF A RIGHT TO SERVE, OR TO RELY UPON, A NOTICE

4.2   A waiver or an estoppel may result in the loss of an entitlement to serve a notice. In *Datlow v Jones*,[5] in return for an agreement by a tenant of an agricultural holding to an amalgamation scheme proposed by his landlord, the landlord agreed to safeguard the tenant against future encroachment on his farm for the purpose of afforestation. The landlord thereby became estopped from being able to serve and rely upon a notice to quit in respect of part of the tenant's holding in order to obtain land for afforestation. Similarly, in *John v George*[6] a tenant of an agricultural holding supported an application made by his landlord for planning permission to convert some old farm buildings into a dwelling in order to enable the landlord to sell those buildings and use the proceeds to build new buildings for the tenant. After planning permission had been granted, the landlord transferred the buildings to a family trust but refused to build the new buildings. An estoppel by convention was held to preclude the landlord from relying upon the service of a notice to quit which relied upon the fact that planning permission, which would not have been granted in the absence of the tenant's support, had authorised a change of use for the farm buildings.

4.3   Alternatively, the server of a notice may, as a result of a waiver or estoppel, *become* disentitled from relying upon (what had hitherto been) an effective notice. In *Milne-Berry & Madden v Tower Hamlets LBC*[7] a local authority served a tenant who had exercised the 'right to buy' with a notice under the Housing Act 1980, s 16(6) requiring the tenant to complete within 56 days. The local authority was held to have waived any entitlement to rely upon that notice because, seven days before the expiry of the notice, a local authority employee had informed the tenant's solicitor that, notwithstanding the notice, the tenant's right to buy 'could continue'. In some circumstances, the service of a subsequent notice might create an estoppel preventing reliance upon an earlier notice if the subsequent notice has not been served 'without prejudice' to the earlier notice. In *Cordon Bleu Freezer Food Centres Ltd v Marbleace Ltd*[8], which concerned notices served under rent review provisions in a lease, Judge Paul Barker QC said[9] that:

> '[Counsel submitted that] [i]f the party serving the notice, the tenant in this case, serves two notices, having served the second one you cannot go back to them with the first one unless the second one is served without prejudice to the other ...In the ordinary way I would accede to that. That perhaps

---

5   [1985] 2 EGLR 1.
6   (1995) 71 P&CR 375.
7   (1995) 28 HLR 225.
8   [1987] 2 EGLR 143.
9   At p 146.

would raise an estoppel. The notice itself is some sort of representation that the landlord is entitled to act on it.'[10]

4.4   Another possibility is that the conduct of the server gives rise to a waiver or an estoppel that has the effect of *suspending* the operation of a notice. In *Hughes v Metropolitan Railway Co*[11] the landlord of commercial premises served a notice requiring his tenant to carry out repairs to the demised premises. The parties then entered into negotiations for the surrender of the lease and, as a result of those negotiations, the tenant – with the concurrence of the landlord – postponed carrying out any repairs. The landlord was held to have thereby waived any entitlement to rely upon the notice in respect of the period during which the negotiations were ongoing.

LOSS OF A RIGHT TO DISPUTE THE VALIDITY OF A NOTICE

Loss by a recipient of an entitlement to dispute the validity of a notice

4.5   In *Swanson's Agreement, Hill v Swanson*,[12] Evershed J said[13] that:

'It is clearly established that where an invalid notice ... is given, the party to whom it is given may, as the result of his conduct, be estopped from asserting the true fact, namely, that the notice was insufficient.'

Equally, a recipient can conduct himself so as to waive a right that he would otherwise have had to dispute the validity of a notice.

---

[10]   However, in *Lowenthal v Vanhoute* [1947] 1 KB 342 it was held that, by serving a second notice to quit after a tenancy had already been determined by an earlier notice to quit, the landlord had not waived his entitlement to contend that the earlier notice to quit had put an end to the tenancy. Denning J said at pp 344 –5 that: 'Passages were cited to me, from Woodfall's *Landlord and Tenant*, 24th ed., p 981, and *Halsbury's Laws of England*, 2nd ed., vol.20, p 142, to the effect that generally speaking, giving a second notice to quit amounts to a waiver of a notice previously given. In my judgment that statement in the text-books is not accurate. It is based upon *Brierly v Palmer* 16 East 53, 56. But when that case is examined it does not support the proposition. In my opinion the law is now well settled that where a tenancy is determined by a notice to quit, it is not revived by anything short of a new tenancy and in order to create a new tenancy there must be an express or implied agreement to that effect. A subsequent notice to quit is of no effect unless, with other circumstances, it is the basis for inferring an intention to create a new tenancy after the expiration of the first. Applying that test in the present case it is plain that there was no agreement, express, or implied or to be inferred, for the creation of a new tenancy.'
[11]   (1887) 2 App Cas 439.
[12]   [1946] 2 All ER 628.
[13]   At p 633.

Service by the wrong person

4.6   In *Dun & Bradstreet Software Services (England) Ltd v Provident Mutual Life Assurance Association*[14] it was held that a landlord had become estopped from disputing the validity of break notices by relying upon the fact that they had been served, not by the tenant, but by the tenant's parent company as a result of the landlord's surveyor having given an unequivocal assurance that the notices were acceptable and the tenant relying upon that assurance by not serving replacement notices.

Service after a contractual deadline

4.7   In *Fifield v W&R Jack Ltd*[15] a lease provided that a tenant's counter-notice under rent review machinery was required to be served within 28 days of the landlord's notice triggering the rent review and, in default of the service of a counter-notice by that deadline, the lease provided that the rent would be increased to the amount proposed in the landlord's notice. The Privy Council held that the landlord had waived its entitlement to complain about the fact that the tenant's counter-notice was served out of time because it had treated the counter-notice as valid and it had entered into negotiations over the amount of the new rent.

Incorrect date for the expiry of a notice

4.8   In *Swanson's Agreement, Hill v Swanson*[16] the landlord was entitled to terminate a contractual tenancy of residential premises by giving three months' notice. The landlord served a notice of less than three months and, when the tenant pointed out the mistake, the landlord apologised for the error and invited the tenant to regard the notice as referring to the correct date. The tenant was held to have become estopped from disputing the validity of the notice because, whilst he failed to respond to that letter, he had paid the rent that would have been payable under a statutory tenancy that would have come into existence had the contractual tenancy been terminated.

Defective contents

4.9   In *Keepers and Governors of the Free Grammar School of John Lyon v Mayhew*[17] it was held that, by serving a counternotice and commencing proceedings for a new tenancy, a tenant had impliedly represented that he would not dispute the validity of a notice served under the Landlord and Tenant Act 1954, s 25 to terminate a business tenancy on the ground that the notice was not in the prescribed form.

---

14   [1998] 2 EGLR 175.
15   [2001] L&TR 4.
16   [1946] 2 All ER 628.
17   [1997] 1 EGLR 88.

Leggatt LJ said[18] that 'the counternotice assumed the validity of the section 25 notice' and the landlord had suffered detriment, in reliance on a belief that the notice was valid, by incurring professional fees and from refraining from serving another section 25 notice in the correct form. Equally, in *Tennant v London County Council*,[19] it was held that a tenant, by serving a counter-notice and issuing proceedings for a new tenancy, had lost a right to complain that a section 25 notice was invalid on the ground that it was not properly signed.

4.10   In *Sidnell v Wilson*[20] Denning MR said,[21] obiter, that the service by a tenant of a counter-notice claiming the benefit of the Leasehold Property (Repairs) Act 1938 in response to a notice served under the Law of Property Act 1925, s 146 would give rise to a waiver precluding the tenant from disputing the validity of the section 146 notice. However, in *BL Holdings Ltd v Marcolt Investments Ltd*[22] it was held that the service by a tenant of such a counter-notice had not created an estoppel preventing the tenant from disputing the validity of the landlord's section 146 notice on the ground that it failed to contain prescribed information. Stephenson LJ said that:[23]

> '[The counter-notice] cannot be considered as more than a statement of intention to go ahead with the service of the counternotice and to go ahead with the claim for the benefit of the Act, and it does not involve any promise or representation never to withdraw that intention or never to take any point on the validity of the notice. It was a wise move to preserve the position created by the serving of the notice, however defective, by putting in a counternotice, and this was done within a week of the notice being sent.'

Loss by the server of a right to dispute the validity of a notice

4.11   Sometimes it will be in the interests of the server of a notice to dispute the validity of his own notice. However, a waiver or an estoppel mightpreclude the server of the notice from doing so.

4.12   In *Elsden v Pick*[24] the tenant of agricultural holding served a notice to quit on his landlord. The notice to quit was invalid because, contrary to the Agricultural Holdings Act 1948, s 23(1) it purported to terminate the tenancy before the expiration of 12 months from the end of the current year of the tenancy. The tenant disputed the validity of his own notice. However, he was held to be estopped from doing so

---

18   At p 89.
19   (1957) 55 LGR 421.
20   [1962] 2 QB 67.
21   At p 77.
22   [1979] 1 EGLR 97.
23   At p 100.
24   [1980] 1 WLR 898.

because, after serving the notice, he had agreed with his landlord that – notwithstanding short service – the notice would be valid. Brightman LJ said[25] that: 'If the parties so agree, the tenancy will come to an end on the agreed date by virtue of the defective notice to quit which it is agreed shall be treated as valid.'

4.13 The service of (what purports to be) a notice may be regarded as constituting an implied representation that the notice is valid.[26] Accordingly, if the recipient has relied to his detriment upon a belief – created by the service of the notice – that the notice was indeed valid, an estoppel might preclude the server from disputing the validity of his own notice. In *Farrow v Orttewell*[27] an assignee of a landlord's leasehold estate in a farm served a notice to quit before completion. After the tenant had vacated the farm and sold his stock, the assignee disputed the validity of the notice to quit on the ground that he was unable to serve a valid notice because, at the date of service, he had only an equitable interest. Lord Hanworth MR said[28] that: 'I think if ever there was a case where the doctrine of estoppel applied and was necessary to do justice, it is the present case.'

LIMITATIONS ON THE APPLICATION OF ESTOPPEL AND WAIVER

An estoppel cannot be used as 'a sword' to create a cause of action

4.14 The role of the law of estoppel in the context of notices is circumscribed by the fact that an estoppel[29] cannot create substantive rights and will not, in the proper sense of the word, create a cause of action. In other words, whilst an estoppel can deprive a person of a defence, thereby enabling a claimant to succeed on a claim that he would otherwise have lost, the facts constituting any cause of action must exist independently of any estoppel.[30] In *Aristocrat Property Investments v Harounoff*[31] a landlord of a statutory tenancy contended, in possession

---

25   At p 907.

26   Although, in *Sinclair Gardens Investments (Kensington) Ltd v Poets Chase Freehold Co Ltd* [2007] EWHC 1776, Morgan J said at para 70 that there was 'something to be said' for the argument that the service of a purported notice under the Leasehold Reform, Housing and Urban Development Act 1993, s 13 (ie a notice to exercise a right to collective enfranchisement) did not imply a representation that the notice was valid.

27   [1933] 1 Ch 480.

28   At p 499.

29   Other than a proprietary estoppel (being a type of estoppel that is unlikely to have any application to the validity of notices).

30   Save in the 'special circumstances' of an estoppel by convention resulting in a conventional interpretation of a contract (see *Riverside Housing Association Ltd v White* [2005] EWCA Civ 1385, [2006] 1 EGLR 45, per Sir Peter Gibson at p 52).

31   (1982) 2 HLR 102.

proceedings relying upon alleged rent arrears, that the tenant was estopped from disputing the validity of notices that had purported to increase the rent because the tenant had, for a time, paid the rent at the increased amount. The Court of Appeal held that the landlord was attempting – illegitimately – to use an estoppel as a sword. Oliver LJ said that:[32]

> '[H]ere, in order to succeed, the landlord ... has ... to make an estoppel (because this, it seems to me, is an estoppel or nothing) the foundation of the positive case for the recovery of rent which he seeks to make.'[33]

Public policy may prevent a waiver or an estoppel from defeating a statutory right

4.15 Some statutes are properly interpreted as precluding, on public policy grounds, a person from contending that a right to serve a notice, or a right to object to a defect in a notice, has been lost as a result of a waiver or an estoppel. In *Aristocrat Property Investments v Harounoff*[34] it was held that stipulations in the Rent Act 1977, Part III should be interpreted as imposing conditions precedent to the operation of an increase of rent which could not be overridden either by an agreement or a waiver. The fact that a statute speaks in terms of illegality ('it shall be unlawful'), rather than mere invalidity, might indicate that there is an element or public interest involved that would preclude a requirement from being overridden by a waiver or an estoppel.[35] Moreover, a waiver or an estoppel cannot confer upon the court a jurisdiction denied by Parliament.[36]

WITHDRAWAL OF NOTICES

4.16 In *May v Borup*[37] AT Lawrence J said that:[38]

> 'A tenant who has given a good notice to quit cannot subsequently cancel it without the consent of the landlord. If the tenant desires to continue his tenancy after giving notice it is a matter for negotiation with the landlord, who can accept or reject the tenant's proposals as he pleases.'[39]

---

[32] At p 115.
[33] See also *Riverside Housing Association v White* [2005] EWCA Civ 1385, [2006] 14 EG 176.
[34] (1982) 2 HLR 102.
[35] *Elsden v Pick* [1980] 1 WLR 898, per Shaw LJ at p 906.
[36] *Daejan Properties Ltd v Mahoney* [1995] 2 EGLR 75, per Sir Thomas Bingham MR at p 77, and *Lafiti v Colherne Court Freehold Ltd* [2002] EWHC 2873, [2003] 1 EGLR 78.
[37] [1915] 1 KB 830.
[38] At p 832.
[39] See also *Norfolk County Council v Child* [1918] 2 KB 805. Note that an agreement

If a notice is served under a statutory or contractual provision whether the notice is *capable* of being withdrawn by the server after it has been served is, ultimately, a question turning on the proper interpretation of the statute or contract. However, in the absence of any express provision permitting the server to withdraw a notice, the service of a notice is likely to be treated as irrevocable.

4.17   For example, it has been held that a business tenant with security of tenure under the Landlord and Tenant Act 1954, Part II cannot withdraw a 'section 26 notice' requesting a new tenancy[40] or withdraw a 'positive counter-notice' – served in response to a landlord's 'section 25 notice' – stating that the tenant is willing to give up possession.[41] In *Kinch v Bullard*[42] Neuberger J held,[43] in respect of a notice served under the Law of Property Act 1925, s 36(2) to determine a beneficial joint tenancy, that: 'Once the sender has served the requisite notice, the deed is done and cannot be undone.' The learned judge added that:

> 'The position is the same as with a contractual right to determine a lease, which normally entitles either or both of the parties to serve notice to determine the lease if it desires to put an end to the term. Once the procedure has been set in train, and the relevant notice has been served, it is not open to the giver of the notice to withdraw the notice ...'.

4.18   However, a server of a notice may be able to 'countermand' a notice that has been posted to the recipient if he informs the recipient of his desire to revoke the notice before the notice is deemed to have been served. In *Kinch v Bullard*[44] Neuberger J said:[45]

> 'I am inclined to think that the [notice could be countermanded] if, before the notice was "given", the sender had informed the addressee that he wished to revoke it. In such a case, it appears to me that the notice would have been withdrawn before it had been "given"... Accordingly, it seems to me that, while the notice is still in the post, it has not been given, and, until it is given, the sender has in effect a locus poenitentiae whereby he can withdraw the notice, but only provided his withdrawal is communicated to the addressee before the notice is given to, or served on, the addressee. I should emphasise, however, that this is no more than a tentative view.'

---

between landlord and tenant that a notice to quit shall be 'withdrawn' creates a *new* tenancy (see *Tayleur v Wildin* (1868) LR 3 Exch 303 and *Lower v Sorrell* [1963] 1 QB 959).

[40]   *Stile Hall Properties Ltd v Gooch* [1979] 3 All ER 848.
[41]   *Shaws (EAL) Ltd v Pennycrook* [2004] EWCA Civ 100, [2004] Ch 296.
[42]   [1998] 4 All ER 650.
[43]   At p 655.
[44]   [1998] 4 All ER 650.
[45]   At p 656.

Chapter 5

SERVICE AT COMMON LAW

INTRODUCTION

5.1   The common law regards a contractual or statutory requirement that a notice be 'served' or 'given',[1] or a requirement under the common law for the service of a notice,[2] as requiring the person entitled to serve the notice (or the server's properly authorised agent) to cause the notice to be *received by*, or *to come to the attention of*, the recipient (or the recipient's properly authorised agent).

5.2   It is, however, often difficult for the server of a notice to ensure that the notice is received by, or comes to the attention of, the recipient. Even if service in that sense can been effected, the server of a notice – when faced with a denial by the recipient that he has been served – may be unable to *prove* service because, whether or not a notice has been served in that sense, often depends upon facts that are known only to the recipient. To address those problems, statutory and contractual provisions have extended the common law definition of service to enable certain types of notice to be served by methods that do not require a notice to have been received by, or to have come to the attention of, the recipient. In *Blunden v Frogmore Investment Ltd*,[3] Robert Walker LJ said[4] that:

> 'Notice is not the same as knowledge. But the evident purpose of requiring notice to be given to a particular person is that the contents of the notice should be communicated to, and become known by, that person. Nevertheless there is no doubt that both statutory and contractual provisions may lead to the position that a valid notice has been given even though the intended recipient does not know of the notice (and is not at fault in not knowing about it).'

5.3   This chapter addresses issues relating to the common law's definition of service, whilst the extension of the common law's definition of service by contractual and statutory provisions is discussed, respectively, in Chapters 6 and 7 below.

---

[1]   There is no distinction between 'serving' and 'giving' a written notice (see *Re Berkeley Road* [1971] 1 Ch 648, *Holwell Securities Ltd v Hughes* [1974] 1 WLR 155, and *Kinch v Bullard* [1999] 1 WLR 423, per Neuberger J at p 425).

[2]   For example, the requirement for the service of a notice to quit.

[3]   [2002] EWCA Civ 573, [2002] L&TR 31.

[4]   At p 505.

SERVICE BY THE PERSON ENTITLED TO SERVE THE NOTICE (OR HIS AGENT)

Service by agents

5.4   A person entitled to serve a notice is entitled to delegate the service of the notice to an agent;[5] indeed a company is able to serve a notice (or, for that matter, do anything else) only through agents. The law of agency, and in particular the principles relating to express authority and implied agency (ie where an agency can be inferred from the circumstances), determine whether a person was properly authorised to serve a notice on behalf of someone else.[6]

5.5   In *Jones v Phipps*[7] and *Re Knight and Hubbard's Underlease*[8] equitable owners of landlords' reversionary interests who had managed demised premises for several years were held to have authority to serve notices to quit on behalf of the landlord; such authority being held, in the absence of any express authorisation, to have been incidental to their authority to manage the premises. In *Townsends Carriers Ltd v Pfizer Ltd*[9] an associated company of the tenant, which had occupied the demised premises and which was authorised to deal – in all respects – with the tenancy, was held to have an implied authority to serve a tenant's break notice.

5.6   In some circumstances a notice will have been properly served by an agent on behalf of the person entitled to serve the notice even if the agent, due to a misapprehension about the identity of the person entitled to serve the notice, has, in the contents of the notice, misidentified the server. In *Proctor & Gamble Technical Centres Ltd v Brixton plc*[10] a firm of solicitors served a break notice that was stated to have been served on behalf of a company in the Procter & Gamble group that the solicitors believed to be the tenant under the lease. In fact, the tenant was another company in that group. Nevertheless, it was held that the solicitors had served the notice on behalf of the tenant: the solicitors' instructions had been supplied by a team of people called EMEA to whom all companies in the Procter & Gamble group had delegated responsibility for estate transactions. Neuberger J said that:[11]

> 'It seems to me that the solicitor had been instructed by EMEA, which was acting on behalf of the tenant, whichever that was. EMEA was therefore

---

[5]   *Procter & Gamble Technical Centres Ltd v Brixton plc* [2003] 2 EGLR 24, per Neuberger J at p 26.

[6]   Note that whether a notice can be served in the agent's own name, which is an issue relating to the *contents* of notices, is discussed at paras **3.62–3.65** above.

[7]   (1868) LR 3 QB 567.

[8]   [1923] 1 Ch 130.

[9]   (1977) 33 P&CR 361.

[10]   [2002] EWHC 2835 (Ch), [2003] 2 EGLR 24.

[11]   At p 26.

acting on behalf of the tenant ...when EMEA instructed [the solicitor], and it was therefore [the tenant] that was [the solicitor's] client.'

5.7   Similarly, in *Lay v Ackerman*[12] a solicitor served a counter-notice in response to a notice served by a leaseholder under the Leasehold Reform, Housing and Urban Development Act 1996, s 42 exercising a right to new long lease of a flat. The counter-notice was *stated* to have been served on behalf of the 'Trustees of the Portman Collateral Settlement', even though the landlord was, in fact, the 'Portman Trustees'. It was nevertheless conceded by the leaseholder that the solicitors had served the notice on behalf of the correct landlord. Neuberger J said that:[13]

> 'It seems to me that that concession is entirely realistic. It is clear from the evidence, and, indeed, wholly in accordance with common sense, that, in relation to relatively routine, albeit very important, matters such as the service of statutory and contractual notices in relation to properties on the Portman Estate, the legal owners of the properties have left day-to-day decisions and actions in relation to notices in the hands of their solicitor ...'.

Service by sub-agents

5.8   There are numerous instances of notices being held to have been validly served by sub-agents, frequently solicitors acting for agents of the person entitled to serve a notice. There will usually be no legal impediment to the delegation to a sub-agent of the role of serving a notice, so long as the decision to serve the notice is taken by the agent: although, where a principal places confidence in an agent, that in respect of which the principal places such confidence must be done by the agent personally (unless either expressly or inferentially the agent is authorised to employ a sub-agent), *the role of physically serving a notice on instructions* is a purely ministerial act that is always capable of being delegated to a sub-agent.[14]

A notice served by the wrong person cannot retrospectively be 'validated'

5.9   If a notice has been served by the wrong person it cannot retrospectively be 'validated' or 'ratified' by the person entitled to serve the notice. In *Thompson v McCullough*[15] it was submitted that such a validation had occurred by a process of 'relation back'. A notice to quit, being a notice that can be served only by the person in whom the legal

---

12   [2004] EWCA Civ 184, [2005] 1 EGLR 139.
13   At p 141.
14   *Allam & Co Ltd v Europa Poster Services Ltd* [1968] 1 All ER 826, per Buckley J at p 832.
15   [1947] 1 KB 447.

estate of the reversion is vested, was served, instead, by the assignee of the landlord's freehold interest before completion of the assignment and the vesting of the legal estate in the assignee. Morton LJ said that:[16]

> '[The landlord contended] that ... the delivery of the conveyance relates back so as to make his notice to quit ... effective. [T]hat would seem to me a very startling proposition. It involves [saying] that a man can effectively as landlord give a notice to a tenant at a time when it is quite uncertain whether he, the giver of the notice, will ever be the landlord in fact ... For relation back to have such an effect as that would render the position of a tenant quite intolerable.'

SERVICE *ON* THE RECIPIENT (OR HIS AGENT)

A notice must be received by, or come to the attention of, the recipient

5.10 At common law, a notice is regarded as having been served only if it has been received by, or if it has come to the attention of, the recipient (or his properly authorised agent).[17] In *Hogg v Brooks*[18] the plaintiff let a shop in Regent Street under a lease that contained a break clause. The lessee mortgaged the lease and the mortgagee took possession of the shop and granted a sub-lease. The plaintiff wanted to exercise his entitlement to break the lease but the lessee had disappeared and could not be found. Nevertheless, the plaintiff sent a break notice to the lessee's last known address (which was returned undelivered) and he also sent the notice – addressed to the sub-tenant, the occupier and the lessee – to the demised premises. The break notice was held not to have been served on the ground that it had not been received by the lessee. The disappearance of the lessee meant that there was simply no means of serving a break notice so as to terminate the lease.

5.11 Indeed, unless it can be established that a notice was in fact received by, or came to the attention of, the recipient (or his properly authorised agent), the common law does not regard a notice as having been served merely because the notice has been posted to the recipient at a home or business address;[19] left at the recipient's house;[20] or posted under the door of the recipient's house.[21]

---

16   At p 454.
17   *Galinski v McHugh* [1989] 1 EGLR 109, per Slade at p 111, and *Yenula Properties Ltd v Naidu* [2003] L&TR 9, per Robert Walker LJ at pp 116–7.
18   (1885) 15 QB 256.
19   *New Hart Builders v Brindley* [1975] 1 Ch 342, per Goulding J at pp 353–4, *Chiswell v Griffon Land and Estates* [1975] 2 All ER 665, *Minay v Sentongo* (1982) 45 P&CR 190, per Ackner LJ at p 193, and *Beanby Estates Ltd v Egg Stores (Stamford Hill) Ltd* [2003] EWHC 1252, [2003] 1 WLR 2064, per Neuberger J at p 2075.
20   *Doe d Buross v Lucas* (1804) 5 Esp 153.
21   *Alford v Vickery* (1842) Car & M 280.

5.12 However, a notice will be treated as having come to the attention of the recipient if it has being identified as such and left in his presence. In *New Hart Builders Ltd v Brindley*,[22] it was (perhaps surprisingly) held that a notice to renew an option had been validly served when an agent of the recipient failed to accept delivery of a registered letter which he knew, or at least strongly suspected, contained the notice. It is likely – so long as the notice is received by, or comes to the attention of, the recipient (or his properly authorised agent) – that service of a notice at common law can be effected electronically by email or fax.[23]

The presumed sequence in which notices are deemed to have been served

5.13 In *Keith Bayler Rogers & Co v Cubes Ltd*[24] Templeman J said[25] that,

> 'where a landlord has power to serve two notices in sequence ... and he launches both notices on the same day, it is to be assumed that the notices were delivered in the correct sequence and it is not necessary to pest the postman to see which notice was delivered first.'

Service on an agent of the recipient

5.14 At common law, a written notice can be validly served on an agent of the recipient so long as the scope of the agency extends to accepting service of the notice. In accordance with the general law of agency, an authorisation permitting an agent to accept service of a notice can arise:

- from an *express* authorisation given by the recipient to the agent;

- from an *implied* authorisation given by the recipient to the agent (ie an authorisation to be inferred from the circumstances of the case);

- under the doctrine of ostensible authority if recipient has made a representation to the server to the effect that the agent is authorised to accept service, and, in reliance upon that representation, the notice has been served on the agent.

---

[22] [1975] 1 Ch 342.

[23] *Trafford MBC v Total Fitness (UK) Ltd* [2002] EWCA Civ 1513, [2003] 2 P&CR 2 a break notice which had been served by fax was held to be valid. See also *EAE (RT) Ltd v EAE Property Ltd* 1994 SLT 627 (rent review notice validly served by fax), *Hastie & Jenkerson v McMahon* [1990] 1 WLR 1574 (list of documents validly served by fax for the purposes of the Rules of the Supreme Court) and *PNC Telecom Plc v Thomas* [2002] EWHC 2848 (a faxed letter constituted service of a notice under section 368 of the Companies Act 1985).

[24] (1975) 31 P&CR 412.

[25] At p 416.

5.15 If a notice is served on an agent who *has* been authorised to accept service, the notice will be regarded as having been validly served even if the agent fails to pass on the notice to the recipient. In *Tanham v Nicholson*,[26] Lord Hatherley LC said that:[27]

> 'If once you have constituted your servant your agent for the purpose of receiving such a notice, the question of fact as to whether that servant has performed his duty [to pass the notice on to you] or not, is not one which is any longer in controversy. When once you constitute your servant your agent for that general purpose, service on that agent is service on you – he represents you for that purpose – he is your *alter ego*, and service upon him becomes an effective service upon yourself.'

Solicitors

5.16 It is often wrongly supposed that solicitors typically have authority to accept service of notices on behalf of their clients. In *Re Munro*[28] Walton J said,[29] in relation to a notice served under the bankruptcy rules, that:

> 'It is, of course, a common fallacy to think that solicitors have an implied authority on behalf of their clients to receive notices. They may have express authority so to receive them, but in general a solicitor does not have any authority to accept a notice on behalf of his client.'

5.17 The basis of that fallacy was explained in *Saffron Walden Second Benefit Society v Rayner*,[30] in which the plaintiffs had taken a mortgage of a reversionary share in a testator's estate and had given notice to a firm of solicitors who acted for the trustees in all matters relating to the estate in which professional assistance was required. The Court of Appeal held that the notice had not been validly served. In an important and well-known passage, James LJ said[31] that:

> 'I have had occasion several times to express my opinion about the fallacy of supposing that there is such a thing as the office of solicitor, that is to say, that a man has got a solicitor not as a person to whom he is employing to do some particular business for him, either conveyancing, scrivening, or conducting an action, but as an official solicitor, and that because the solicitor has been in the habit of acting for him, or been employed to do something for him, that solicitor is his agent to bind him by anything he says, or to bind him by receiving notices or information. There is no such officer known to the law. A man has no more a solicitor in that sense than he has an accountant, or a baker, or butcher. A person is a man's accountant, or baker, or butcher, when the man chooses to employ him or

---

[26] (1871) LR 5 HL 561.
[27] At p 568.
[28] [1981] 1 WLR 1358.
[29] At p 1361.
[30] (1880) 14 Ch D 406.
[31] At pp 409–10.

deal with him, and the solicitor is his solicitor when he chooses to employ him and in the matter in which he is so employed. Beyond that the solicitorship does not extend ...

... I am prepared, therefore, to say that before a notice of this kind of a charge upon the property can be of the slightest validity it must be given, if given to a solicitor, to a solicitor who is actually, either expressly or impliedly, authorised as agent to receive such notices ....'

5.18 Accordingly, in *Glen International Ltd v Triplerose Ltd*[32] – in which Munby J said[33] that the above passage was 'laying down nothing that was novel in 1880 and something that is still recognised as sound principle today ...' – it was held that a firm of solicitors instructed by a tenant in relation to dilapidations and insurance was not authorised to accept service of a notice served under the Landlord and Tenant Act 1987, s 48 informing the tenant of the landlord's address in England and Wales for the service of notices. Similarly, in *Holwell Securities Ltd v Hughes*,[34] which concerned an option to purchase land that could be exercised by the service of a written notice, the purchaser served a notice on the vendor's solicitors, and those solicitors, in the course of a telephone conversation, notified the vendor that they had received the notice. It was held that the notice had not been validly served on the vendor. There was no suggestion that the vendor's solicitors were authorised to receive the notice. Moreover, by communicating the contents of the notice to the vendor, the solicitors had not served the notice. Russell LJ said[35] that:

'A person does not give notice in writing to another person by sitting down and writing it out and then telephoning to that other saying "Listen to what I have just written".'

5.19 Nevertheless, in circumstances in which the recipient's solicitors or legal representatives have not been *expressly* authorised to accept service of a notice it will sometimes be possible to conclude that they have an implied authority to accept service. In *Yenula Properties Ltd v Naidu*[36] a tenant who was about to enter into possession of premises under a residential tenancy was held to have impliedly given a licensed conveyancer authority to accept service of a notice under the Housing Act 1988, s 20 by instructing him to do whatever was necessary to get him into the property as quickly as possible. In *Westway Homes Ltd v Moores*[37] a vendor's solicitors was held to have had implied authority to accept service of a notice exercising an option on the ground that they had been instructed 'to deal with all matters relating to the improvement

---

[32] [2007] EWCA Civ 388, [2007] 26 EG 164.
[33] At p 167.
[34] [1974] 1 WLR 155.
[35] At p 159.
[36] [2002] EWCA Civ 719, [2002] L&TR 104.
[37] [1991] 2 EGLR 193.

of his title, or the protection of the title by insurance, or anything else which would enable the property to be developed'.[38] A solicitor does not, however, have an implied authority to accept service of a notice merely on the ground that he is instructed under a retainer creating a duty to pass the notice on to the recipient.[39]

5.20 Alternatively, in the absence of any express or implied authority to accept service of notices on behalf of his client, a solicitor might be held to have had ostensible authority to accept the service. In *Galinski v McHugh*[40] a tenant's solicitor was held to have had authority to accept service of a notice under the Landlord and Tenant Act 1954, s 4 proposing a statutory tenancy because the tenant had informed his landlord that his solicitor 'had full authority to act for the [tenant] and to accept service of the notice'.[41]

Managing agents

5.21 Managing agents appointed by a landlord will usually be 'general agents', namely agents with authority to act on all matters relating to the letting and management of the property, and, if so, they will be taken to have authority to accept service of notices relating to the property.[42]

Servants

5.22 A servant of a house in which his master lives is likely to have implied authority to accept service of notices at the house, with the result that service on such a servant will be effective.[43]

Rent collectors

5.23 In *Pearse v Boulton*[44] it was held that a person who, on behalf of the landlord, merely collected the rent from the tenant was not authorised to accept service from the tenant of a notice to quit.

---

[38] Dillan LJ at p 196.

[39] *Von Essen Hotels 5 Ltd v Vaughan* [2007] EWCA Civ 1349, per Mummery LJ atpara 44.

[40] [1989] 1 EGLR 109.

[41] Slade LJ at p 110.

[42] *Townsends Carriers Ltd v Pfizer Ltd* (1977) 33 P&CR 361, per Megarry V-C at p 365, and *Peel Developments (South) Ltd v Siemens plc* [1992] 2 EGLR 85, per Judge Baker at p 87.

[43] *Tanham v Nicholson* (1872) LR 5 HL 561, and *School Board of London v Peters* (1902) 18 TLR 509.

[44] (1860) 2 F&F 133.

Service on a recipient incapable of understanding a notice

5.24 The fact that the recipient of a notice is, by virtue of some mentally incapacity, unable to understand, or to act upon, a notice will not prevent the notice from being properly served. The Law of Property Act 1925, s 196(2) provides that:

'Any notice required or authorised by this Act to be served on a lessee or mortgagor shall be sufficient ...notwithstanding that any person to be affected by the notice is ...under disability ....'

5.25 Even in cases where the Law of Property Act 1925, s 196(2) does not apply, the mental incapacity of the recipient presents no obstacle to the valid service of a notice. In *Tanham v Nicholson*[45] a landlord was held to have validly served a notice to quit on the agent of a tenant even though the tenant was 'in a weak state of mind'.

5.26 In *Tadema Holdings Ltd v Ferguson*[46] an elderly tenant under an assured tenancy suffered from a mental disorder and was incapable of managing his own affairs. The landlord served a notice on the tenant under the Housing Act 1988, s 13(2) to increase the rent payable under the tenancy. The tenant did not exercise his entitlement to object to the proposed rent increase and, thereafter, he failed to pay the rent at the increased amount. That resulted in the landlord serving a 'section 8 notice' on the tenant relying upon the rent arrears. It was submitted on behalf of the tenant that neither the notice to increase the rent, nor the 'section 8 notice', had been validly served on the ground that it is not possible to serve a statutory notice by delivering it to a person who suffers from a mental disability or who is incapable of dealing with the notice. That submission was rejected by the Court of Appeal. Peter Gibson LJ said[47] that:

'It seems to me that what the Court must do is to construe the meaning of the word "serve" in section 8(1) and section 13(2). I do not think it can be said that the meaning of that word is different in relation to service on a patient from that which it would have in relation to service on a person of full capacity. "Serve" is an ordinary English word connoting the delivery of a document to a particular person. It does not seem to me to imply that the document has to be understood by the person to whom it is delivered. It does not have to be read by the person to whom it is delivered. Indeed it may not even be known to have been delivered to that person if it is delivered to the proper address for service.

In the particular circumstances of this case, [the tenant] did not present to a stranger as a person suffering from mental incapacity. There would have

---

[45] (1871) LR5 HL 561.
[46] (2000) 32 HLR 866.
[47] (2000) 32 HLR 866.

been nothing to put [the landlord] on notice, when dealing as landlord with [the tenant], that he was incapable of managing his own affairs by reason of mental incapacity.

Even a contract made by a person who, at the time of the contract, lacked the capacity to make it, is binding on him in every respect, unless it can be shown that the other contracting party know of the incapacity at that time, or knew of such facts and circumstances that he must be taken to have been aware of the incapacity. I do not see why a more rigorous rule should be taken to apply to service of a notice on a tenant. Our attention has been drawn to the fact that by section 196 of the Law of Property Act 1925, notices required or authorised by that Act to be served on a lessee, or mortgagor, may be served even though the lessee or mortgagor is under a disability. That subsection, of course, has no direct application here, but it is an indication that Parliament was not averse to the notion that someone under a disability could properly be served with a notice. If there is to be a special meaning given to "service", when the service is effected on a patient, then that must, I think, be a matter for Parliament to prescribe. In the present case, for the reasons which I have given, it seems to me plain that service was effected on [the tenant], even though, because of his mental incapacity, it would appear, he did not trouble to open any envelope containing such notice or otherwise choose to deal with formal documents served upon him.'

'INDIRECT' SERVICE

5.27 Under the common law, it is immaterial that a notice was not served *directly* upon the recipient, but, instead, passed through the hands of one or more third parties before reaching the recipient. In *Townsends Carriers Ltd v Pfizer Ltd*[48] Megarry V-C said[49] (in relation to the service of a break notice):

'I should add that [counsel] emphasised that [the break clause] requires the tenant to "give" notice to the landlord, and he said that although the landlord had ultimately received the notice, no notice had ever been given to the landlord as such. However, I do not think that a requirement to "give" notice is one that excludes the indirect giving of notice. The question is whether the notice has been given, not whether it has been given directly. If the note emanates from the giver and reaches the ultimate recipient, I do not think that it matters if it has passed through more hands than one in transit.'[50]

---

[48] (1977) 33 P&CR 361.

[49] At p 366.

[50] In *Hussein v Mehlman* [1992] 2 EGLR 85, Judge Paul Baker QC said at p 87 that: 'A notice served on an agent who had not got authority to receive might still be good if it could be shown that the agent was likely to pass it on to the landlord. In the present case, the tenants could not rely on that last point simply because there was not time enough for the notice to have got to the hands of the agents and then be handed on to the landlords, having regard to the fact that the offices of the landlords and their agent were closed on the dates I have already mentioned.'

THE SAME PERSON AS THE SERVER AND THE RECIPIENT

5.28 In principle, there seems to be nothing to prevent a person, in whom is vested the respective interests of the server and also of the recipient, from serving a notice on himself. In *Re Knight and Hubbard's Underlease*[51] the trustees of a friendly society were both the lessor and the lessee under a lease. That fact did not prevent those trustees from serving a valid break notice on themselves. Sargant J said that:[52]

> 'When once merger is abandoned, and the co-existence of the two interests in the society or their trustees is admitted, it seems to me to follow that the society can validly act in respect of either or both of those interests, and that for this purpose, there is nothing absurd or illogical in the society, as the owner of one interest, giving notice to the society, as the owner of another interest. It is said that this cannot be, because there is a necessary "suspension" during the period of common ownership. But this "suspension" seems to me a partial or temporary merger under another name; and no authority has been cited to me to show that any "suspension" of this kind has ever been recognized. No doubt there is a certain awkwardness in the society, in respect of one interest, giving itself notice in respect of another interest. But, in my view, it is awkwardness only and not impossibility.'[53]

---

[51] [1923] 1 Ch 130.

[52] At p 140.

[53] However, in *R v Cardiff City Council, ex p Cross* [1982] 6 HLR 1, it was held that obligations under the Housing Act 1957, Part II in respect of houses that were unfit for human habitation did not apply to the council's own properties because the operative procedures 'can only be initiated by the service by one person (the local authority) of a formal notice on some other person and that the procedures consequent on the service of the notice are ...replete with procedures that can only be operated when two parties are involved' (per Woolf J).

Chapter 6

SERVICE PURSUANT TO CONTRACTUAL PROVISIONS

INTRODUCTION

6.1   Leases, and other contracts under which notices are served, frequently contain provisions authorising methods for the service of notices. That is frequently achieved by expressly incorporating into the contract a statutory provision, usually the Law of Property Act 1925, s 196 (see paras **7.10–7.31** below).[1] On other occasions, the contract will identify specified methods of service for notices in addition to, or in substitution for, the methods of service recognised by the common law.

METHODS OF SERVICE

'By post'

6.2   If a lease, or other contract, provides that a notice can be served by being 'sent to … [the recipient] … by post' that is likely to be interpreted as not imposing any requirement for the notice to be *delivered* to the recipient's address. Accordingly, a notice will be validly served by that method if it has been sent in the post to the recipient in a correctly addressed envelope, even if the notice has been returned by the Post Office undelivered.[2]

At the recipient's 'last known address'

6.3   In *National Westminster Bank Ltd v Betchworth Investments Ltd*[3] a lease provided that notices could be served on the tenant at its 'last known address'. It was held that the address of managing agents who

---

[1]   The provisions of s 196 are likely to be incorporated even if that is not achieved expressly. Subsection (5) of s 196 provides that the provisions in that section relating to service 'shall extend to notices required to be served by any instrument affecting property executed or coming into operation after the commencement of this Act unless a contrary intention appears'.

[2]   *Blunden v Frogmore Investments Ltd* [2002] EWCA Civ 573, [2002] L&TR 31, per Robert Walker LJ at p 511.

[3]   [1975] 1 EGLR 57.

conducted the tenant's business could not constitute the tenant's 'last known address'. Cairns LJ said that:[4]

> 'I am quite unable to accept that when business is conducted by managing agents on behalf of a company the address of the managing agents becomes the address of the company, unless indeed the company were to inform a correspondent "letters may be sent to us addressed care of so-and-so", in which circumstances I think it might become an address within the meaning of this clause.'

DO CONTRACTUAL PROVISIONS DISPLACE THE COMMON LAW?

6.4   An issue that can arise in relation to methods of service authorised by a contract is whether those methods of service are intended to constitute an *exhaustive* account of how notices can be served so as to prevent the server from serving a notice in accordance with an alternative method approved by the common law. That will depend upon (what should be regarded as) the *purpose* of the contractual provision. Is the prescribed method of service intended merely to provide a fail-safe way of serving a notice? Or is the prescribed method intended to identify the *only* method of service that can be adopted so as to exclude what the common law would regard as constituting valid service?

6.5   Two cases illustrate those alternative interpretations that can be placed upon a provision in a contract providing for a method for the service of notices. In *Yates Building Co Ltd v RJ Pulleyn & Sons (York) Ltd*[5] an option provided that any notice exercising the option was 'to be sent by registered or recorded delivery post'. Nevertheless, a notice sent by ordinary post and received by the recipient, was held to have been validly served. The 'requirement' that the notice be sent by registered or recorded delivery, properly understood, simply provided the vendor with a fail-safe method of service and did not preclude the vendor from using an alternative method of service. In contrast, in *Capital Land Holdings Ltd v Secretary of State for the Environment*,[6] a Scottish case, it was held that a clause in a lease which provided that notices served on the landlord 'shall be sent to its registered office' was designed for the benefit of the landlord to ensure that the landlord knew where to look for notices. Accordingly, a notice served at the landlord's business address had not been properly served, even though the landlord had received the notice.

---

4   At p 58.
5   [1976] 1 EGLR 157.
6   1996 SLT 1379.

Chapter 7

METHODS OF SERVICE AUTHORISED BY STATUTE

INTRODUCTION

7.1   The most important statutory provisions authorising methods for the service of notices are:

- Law of Property Act 1925, s 196(3) and (4);

- Landlord and Tenant Act 1927, s 23(1) (which has been incorporated into the Landlord and Tenant Act 1954, Parts I and II,[1] the Leasehold Reform Act 1967,[2] and the Landlord and Tenant (Covenants) Act 1995[3]);

- Agricultural Holdings Act 1986, s 93;

- Agricultural Tenancies Act 1995, s 36.

The purpose of statutory methods of service

7.2   The primary purpose of these statutory provisions is 'to assist the person who is obliged to serve the notice, by offering him choices of mode of service which will be *deemed* to be valid service, *even if in the event the intended recipient does not in fact receive it*'.[4]

> 'The other main purpose is to avoid disputes on issues of fact (especially as to whether a letter went astray in the post or was accidentally lost, destroyed or overlooked after delivery to the premises of the intended recipient) where the true facts are likely to be unknown to the person giving the notice, and difficult for the court to ascertain.'[5]

---

[1]   LTA 1954, s 66(4).
[2]   LRA 1967, s 22(5).
[3]   LT(C)A 1995, s 27(5).
[4]   *Galinski v McHugh* (1988) 57 P & CR 359, per Slade LJ at p 365 (in relation to the Landlord and Tenant Act 1927, s 23(1)).
[5]   *Blunden v Frogmore Investments Ltd* [2002] EWCA Civ 573, [2002] L&TR 31, per Robert Walker LJ at p 506 (in relation to the Landlord and Tenant Act 1927, s 23(1) and the Law of Property Act 1925, s 196(3) and (4)).

Those objectives are said to justify placing the risk of a notice going astray on the recipient.

Human rights

7.3   The public policy benefits of these statutory provisions means that they are unlikely to involve any infringement of the Convention for the Protection of Human Rights and Fundamental Freedoms. In *CA Webber Ltd v Railtrack plc*[6] Longmore LJ said,[7] in relation to the Landlord and Tenant Act 1927, s 23, that:

> 'I am of the view that the rules laid down by statute as construed by the courts are in the public interest, and it is impossible to say that the legislature has attached insufficient importance to the tenant's Convention rights.'[8]

The statutory provisions do not *exhaustively* prescribe how notices can be served

7.4   These statutory provisions do not *exhaustively* prescribe the methods of service that a server of a notice is entitled to adopt. It follows that, notwithstanding the application of any of these provisions, if a notice is actually received by, or comes to the attention of, the recipient (or his properly authorised agent) the notice will be regarded as having been served under the common law (see Chapter 5 above).

Can the statutory provisions relating to service be used 'as an engine of fraud'?

7.5   The statutory provisions relating to the service of notices all identify circumstances in which a notice will be *deemed* to have been served even if, in reality, it has not been received by, or come to the attention of, the recipient or his properly authorised agent.

7.6   This raises the question whether the server of a notice can deliberately select a particular statutory method of service that he knows will mean that the notice will not come to the attention of the recipient, in preference to some other permissible method of service that he knows would result in the notice coming to the attention of the recipient so as to subvert the very purpose of requiring the service of a notice, namely to communicate information to the recipient. Equally, can a person establish the service of a notice by adopting a statutory method of

---

[6]   [2003] EWCA Civ 1167, [2004] 1 WLR 320.
[7]   At p 339.
[8]   See also *Beanby Estates Ltd v Egg Stores (Stamford Hill) Ltd* [2003] EWHC 1252 (Ch), [2003] 1 WLR 2064, per Neuberger J at p 2079–81.

service whilst, at the same time, taking steps – perhaps by physically intercepting the notice – to ensure that the notice does not, in fact, come to the attention of the recipient?

7.7 In *Kinch v Bullard*[9] Neuberger J stated that a statutory provision providing for a deemed method of service cannot be used as an instrument of fraud, or relied upon if the server has taken positive steps to prevent the recipient from receiving the notice. The learned judge said,[10] in relation to the Law of Property Act 1925, s 196(3), that:

> '[W]hatever section 196 provides, it could not be relied on by the sender of a notice as an engine of fraud. The very purpose of serving a notice is to convey information, with legal consequences, on the addressee: it cannot be right that the sender of a notice can take positive steps to ensure that the notice does not come to the attention of the addressee, after it has been statutorily deemed to have been served, and then fall back on the statute to allege that service has none the less been effected.'

7.8 However, in *Blunden v Frogmore Investments Ltd*[11] Robert Walker LJ expressed his disagreement with that view. In that case, a landlord contended that it had validly served a break notice under the Law of Property Act 1925, s 196(3) by attaching the notice to demised premises that had been damaged by an IRA bomb. The landlord had, on the ground that the demised premises had been rendered dangerous by the bomb damage, previously exercised an entitlement to exclude the tenant from the premises. So the statutory method of service adopted meant that there was no prospect that the notice would, as a result of that method of service, come to the tenant's attention. Robert Walker LJ, in holding that the notice had been validly served, said[12] that it was,

> '[not] open to the court to conjure up a doctrine which overrides the effect of a statutory provision, as the Court of Chancery developed the doctrine of part performance in order to circumvent the operation of the Statute of Frauds. Even in the recondite area of artificial tax avoidance the House of Lords (in *MacNiven v Westmoreland Investments Ltd* [2001] STC 237 at 255) has recently reiterated "the paramount necessity of giving effect to the statutory language".'

7.9 However, a majority of the Court of Appeal (Carnwath and Schiemann LJJ) did not express a concluded view on that issue (the landlord having adopted other methods of service which were held to have been valid). Indeed, Schiemann LJ said that:[13]

---

[9] [1999] 1 WLR 423.
[10] At p 431, Carnwath and Schiemann LJJ preferred not to express any view on the issue.
[11] [2002] EWCA Civ 573, [2002] L&TR 31.
[12] At p 513.
[13] At p 514.

'Had the landlord in the present case only been able to rely upon the affixing of the notice in the circumstances described then I would have felt it unjust to find in his favour. Whether more general considerations should lead to a different conclusion I …would prefer to leave to another day.'

Carnwath LJ said that:[14]

'I would not wish to encourage a landlord in a similar case to think that it is sufficient to fix a notice to a door when everyone knows that it is impossible for the tenant, or anyone on his behalf, to see it.'

LAW OF PROPERTY ACT 1925, S 196

7.10 The most important of the statutory provisions authorising methods for the service of property notices are contained in the following subsections of the Law of Property Act 1925, s 196:[15]

'(3) Any notice required or authorised by this Act to be served shall be sufficiently served if it is left at the last-known place of abode or business in the United Kingdom of the lessee, lessor, mortgagor, or other person to be served, or, in the case of a notice required or authorised to be served on a lessee or mortgagor, is affixed or left for him on the land or any house or building comprised in the lease or mortgage, or, in the case of a mining lease, is left for the lessee at the office or counting-house of the mine.

(4) Any notice required or authorised by this Act to be served shall also be sufficiently served, if it is sent by post in a registered letter addressed to the lessee, lessor, mortgagor, or other person to be served, by name, at the aforesaid place of abode or business, office, or counting-house, and if that letter is not returned by the postal operator (within the meaning of the Postal Services Act 2000) concerned undelivered; and that service shall be deemed to be made at the time at which the registered letter would in the ordinary course be delivered.

(5) The provisions of this section shall extend to notices required to be served by any instrument affecting property executed or coming into operation after the commencement of this Act unless a contrary intention appears.

(6) This section does not apply to notices served in proceedings in the court.'

To what types of notice does s 196 apply?

7.11 The Law of Property Act 1925, s 196 applies to two categories of notice:

---

[14] Also at p 514.
[15] Replacing, with no significant amendments, the Conveyancing Act 1881, s 67.

- notices required or authorised by the Law of Property Act 1925 to be served;[16]

- notices required to be served by any instrument affecting property executed or coming into operation after the commencement of [the Law of Property Act 1925] unless a contrary indication appears.[17]

(i) Notices required or authorised by the Law of Property Act 1925 to be served

7.12 The Law of Property Act 1925, s 196 applies to notices 'required or authorised by [the Law of Property Act 1925] to be served'. Accordingly, it will apply to: (i) a notice served under section 36 to sever a beneficial joint tenancy;[18] (ii) a notice served by a mortgagee under section 103(i) requiring payment of the mortgage money (as a pre-condition of exercising a power of sale); (iii) a counter-notice served by a tenant under section 140(2) to determine a tenancy following the service by the landlord of a notice to determine the tenancy in so far as it relates to part only of the demised premises; and (iv) a notice served under section 146(1) as a pre-condition to the forfeiture of a lease.

(ii) Notices required to be served by any instrument affecting property executed or coming into operation after the commencement of [the Law of Property Act 1925] unless a contrary indication appears

7.13 Subsection (5) of the Law of Property Act 1925, s 196 extends the operation of s 196 'to notices required to be served by any instrument affecting property executed or coming into operation after the commencement of this Act unless a contrary intention appears'. The purpose of extending the operation of s 196 to such instruments was to obviate the need, when drafting such instruments, to include a provision dealing with the service of notices. It is nevertheless very common for leases and other instruments affecting property to contain a clause expressly incorporating s 196.

7.14 An 'instrument affecting property' includes a lease, a mortgage, a contract of sale of land, a transfer of land, an option, a trust deed relating to land etc. In *Wandsworth LBC v Attwel*[19] it was held that an

---

[16] Subsections (3) and (4).
[17] Subsection (5).
[18] Section 196 applies to such notices even though s 36(2), instead of providing that a joint tenant can 'serve' a notice of severance, provides that a joint tenant can 'give' such a notice. That is because there is no distinction between 'serving' and 'giving' a notice (*Kinch v Bullard* [1999] 1 WLR 423, per Neuberger J at p 425).
[19] [1996] 1 EGLR 57.

'acceptance of offer' document, which set out the terms of a tenancy, was 'an instrument affecting property'. A statute is not an 'instrument' unless it creates a settlement.[20]

7.15 The Law of Property Act 1925, s 196 applies to notices served under instruments affecting property whether the instrument requires a notice to be 'served' or requires a notice to be 'given' because there is no difference between 'serving' a notice and 'giving' a notice.[21]

7.16 However, sub-s (5) extends the operation of the Law of Property Act 1925, s 196 only to notices 'required' by an instrument affecting property to be served'. That contrasts with the reference in sub-ss (3)–(4) to notices 'required *or authorised*' by the Law of Property Act 1925 to be served. Nevertheless, s 196 probably applies to a notice to be served under an instrument which affords someone a *choice* over whether or not to serve a particular type of notice. In *Enfield LBC v Devonish*[22] a clause in a tenancy agreement provided that the tenancy could be terminated on not less than four weeks' written notice. Whilst not deciding the issue, Kennedy LJ said[23] that:

> '... I incline to the view that in reality the wording of [the tenancy] was sufficiently mandatory to come within the scope of s 196(5). It provided that if a tenancy was to be ended written notice as prescribed had to be given.'

7.17 Nevertheless, sub-s (5) will apply the Law of Property Act 1925, s 196 only if *an instrument affecting property* provides for the service of a particular type of notice. It does not, for example, operate to apply s 196 to notices that can be served under the common law or statute in relation to the interest created by such an instrument. In *Wandsworth LBC v Attwell*[24] it was held that a notice to quit was not 'required' to be served by a tenancy agreement which made no reference to the parties' right to determine the tenancy by serving such a notice. Waite LJ said[25] that the phrase 'notices required to be served by any instrument' provides,

> 'a plain indication that the subsection is only to apply in cases where the requirement of service is one that appears explicitly on the face of the instrument. Those words would not be apt to describe a case where the requirement of service is merely implied at common law, or is imported by statute, for example under s 5 of the Protection from Eviction Act 1977.'

---

[20]   Law of Property Act 1925, s 205(viii).
[21]   *Re 88 Berkeley Road* [1971] 1 Ch 648, per Plowman J at pp 652–3, *Holwell Securities Ltd v Hughes* [1974] 1 WLR 155, per Russell and Lawton LJJ at pp 158 and 161, and *Kinch v Bullard* [1999] 1 WLR 423, per Neuberger J at p 426.
[22]   (1996) 74 P&CR 288.
[23]   At p 294.
[24]   [1996] 1 EGLR 57.
[25]   At p 59.

The methods of service authorised by the Law of Property Act 1925, s 196

(i) Leaving the notice at the last-known place of abode or business in the United Kingdom of the person to be served

7.18 Subsection (3) of the Law of Property Act 1925, s 196 provides that a notice shall be sufficiently served 'if it is left at the last-known place of abode or business in the United Kingdom of the lessee, lessor, mortgagor, or other person to be served ...'.

7.19 The reference to the 'last-known' place of abode or business 'is designed to deal with a situation where the server is unaware of a change of address; in such a case a notice will be properly served if it is left at the last place of which the server knew to be the recipient's address'.[26] For the purposes of identifying the 'last known address', information known by an agent may sometimes be imputed to the server. For example, in *Arundel Corn v Khokher*[27] a notification to a landlord's solicitor of a change of the tenant's registered office was imputed to the landlord, even though the solicitor had forgotten that information and had failed to pass it on to the landlord, with the result that the landlord had served a rent review trigger notice at the previous registered office. That was on the ground that a principal is deemed to have knowledge of any fact that came to the attention of his agent in the course of a matter in which he was employed to act if the agent was under a duty to communicate that information back to the principal.

7.20 The Landlord and Tenant Act 1987, s 49 provides, in respect of a notice served by a tenant of residential premises on his landlord, that 'the last known place of abode or business' shall included a reference to: (i) the address last furnished to the tenant by the landlord in accordance with s 48 (being the address in England and Wales for the service of notices); or (ii) if no such address has been so furnished, the address last furnished to the tenant in accordance with s 47 (the landlord's name and address in a demand for rent or other sum).

7.21 It does not matter *how* the notice came to be 'left at' the last-known place of abode or business of the person to be served. In particular, there is no requirement that the server hand-deliver the notice to those premises. So a notice will be 'left at' premises if it is *posted* to those premises and, as a result, is delivered to the premises by the Post Office.[28]

---

[26] *Price v West London Investment Building Society Ltd* [1964] 1 WLR 616.
[27] [2003] EWCA Civ 1784.
[28] *Kinch v Bullard* [1999] 1 WLR 423, per Neuberger J at p 427 ('there is no suggestion that it matters how that service is effected, ie whether it is by the giver of the notice, his agent, courier service, ordinary post, recorded delivery, or some other method'). See also *Sharpley v Manby* [1942] 1 KB 217 (in relation to a similar provision in the

7.22   Nevertheless, to be 'left at' premises, a notice 'must be left there in a proper way; that is to say, in a manner that a reasonable person, minded to bring the document to the attention of the person to whom the notice is addressed, would adopt'.[29] A notice will be 'left at' the last-known place of abode of a person if it is left at the furthest point that a member of the public or postman can go to communicate to a tenant residing there. In *Henry Smith's Charity Trustees v Kyriakou*[30] it was held that it was sufficient that a notice had been posted through the letter-box of the front door of a building in which demised premises consisting of a bed-sitting-room were situated. A notice can also be 'left at' premises by entrusting it to a person present at the premises. In *Cannon Brewery Co v Signal Press Ltd*,[31] Humphreys J said that:[32]

> 'In my view, the expression "left for him" includes the case of a notice which is left in the hands of some person who is in fact on the premises, and in regard to whom there is reasonable ground for supposing that he or she will hand it to the lessee, if the lessee should be available for that purpose.'

Nevertheless, the learned judge added that:

> 'I do not say that there is necessarily a good service of a notice if it is left in the hands of a person who, to the knowledge of the parties, is a mere visitor to the premises and happens at the moment to be leaving the house.'[33]

7.23   A notice can obviously be 'left at the last known place of abode or business' of the recipient, and thereby validly served, even if it never comes to the attention of the recipient or his agent. In *Kinch v Bullard*[34] a husband and wife were beneficial joint tenants of the freehold of a house. The wife was terminally ill and she decided to sever the joint tenancy to ensure that her beneficial interest would not automatically vest in the husband when she died. The wife's solicitors duly sent a

---

Agricultural Holdings Act 1923, s 53) and *Stylo Shoes Ltd v Prices Tailors Ltd* [1960] 1 Ch 396 (in relation to a similar provision in the Landlord and Tenant Act 1927, s 23(1)).

[29]   See *Lord Newborough v Jones* [1975] 1 Ch 90, in relation to the Agricultural Holdings Act 1948, s 92 which enables notices to be served 'at [the recipient's] proper address', in which the notice was slipped under the door of the premises, but, according to the recipient, passed under some linoleum and did not come to the recipient's attention. In *Blunden v Frogmore Investments Ltd* [2002] EWCA Civ 573, [2002] L&TR 31, Robert Walker LJ said at p 513: 'If the landlord had deliberately concealed his notice under the linoleum in *Newborough v Jones*, he would not have left the notice at the tenant's house in a proper way ...'.

[30]   [1989] 2 EGLR 110.

[31]   (1929) 139 LT 384.

[32]   At p 385.

[33]   See also *Warborough Investment Ltd v Central Midlands Ltd* [2006] EWHC 2622 (Ch), [2007] L&TR 10 (in relation to a provision in a lease permitting notices to be 'left ... on the demised premises').

[34]   [1999] 1 WLR 423.

notice of severance, addressed to her husband, to the house by ordinary first class post. However, before the Post Office had delivered the notice, the husband had a heart attack and – given that it now appeared that her husband would predecease her – the wife no longer desired to sever the joint tenancy. So, when the postman put the notice through the letter box the wife destroyed the notice thereby ensuring that it never came to her husband's attention. Nevertheless, it was held that the notice had been properly served. The delivery of the notice to the property meant that – for the purposes of the Law of Property Act 1925, s 196 – the notice had been 'left at' the last-known place of abode of the husband.

7.24 A notice served in accordance with this method of service will be served at the time when it is 'left at' the last know place of place of abode or business of the person to be served.

(ii) Affixing or leaving a notice at demised or mortgaged premises, or the office or counting-house of a mine

7.25 Subsection (2) of the Law of Property Act 1925, s 196 provides that a notice shall be sufficiently served if,

> 'in the case of a notice required or authorised to be served on a lessee or mortgagor [it] is affixed or left for him on the land or any house or building comprised in the lease or mortgage, or, in the case of a mining lease, is left for the lessee at the office or counting-house of the mine.'

7.26 The case-law referred to above in relation to the notices 'left at' the last-known place of abode or business will be relevant when establishing whether a notice has been 'left for [the recipient] on the land or any house or building comprised in the lease or mortgage' or 'left for the lessee at the office or counting-house of the mine'. In *Blunden v Frogmore Investments Ltd*,[35] Robert Walker LJ said[36] that if a notice was put up at the premises for only a few minutes and then taken down again 'the court would have little difficulty in concluding that it had not been 'affixed' within the meaning of the statute, and that it was not good service'.

7.27 *Van Haarlam v Kasner*[37] illustrates how a notice can be validly served by this method of service even if the notice does not come to the attention of the recipient. A tenant of a residential flat was imprisoned for committing offences under the Official Secrets Act 1920. The landlord posted a 'section 146 notice' through the front door of the flat. Service was challenged by the tenant, who did not receive the notice in time to act upon it, on the ground that it was not a proper or reasonable

---

[35] [2002] EWCA Civ 573, [2002] L&TR 31.
[36] At p 513.
[37] (1992) 64 P&CR 214.

method of service to adopt given that the landlord knew that the tenant was in prison and that he had authorised solicitors to receive legal documents. Harman J said that:[38]

> 'In my judgment that is unarguably not correct. [The method of service was] perfectly lawful, it may not be very attractive but is perfectly lawful according to the letter of the law which is sufficiently complied with, to serve this notice by serving it through the doorway.'[39]

(iii) Sending the notice by registered post or recorded delivery

7.28 Subsection (4) of the Law of Property Act 1925, s 196 provides that a notice shall be sufficiently served,

> 'if it is sent by post in a registered letter addressed to the lessee, lessor, mortgagor, or other person to be served, by name, at the aforesaid place of abode or business, office, or counting-house, and if that letter is not returned by the postal operator (within the meaning of the Postal Services Act 2000) concerned undelivered; and that service shall be deemed to be made at the time at which the registered letter would in the ordinary course be delivered.'

7.29 Although sub-s (4) of the Law of Property Act 1925, s 196 refers to the sending of the notice by registered letter, a notice can also be served by sending it by recorded delivery. Section 1 of the Recorded Delivery Service Act 1962 provides that,

> 'any enactment which makes any ... provision in relation to the sending of a document or other thing by registered post or to a thing so sent shall have effect as if it made the like provision in relation to the sending of that thing by the recorded delivery service or as the case may be, to a thing sent by that service.'

The reference to the letter '... not [being] returned through the post office undelivered' refers to the ordinary case of the Post Office being unable to effect delivery at the address of the letter for some reason or other, such as that the addressee has gone away or the house is shut or empty. It does not cover a case where the Post Office delivers the notice at the address to which it was sent, but where, as it happens, the server of the notice signs to accept its receipt.[40]

7.30 *Re 88 Berkeley Road, NW9*[41] illustrates how this method of service may result in the valid service of a notice even if the notice does not come to the attention of the recipient. In that case, the beneficial

---

[38] At p 221.
[39] However, see paras **7.5–7.9** above.
[40] *Re 88 Berkeley Road* [1971] 1 Ch 648.
[41] [1971] 1 Ch 648.

interest of the freehold of a house was vested in Mrs Rickwood and Miss Goodwin as joint tenants. Miss Goodwin sent a notice of severance to the house by recorded delivery, addressed to Mrs Rickwood. However, when the notice was delivered, Mrs Goodwin signed for the notice and failed to pass the notice on to Mrs Rickwood. Nevertheless, it was held that the notice had been properly served.

7.31 Service of a notice under sub-s (4) of the Law of Property Act 1925, s 196 is 'deemed to be made at the time at which the registered letter would in the ordinary course be delivered'. The phrase 'in the ordinary course' means 'in the ordinary course of post'. In *WX Investment Ltd v Begg*[42] Patten J held that, given that effective service does not require the notice to have come to the recipient's attention, there was no requirement to establish evidence of a signed receipt and that, to make the presumption about the time of service an effective one, it is necessary to assume that an available recipient on the likely date of delivery.[43] In other words, sub-s (4) provides for a deemed date of delivery irrespective of when, or whether, the delivery was actually effected. The learned judge said that:[44]

'The date of such delivery is governed by what the court finds to have been the time when delivery in the ordinary course of post would take place, but this is judged by normal practice and expectations, not by the circumstances and whims of the addressee at the time.'

LANDLORD AND TENANT ACT 1927, S 23

7.32 The Landlord and Tenant Act 1927, s 23 provides that:

'(1) Any notice ... under this Act shall be in writing and may be served on the person on whom it is to be served either personally, or by leaving it for him at his last known place of abode in England and Wales, or by sending it through the post in a registered letter addressed to him there, or, in the case of a local or public authority or a statutory or a public utility company, to the secretary or other proper officer at the principal office of such authority or company, and in the case of a notice to the landlord, the person on whom it is to be served shall include any agent of the landlord duly authorised in that behalf.

(2) Unless or until a tenant of a holding shall have received notice that the person theretofore entitled to the rents and profits of the holding (hereinafter referred to as 'the original landlord') has ceased to be so entitled, and also notice of the name and address of the person who has become entitled to such rents and profits, any ... notice ... which the

---

[42] [2002] EWHC 925, [2002] 3 EGLR 47.
[43] The learned judge did not regard himself as bound by the contrary decision in *Stephenson v Orca Properties Ltd* [1989] 2 EGLR 129.
[44] At p 50.

tenant shall serve upon or deliver to the original landlord shall be deemed to have been served upon or delivered to the landlord of such holding.'

To what notices does the Landlord and Tenant Act 1927, s 23 apply?

7.33   The Landlord and Tenant Act 1927, s 23 applies to notices served under that Act. Importantly, it has also been incorporated into: (i) the Landlord and Tenant Act 1954, Parts I and II;[45] (ii) the Leasehold Reform Act 1967;[46] and (iii) the Landlord and Tenant (Covenants) Act 1995.[47] The reference to the 'person' to be served includes a company incorporated under the Companies Act.[48]

Methods of service authorised by the Landlord and Tenant Act 1927, s 23

(i) Personal service

7.34   The Landlord and Tenant Act 1927, s 23(1) provides that a notice 'may be served on the person on whom it is to be served ...personally'. It seems that this method of service precludes service on an agent and, for that reason, is confined to service on a natural person. In *Stylo Shoes Ltd v Prices Tailors Ltd*,[49] which concerned the service of a notice to quit on a business tenant, Wynn-Parry J said[50] that:

> 'As the plaintiffs are a company incorporated under the Companies Act 1929, the first method, namely, personal service, could not be effected.'

(ii) Leaving the notice at the recipient's last known place of abode in England and Wales

7.35   A notice '... may be served on the person on whom it is to be served ... by leaving it for [the recipient] at his last known place of abode in England and Wales ...'.

7.36   In *Price v West London Investment Building Society Ltd*[51] it was held that, for the purposes of the service of notices on business tenants

---

[45]   See LTA 1954, s 66(4).

[46]   See LRA 1967, 22(5), incorporating the Landlord and Tenant Act 1954, s 66(4) (by incorporating the Landlord and Tenant Act 1954, section 66(4)).

[47]   See LT(C)A 1995, s 27(5).

[48]   *Stylo Shoes Ltd v Prices Tailors Ltd* [1960] 1 Ch 396, per Wynn-Parry J at p 403.

[49]   [1960] 1 Ch 396.

[50]   At p 403.

[51]   [1964] 1 WLR 616. See also *Stylo Shoes Ltd v Prices Tailors Ltd* [1060] 1 Ch 396, per Wynn-Parry J at p 405, *Beanby Estates Ltd v Egg Stores (Stamford Hill) Ltd* [2003] EWHC 1252 (Ch) [2003] 1 WLR 2064, per Neuberger J at p 2066, and *Webber Ltd v Railtrack plc* [2003] EWCA Civ 1167, [2004] 1 WLR 320, per Peter Gibson LJ at p 324.

under the Landlord and Tenant Act 1954, Part II (Landlord and Tenant Act 1927, s 23(1) being incorporated into that Act by virtue of Landlord and Tenant Act 1954, s 66(4)),

> '[place of abode] must have a meaning wider than [a person's private residence], and the most sensible and natural meaning is not the residence of the person concerned, of which the landlords may very well be entirely ignorant, but the business address, which the landlords are much more likely to know and where for the purposes of the provisions of the Act the tenant is much more likely to be found.'[52]

In *Italica Holdings SA v Bayadea*,[53] which related to whether a landlord had served a notice under the Landlord and Tenant Act 1954, Part II, s 25 to terminate a tenancy, it was held that the tenant's hotel, which operated from the premises demised by a lease, was his 'last known place of abode in England and Wales'.

7.37 The reference to the 'last known' place of abode in England and Wales is designed to deal with the situation where the server is unaware of the change of address; in such a case a notice will be properly served if it is left at the last place of which the server knew to be the recipient's address.[54]

7.38 If this method of service is adopted, the notice must be left at the last-known place of abode in England and Wales, 'in a proper way; that is to say in a manner which a reasonable person, minded to bring the document to the attention of the person to whom the notice is addressed, would adopt'.[55] A notice will be 'left at' a place of abode if it is left at the furthest point that a member of the public or postman can go to communicate to a person residing there. In *Henry Smith's Charity Trustees v Kyriakou*,[56] in relation to a similar method of service authorised by the Law of Property Act 1925, s 196(3), it was held that it was sufficient that a notice had been posted through the letter-box of the front door of a building in which the demised premises, which consisted of a bed-sitting-room, were situated. Moreover, a notice may be 'left at' premises if it entrusted to a person present at those premises. In *Cannon Brewery Co v Signal Press Ltd*,[57] being another case on the Law of Property Act 1925, s 196(3) Humphreys J held that:[58]

---

[52]   Per Danckwerts LJ at p 622.
[53]   [1985] 1 EGLR 70.
[54]   *Price v West London Investment Building Society Ltd* [1964] 1 WLR 616, per Diplock LJ at p 623.
[55]   See *Lord Newborough v Jones* [1975] 1 Ch 90, a case concerning the Agricultural Holdings Act 1948, s 92(1) which enables notices served under that Act to be 'left at [the recipient's] proper address'.
[56]   [1989] 2 EGLR 110.
[57]   (1929) 139 LT 384.
[58]   At p 385.

'In my view, the expression "left for him" includes the case of a notice which is left in the hands of some person who is in fact on the premises, and in regard to whom there is reasonable ground for supposing that he or she will hand it to the lessee, if the lessee should be available for that purpose.'

7.39 It does not matter *how* the notice came to be 'left at' the last-known place of abode. In particular, there is no requirement that the notice be hand-delivered by the server and a notice will be properly served if the notice is posted by ordinary post and then delivered by the post office to the premises (see *Stylo Shoes Ltd v Prices Tailors Ltd*[59]). However, in *Rostron v Michael Nairn & Co Ltd*[60] it was held, in relation to a husband and wife who were joint tenants, that a notice served under the Landlord and Tenant Act 1954, s 25 to terminate a business tenancy had not be validly served on the wife under this provision by being sent by registered post in a letter addressed to her husband.

7.40 A notice may be validly served using this method of service even if the notice never comes to the attention of the recipient.[61] The time of service when this method of service is adopted will be the time that the notice is left at the premises.

(iii) Sending the notice by registered post or recorded delivery

7.41 A notice may be served,

'... by sending it through the post in a registered letter addressed to [the recipient at his last known place of abode in England and Wales], or, in the case of a local or public authority or a statutory or a public utility company, to the secretary or other proper officer at the principal office of such authority or company ....'

7.42 Although the Landlord and Tenant Act 1927, s 23(1) refers to the sending of the notice by registered post, the notice can also be sent by recorded delivery. The Recorded Delivery Service Act 1962, s 1 provides that,

'any enactment which makes any other provision in relation to the sending of a document or other thing by registered post or to a thing so sent shall

---

59   [1960] 1 Ch 396, per Wynn-Parry J at p 404-405. See also *Kinch v Bullard* [1999] 1 WLR 432, per Neuberger J at p 427 (in relation to the similar provision in the Law of Property Act 1925, s 196(3)), and *Sharpley Manby* [1942] 1 KB 217 (in relation to the similar provision in the Agricultural Holdings Act 1923, s 53).

60   [1962] EGD 284

61   See *Kinch v Bullard* [1999] 1 WLR 423 (concerning a similar provision in the Law of Property Act 1925, s 193(3)).

have effect as if it made the like provision in relation to the sending of that thing by the recorded delivery service or as the case may be, to a thing sent by that service.'

7.43 A 'statutory company' means 'any company constituted by or under an Act or Parliament to construct, work or carry on any tramway, hydraulic power, dock, canal or railway undertaking, whilst a 'public utility company' refers to,

> 'any company within the meaning of the Companies (Consolidation) Act 1908, or a society registered under the Industrial and Provident Societies Acts 1893 to 1913, carrying on any such undertaking.'[62]

7.44 A notice may be validly served using this method even if the notice does not come to the attention of the recipient. Indeed, a notice can be 'sent' by registered post or recorded delivery, and thereby validly served, even if the notice is lost in the post. Moreover, in contrast to service under the Law of Property Act 1925, s 196(4) (see above), a notice can be 'sent' by registered post or recorded delivery, and thereby validly served, even if it has been returned through the post undelivered (see *Chiswell v Griffon Land & Estates Ltd*,[63] *Italica Holdings SA v Bayadea*,[64] *Galinski v McHugh*,[65] *Railtrack v Gojra*,[66] *Commercial Union Life Assurance Co Ltd v Moustafa*,[67] *Blunden v Frogmore Investments Ltd*,[68] and *CA Webber Ltd v Railtrack plc*[69]).

7.45 Since effective service using this method does not depend upon receipt, service of a notice will be effected on the date on which the notice is *sent* by registered post or recorded delivery, rather than the date, if any, on which the notice was delivered to the premises.[70]

---

62 Section 25(1).
63 [1975] 1 WLR 1181, per Megaw LJ at pp 1188–9.
64 [1985] 1 EGLR 70, per French J at p 71.
65 (1989) 57 P&CR 354, per Slade LJ at p 365.
66 [1998] 1 EGLR 63, per Wilson J at p 65.
67 [1999] 2 EGLR 44.
68 [2002] EWCA Civ 573, [2002] L&TR 31.
69 [2003] EWCA Civ 1167, [2004] 1 WLR 320, per Peter Gibson LJ at p 333, in which the Court of Appeal rejected a submission that 'sending' through the post implied that some sort of onward transmission was required.
70 *Sun Alliance and London Assurance Co Ltd v Hayman* [1975] 1 WLR 177, per Stephenson LJ at p 183, *Railtrack v Gojra* [1998] 1 EGLR 63, per Wilson J at p 65, *Beanby Estates Ltd v Egg Stores (Stamford Hill) Ltd* [2003] 1 WLR 2064, *CA Webber Ltd v Railtrack plc* [2003] EWCA Civ 1167, [2004] 1 WLR 320. In *Price v West London Investment Building Society Ltd* [1964] 1 WLR 616, Dankwerts LJ was wrong to say, at p 623, that: 'It seems to me, therefore, that the giving of the notice was complete when the registered letter was taken in and signed for ...'.

(iv) Service upon the landlord's predecessor in title

7.46 By virtue of sub-s (2) of the Landlord and Tenant Act 1927, s 23 the application of which appears to be confined to notices served under that Act,[71] a tenant who serves a notice on his landlord's predecessor in title will be deemed to have served the notice upon his current landlord, unless the tenant has received: (i) notice that the original landlord has ceased to be entitled to the rents and profits of the holding; and (ii) notice of the name and address of the person who has become entitled to such rent and profits.

Methods of service not exhaustive

7.47 The fact that these methods of service are not exhaustive is confirmed by the fact that, whilst a notice served under the Landlord and Tenant Act 1927 *shall* be in writing, it *may* be served by one of the three methods set out in s 23(1). Accordingly, a notice authorised to be served under Landlord and Tenant Act 1927, s 23(1) may be properly served if, instead of adopting one of those methods of service, the server adopts an alternative method of service permitted at common law or by some other statutory provision.[72]

Service on the agent of a tenant

7.48 In *Galinski v McHugh*[73] it was held that the fact that Landlord and Tenant Act 1927, s 23(1) expressly authorises service on a duly authorised agent of a landlord does not – by implication – preclude service on the properly authorised agent of a tenant. Slade LJ said[74] that:

> 'Whilst this must be a matter for speculation, we can think of certain reasons why Parliament, in drafting section 23(1), might have chosen to make express reference to service by the tenant upon the landlord's duly authorised agent and not vice versa. Landlords are more likely to have agents than tenants. Furthermore, in many cases the tenant may be more accustomed to deal with the landlord's agent than with the landlord himself. It appears to us by no means improbable that in extending the "deemed service" provisions of section 23(1) to the duly authorised agent of a landlord, the legislature regarded as similar extension to the agent of a tenant as simply unnecessary. Be this as it may ... we are of the opinion that this omission does not operate to render actual service on the duly authorised agent of a tenant invalid service on the tenant.'

---

[71]   Save where s 23 is incorporated into other statutes or contracts (see above).

[72]   *Stylo Shoes Ltd v Prices Tailors Ltd* [1960] 1 Ch 396, per Wynn-Parry J at pp 405–6, and *Galinski v McHugh* (1988) 57 P&CR 359, per Slade LJ at pp 364–5.

[73]   (1988) 57 P&CR 359.

[74]   At pp 367–8.

The relationship between the Landlord and Tenant Act 1927, s 23(1) and the Interpretation Act 1978, s 7

7.49   The Interpretation Act 1978, s 7 provides that:

'Where an Act authorises or requires any document to be served by post (whether the expression "serve" or the expression "give" or "send" or any other expression is used) then, unless the contrary intention appears, the service is deemed to be effected by properly addressing, pre-paying and posting a letter containing the document and, unless the contrary is proved, to have been effected at the time at which the letter would have been delivered in the ordinary course of post.'

7.50   In *Commercial Union Life Assurance Co Ltd v Moustafa*,[75] *Beanby Estates Ltd v Egg Stores (Stamford Hill) Ltd*[76] and *CA Webber Ltd v Railtrack plc*[77] it was held that the Interpretation Act 1978, s 7 does not apply to a case where service is authorised under the Landlord and Tenant Act 1927, s 23(1). Where s 23(1) applies a 'contrary intention appears' so as to dis-apply the Interpretation Act 1978, s 7. In *Lex Services plc v Johns*[78] the Court of Appeal were wrong to proceed on the basis of the contrary assumption.

THE AGRICULTURAL HOLDINGS ACT 1986, S 93

7.51   The Agricultural Holdings Act 1986, s 93 provides that:

'(1) Any notice, request, demand or other instrument under this Act shall be duly given to or served on the person to whom it is to be given or served if it is delivered to him, or left at his proper address, or sent to him by post in a registered letter or by the recorded delivery service.

(2) Any such instrument shall be duly given to or served on an incorporated company or body if it is given or served on the secretary or clerk of the company or body.

(3) Any such instrument to be given to or served on a landlord or tenant shall, where an agent or servant is responsible for the control of the management or farming, as the case may be, of the agricultural holding, be duly given or served if given to or served on the servant or agent.

(4) For the purposes of this section and of section 7 of the Interpretation Act 1978 (service by post), the proper address of any person to or on whom any such instrument is to be given or served shall, in the case of the secretary or clerk of an incorporated company or body, be that of the

---

[75]   [1999] 2 EGLR 44.
[76]   [2003] EWHC 1252, [2003] 1 WLR 2064.
[77]   [2003] EWCA Civ 1167, [2004] 1 WLR 320.
[78]   [1990] 1 EGLR 92, [1990] 10 EG 67.

registered or principal office of the company or body, and in any other case be the last known address of the person in question.

(5) Unless or until the tenant of an agricultural holding has received –

(a)   notice that the person who before that time was entitled to receive the rents and profits of the holding ("the original landlord") has ceased to be so entitled, and

(b)   notice of the name and address of the person who has become entitled to receive the rents and profits,

any notice or other document served upon or delivered to the original landlord by the tenant shall be deemed for the purposes of this Act to have been served upon or delivered to the landlord of the holding.'

Methods of service authorised by the Agricultural Holdings Act 1986, s 93

7.52   The Agricultural Holdings Act 1986, s 93, which applies to any notice served under that Act,[79] authorises the methods of service set out below. Those methods of service, which do not require the recipient to have actually received the notice,[80] are not exhaustive. Accordingly, it remains possible to serve a notice under the Agricultural Holdings Act 1986 by adopting a method of service authorised by the common law or by a contract.

(i) Delivering the notice to the recipient

7.53   Subsection (1) of the Agricultural Holdings Act 1986, s 93 provides that a notice 'shall be duly given to or served on the person to or on whom it is to be given or served if it is delivered to him ...'. This appears to be a reference to delivery to the recipient personally, rather than to his agent. A notice would be 'delivered to' the recipient if it was physically handed to him or, if the recipient refused to take the notice, if it was identified as a notice and left in his presence.

(ii) Leaving the notice at the recipient's proper address

7.54   Service will be effected if a notice is 'left at [the recipient's] proper address',[81] namely,

'in the case of the secretary or clerk of an incorporated company or body,... the registered or principal office of the company or body, and in any other case ... the last known address of the person in question'.[82]

---

[79]   AHA 1986, s 93(1).
[80]   *Newborough (Lord) v Jones* [1975] 1 Ch 90.
[81]   See sub-s (1).
[82]   See sub-s (4).

The entitlement to serve a notice at 'the last known' address is designed to deal with a situation where the server is unaware of a change of address; in such a case a notice will be properly served is left at the last place of which the server knew to be the recipient's address.[83] The address can probably be either a home address or a business address.[84]

7.55 It does not matter *how* the notice came to be 'left at' the recipient's 'proper address'. In particular, this method of service does not impose a requirement that the server hand-deliver the notice to the recipient's proper address, and so a notice would be 'left at' those premises if it was, for example, posted by ordinary post to those premises, and, as a result, delivered to the premises by the post office.[85]

7.56 In *Newborough (Lord) v Jones*[86] a landlord visited his tenant's farmhouse to serve a notice to quit. He knocked on the door that was most often used by the tenant but received no answer. There was no slit or letterbox in the door and so the landlord slipped the notice under the bottom of that door. However, the notice slipped under the linoleum and did not come to the attention of the tenant. The tenant contended that the notice had not been served on the ground that a notice is only 'left at' the recipient's address if, as a fact, it is left in a place which makes the notice likely to be observable. The Court of Appeal rejected that submission and held that the notice had been properly served. Russell LJ said[87] that:

> 'I have formed the view that, the subject matter being a notice, it is implicit in the provisions of section 92 that, if served by leaving at the proper address of the person to be served, it must be left there is a proper way; that is to say, in a manner which a reasonable person, minded to bring the document to the attention of the person to whom the notice is addressed, would adopt. That is, to my mind, the only qualification (or gloss, if you please) properly to be placed on the express language of the statutory provision).

---

[83] *Price v West London Investment Building Society Ltd* [1964] 1 WLR 616, per Diplock LJ at p 623 (in relation to a similar provision in the Landlord and Tenant Act 1927, s 23).

[84] In *Price v West London Investment Building Society Ltd* [1964] 1 WLR 616 it was held that 'place of abode', for the purposes of the Landlord and Tenant Act 1927, s 23(1) as incorporated into Part II of the Landlord and Tenant Act 1954 by s 66(4) of that Act, was capable of referring either to a person's home address or to his business address.

[85] See *Sharpley v Manby* [1942] 1 KB 217 (in relation to a similar provision in the Agricultural Holdings Act 1923, s 53), *Kinch v Bullard* [1999] 1 WLR 423 (in relation to a similar provision in the Law of Property Act 1925, s 196(3)), and *Stylo Shoes Ltd v Prices Tailors Ltd* [1960] 1 Ch 396 (in relation to a similar provision in the Landlord and Tenant Act 1927, s 23(1)).

[86] [1975] 1 Ch 90.

[87] At p 94.

In the present case it is quite impossible to say that the action of the landlord in putting the notice under the door was other than leaving it at the proper address in a manner which a reasonable person, minded to bring the document to the attention of the tenant would adopt. Consequently, it appears to me that [the notice was properly served].'

7.57 A notice will be 'left at' the proper address, if that address is a residential address, if it is left at the furthest point that a member of the public or a postman can go to communicate to a person living there.[88] A notice can be served using this method if the notice is entrusted with a person present at the premises so long as 'there is reasonable ground for supposing that he or she will hand it to the [recipient], if the [recipient] should be available for that purpose'.[89]

(iii) Sending the notice to the recipient by post in a registered letter or by the recorded delivery service

7.58 A notice will be validly served if it is 'sent to [the recipient] by post in a registered letter or by the recorded delivery service'.[90] In *Hallinan (Lady) v Jones*[91] it was held by Mr Peter Langdon-Davies, sitting as an Assistant Recorder at Aberystwyth county court, that a notice sent by registered post or recorded delivery, but returned to the server undelivered, had not been served. That was on the ground that the following provision, namely the Interpretation Act 1978, s 7 applies to a notice served by registered post or recorded delivery under the Agricultural Holdings Act 1986, s 93(1):

'Where an Act authorises or requires any document to be served by post (whether the expression "serve" or the expression "give" or "send" or any other expression is used) then, unless the contrary intention appears, the service is deemed to be effected by properly addressing,[92] pre-paying and posting a letter containing a document and, unless the contrary is proved, to have been effected at the time at which the letter would be delivered in the ordinary course of post.'

7.59 In respect of the Landlord and Tenant Act 1927, s 23(1) which enables a notice to be served 'by sending [the notice] though the post in a

---

[88]   *Henry Smith's Charity Trustees v Kyriakou* [1989] 2 EGLR 110 (in relation to a similar provision in the Law of Property Act 1925, s 196).

[89]   *Cannon Brewery Co v Signal Press Ltd* (1929) 139 LT 384, per Humphreys J at p 385 (in relation to a similar provision in the Law of Property Act 1925, s 193(3)). See also *Warborough Investment Ltd v Central Midlands Estates Ltd* [2006] EWHC 2622 (Ch), [2007] L&TR 10 (in relation to a provision in a lease permitting notices to be 'left … on the demised premises').

[90]   Subsection (1).

[91]   [1984] 2 EGLR 20.

[92]   Pursuant to the Agricultural Holdings Act 1986, s 93(4) this refers to 'in the case of the secretary or clerk of an incorporated company or body,… that of the registered or principal office of the company or body, and in any other case … the last known address of the person in question.'

registered letter', it has been held that, by permitting that method of service, 'a contrary intention appears' so as to dis-apply the Interpretation Act 1978, s 7.[93] However, sub-s (4) of the Agricultural Holdings Act 1986, s 93 defines 'the proper address' for the purposes of *both* the Agricultural Holdings Act 1986, s 93 and the Interpretation Act 1978, s 7. That is a clear indication that the Interpretation Act 1978, s 7 was intended to apply to notices served by registered post or recorded delivery under sub-s (1). Subsection (4) must be referring to notices served under the Agricultural Holdings Act 1986 to which the Interpretation Act 1978, s 7 applies and that can only be reference to notices served by registered post or recorded delivery under sub-s (1). In *Beanby Estates Ltd v Egg Stores (Stamford Hill) Ltd*,[94] Neuberger J said[95] that:

> 'I do not consider that the mere fact that a statute requires or permits service of, sending, or giving a notice or other document without any reference to posting brings it within s 7.'

7.60 The consequence of the application of the Interpretation Act 1978, s 7 in relation to notices served under the Agricultural Holdings Act 1986, s 93 by registered post or recorded delivery is that it is open to the recipient, *if the notice is required to be served by a certain time*, to dispute service on the ground that the notice was not received in time or at all. That follows from the Court of Appeal's decision in *R v County of London Quarter Sessions Appeal Committee, ex p Rossi*,[96] in which Parker LJ said that:[97]

> '[The Interpretation Act 1978, s 7], it will be seen, is in two parts. The first part provides that the dispatch of a notice or other document in the manner laid down shall be deemed to be service thereof. The second part provides that, unless the contrary is proved, that service is effected on the day when in the ordinary course of post the document would be delivered. This second part, therefore, dealing as it does with delivery, comes into play, and only comes into play, in a case where under the legislation to which the section is being applied the document has to be received by a certain time. If in such a case 'the contrary is proved', ie that the document was not received by that time or at all, then the position appears to be that, though under the first part of the section the document is deemed to have been served, it has been proved that it was not served in time.'

---

[93] *Commercial Union Life Assurance Co Ltd v Moustfa* [1999] 2 EGLR 44, *Beanby Estates Ltd v Egg Stores (Stamford Hill) Ltd* [2003] EWCA 1252, [2003] 1 WLR 2064, and *CA Webber Ltd v Railtrack plc* [2003] EWCA Civ 1167, [2004] 1 WLR 320. *Lex Services plc v Johns* [1990] 1 EGLR 92 was incorrectly decided in so far as it held the contrary.
[94] [2003] 1 WLR 2064.
[95] At p 207.
[96] [1956] 1 All ER 670.
[97] At p 681.

7.61   In *Lex Services plc v Johns*,[98] which – it should be noted – has been held to have been wrongly decided insofar as it held that Interpretation Act 1978, s 7 applied to notices served under the Landlord and Tenant Act 1927, s 23 Glidewell LJ said[99] that:

> 'In my judgment, what for this purpose is necessary to prove the contrary ... if it be sent by registered or recorded delivery post [is] that there is no acknowledgement or its ever having been received by the recipient. If there was some evidence of such a document having been received by some person but it were proved that that person was not the person upon whom the document was required to be served and that the person who received the document had not brought it to the attention of the person upon whom it was required to be served, then that, I would accept, would prove that the document had not been properly served. But in the absence of such evidence then, in my judgment, the contrary is not proved. In other words, the statutory provisions are there to entitle those who have to serve documents by taking the steps laid down by the statute, unless the document is returned to them, to be satisfied that service has been effected. It is not sufficient thereafter for the person upon whom service is required to be made to assert that the document has not been served upon him, albeit somebody has acknowledged receipt of the document required to be served.'

7.62   However, in that same case, Balcombe LJ said at p 95 that,

> '... for my part, I would be reluctant to go wider than *Rossi* and would simply say that in a case where time is relevant ... then the contrary may be proved ... It is not sufficient for [the recipient] merely to deny having received the letter. If it were otherwise, the very convenient provisions enabling service in so many cases to be effected by one form of post or another, or by leaving at the person's last known place of abode, would be rendered nugatory, because anyone could always say "I did not receive this notice" and thus raise a triable issue.'

Service on agents and servants

7.63   The Agricultural Holdings Act 1986, s 93 contains two provisions relating to service on an agent or servant of the recipient. First, a notice is to be treated as having been properly served on an incorporated company or body if it is given or served on the secretary or clerk of the company or body.[100] Secondly, where a notice is to be served on a landlord or tenant and an agent or servant is responsible for the control of the management or farming, the notice can be served on that agent or

---

[98]   [1990] 1 EGLR 92, [1990] 10 EG 67.
[99]   At p 95.
[100]   Subsection (2).

servant.[101] In either event, the server would be entitled to adopt the methods of service identified in sub-s (1).

Change of landlord

7.64 A notice is deemed to have been validly served on a landlord, even if it has – in fact – been served on the landlord's predecessor in title, unless the tenant of an agricultural holding has received notice: (i) that the person who before that time was entitled to receive the rents and profits of the holding has ceased to be so entitled; and (ii) notice of the name and address of the person who has become entitled to receive the rents and profits.[102]

AGRICULTURAL TENANCIES ACT 1995, S 36

7.65 The Agricultural Tenancies Act 1995, s 36 provides as follows:

'(1) This section applies to any notice or other document required or authorised to be given under this Act.

(2) A notice or other document to which this section applies is duly given to a person if-

(a)   it is delivered to him,
(b)   it is left at his proper address, or
(c)   it is given to him in a manner authorised by a written agreement made, at any time before the giving of the notice, between him and the person giving the notice.

(3) A notice or other document to which this section applies is not duly given to a person if its text is transmitted to him by facsimile or other electronic means otherwise than by virtue of subsection (2)(a) above.

(4) Where a notice or other document to which this section applies is to be given to a body corporate, the notice or document is duly given if it is given to the secretary or clerk of that body.

(5) Where –

(a)   a notice or other document to which this section applies is to be given to a landlord under a farm business tenancy and an agent or servant of his is responsible for the control of the management of the holding, or

---

[101]   In contrast to the position where a notice is served under the common law, there is no need for the agent or servant to be authorised to receive notices of the type that is to be served.

[102]   Subsection (5).

(b)   such a document is to be given to a tenant under a farm business tenancy and an agent or servant of his is responsible for the carrying on of a business on the holding,

the notice or document is duly given if it if given to that agent or servant if it is given to that agent or servant.

(6) For the purpose of this section, the proper address of any person to whom a notice is given is:

(a)   in the case of the secretary or clerk of a body corporate, the registered or principal office of that body, and
(b)   in any other case, the last known address of the person in question.

(7) Unless or until the tenant under a farm business tenancy has received-

(a)   notice that the person who before that time was entitled to receive the rents and profits of the holding ('the original landlord') has ceased to be so entitled, and
(b)   notice of the name and address of the person who has become entitled to receive the rents and profits,

any notice or other document given to the original landlord by the tenant shall be deemed for the purposes of this Act to have been given to the landlord under the tenancy.'

Methods of service authorised by the Agricultural Tenancies Act 1995, s 36

7.66   This provision, which applies to any notice required or authorised to be given under the Agricultural Tenancies Act 1995,[103] reproduces the Agricultural Holdings Act 1986, s 93 (see above) but with the following two substantive changes.

7.67   First, sending the notice to the recipient by post in a registered letter or by recorded delivery service is omitted as an authorised method of service. In its place, sub-s (2) of the Agricultural Tenancies Act 1995, s 95 provides that a notice is duly given to a person if it,

'is given to him in a manner authorised by a written agreement made, at any time before the giving of the notice, between him and the person giving the notice.'

Secondly, sub-s (3) provides that, unless authorised by an agreement between the parties complying with sub-s (2)(c), a notice is not duly given to a person if its text is transmitted to him by facsimile or other electronic means.

---

[103]   Subsection (1).

COMPANIES ACT 2006

7.68 The Companies Act 2006, s 1144, and Sch 4, Part 2 permit documents, including notices[104], to be validly supplied in hard copy form[105] by hand or by posting a prepaid envelope containing the document[106] to:

- an address specified by the company for that purpose;

- the company's registered office;

- an address to which any provision of the Companies Acts authorises the document to be sent or supplied.[107]

7.69 The Companies Act 2006, Sch 4, Part 3 permits documents, including notices,[108] to be validly supplied to a company in electronic form (eg by email or fax or by sending a disk by post[109]) if the company had agreed (generally or specifically) that the document may be sent in that form, or if the company is deemed to have so agreed by a provision in the Companies Acts. Where a document is supplied by electronic means,[110] it may only be supplied to an address specified for the purpose by the company (generally or specifically), or deemed by a provision in the Companies Acts to have been so supplied.[111] Where a document is supplied in electronic form by hand or by post, it must be supplied to an address to which it could be validly sent if it were in hard copy form.[112]

OTHER STATUTES

7.70 Other statutes provide for rules relating to the service of notices. In particular, the Housing Act 1985,[113] the Landlord and Tenant Act 1987,[114] the Leasehold Reform, Housing and Urban Development

---

[104] Section 1148(1).
[105] Ie sent or supplied in a paper copy or similar form capable of being read (see s 1168(2)).
[106] Schedule 4, para 3(2).
[107] Schedule 4, para 4.
[108] Section 1148(1).
[109] Section 1168(4).
[110] 'A document ... is sent ... by electronic means if it is – (a) sent initially and received at its destination by means of electronic equipment for the processing (which expression includes digital compression) or storage of data, and(b) entirely transmitted, conveyed and received by wire, by radio, by optical means or by other electromagnetic means' (see s 1168(4)).
[111] Schedule 4, para 7(1).
[112] Schedule 4, para 7(2).
[113] See s 176(2) and (3).
[114] See s 54(2).

Act 1993,[115] and the Commonhold and Leasehold Reform Act 2002[116] provide that notices can be 'sent by post'. Whilst the Party Wall Act 1996, s 15(1) provides that:

> 'A notice ... required or authorised to be served under this Act may be served on a person –
>
> (a)   by delivering it to him in person;
> (b)   by sending it by post to him at his usual or last-known residence or place of business in the United Kingdom; or
> (c)   in the case of a body corporate, by delivering it to the secretary or clerk of the body corporate at its registered or principal office or sending it by post to the secretary or clear of that body corporate at that office.'

---

[115]   See s 99(1).
[116]   See s 111(1).

Appendix 1

DIRECTORY OF AUTHORITIES ABOUT PROPERTY NOTICES REFERRED TO IN THE TEXT

COMMON LAW PROPERTY NOTICES (OTHER THAN LANDLORD AND TENANT NOTICES)

Notices to complete

Woods v Mackenzie Hill Ltd [1975] 1 WLR 613

A notice to complete was invalid because it had been served by only one of two vendors.

Tennaro Ltd v Majorarch Ltd [2003] EWHC 2601 (Ch), [2003] 47 EG 154 (CS)

A purchaser failed to establish that it had given 'written notification' to complete.

Notices of incumbrance

Saffron Walden Second Benefit Building Society v Rayner (1880) 14 ChD 406

Solicitors instructed by trustees of a testator's estate were not authorised to receive notice of a mortgage of a reversionary share in the testator's estate.

Notices exercising options

Dibbins v Dibbins [1896] 2 Ch 348

A notice purporting to exercise an option, that had been served by a person with no authority to do so, could not be retrospectively ratified by person entitled to exercise the option.

Holwell Securities Ltd v Hughes [1974] 1 WLR 155

A notice exercising an option was not validly served, even though it was received by the recipient's solicitors, who notified the recipient by telephone that they had received the notice.

New Hart Builders Ltd v Brindley [1975] 1 Ch 342

A notice to renew an option was, as a result of the Law of Property Act 1925, s 196(1) and (5), required to be in writing.

Yates Building Company Ltd v Pulleyn & Sons (York) Ltd [1976] 1 EGLR 158

A notice exercising an option was validly served by posting the notice to the recipient even though the agreement containing the option provided that a notice exercising the option was 'to be sent by registered or recorded delivery post to the registered office of [the vendor] or the offices of their said solicitors'.

Westway Homes Ltd v Moores [1991] 2 EGLR 193

A notice exercising an option was valid even though it was headed 'subject to contract' and had been served on the vendor's solicitors.

Taylor v Crotty [2006] EWCA Civ 1364

An option capable of being exercised on three months' notice was validly exercised by a notice stating that the server 'wish to exercise the option' without specifying the date of the expiry of the notice.

Rennie v Wesbury Homes (Holdings) Ltd [2007] EWCA Civ 1401

A letter was held to be a valid notice to extend the period for exercising an option.

Notices determining licences

Australian Blue Metal Ltd v Hughes [1963] AC 74

A notice to determine a licence, that could be brought to an end on reasonable notice, was not invalid on the ground that it failed to identify the date on which it would expire.

Allam & Co Ltd v Europa Poster Services Ltd [1968] 1 All ER 826

A notice to determine a licence was valid even though it had been served by a sub-agent.

COMMON LAW LANDLORD AND TENANT NOTICES

Break notices

Right v Cuthell (1804) 5 East 491

A landlord's break notice was invalid because it had not been served by all of the joint landlords.

Hogg v Brooks (1885) 15 QB 256

Following the disappearance of the lessee, a break notice was not validly served by a landlord by sending it to the lessee's last-known address or to the demised premises.

Re Viola's Indenture of Lease, Humphrey v Stenbury [1909] 1 Ch 244

A break notice was invalid on the ground that it had been served by only one of two joint tenants.

Stait v Fenner [1912] 2 Ch 504

A break notice was invalid because it had not been served by the person in whom the legal estate of the tenancy was vested.

Re Knight and Hubbard's Underlease [1923] 1 Ch 130

A break notice was valid even though it had been served in the name of the lessor's agent.

Hankey v Clavering [1942] 2 KB 326

A break notice was invalid because it had misidentified the date on which the lease could be brought to an end.

Allam & Co Ltd v Europa Posters Services Ltd [1968] 1 All ER 826

A licensor's break notice was held to be valid which required the tenant 'to cease occupation ...at the earliest date after the service of this notice that [the license] can lawfully be terminated'.

National Westminster Bank Ltd v Betchworth Investments Ltd [1975] 1 EGLR 57

A break notice was validly served, pursuant to a provision in the lease permitting service of notices at the tenant's 'last known address', by posting the notice to an address that had ceased to exist because the building in which it was situated had been demolished.

Keith Bayley Rogers & Co v Cubes Ltd (1976) 31 P&CR 412

A break notice was validly served 'without prejudice' to an earlier break notice.

Townsends Carriers Ltd v Pfizer Ltd (1977) 33 P&CR 361

Where a landlord and a tenant, expressly or by implication, left the conduct and management of the reversion and of the tenancy to their agents, matters dealt with by the agents between them would be as validly done as if they were done between the landlord and tenant themselves.

Manorlike Ltd v le Vitas Travel Agency and Consultancy Services Ltd [1986] 1 All ER 573

A lease which could be terminated on 'not less than 3 months' previous notice in writing' was determined by a break notice requiring the tenant to vacate the premises 'within a period of three months from the date of service of the notice'.

Peel Developments (South) Ltd v Siemens plc [1992] 2 EGLR 85

A break notice was valid even though it misidentified the date on which the lease could be determined and it was addressed to the landlord's agents.

Hounslow London Borough Council v Pilling [1993] 1 WLR 1242

A break notice was invalid because it had been served by only one of the two joint tenants.

Mannai Investment Co Ltd v Eagle Star Assurance Co Ltd [1997] AC 749

Break notices were held to be valid even though they had mis-identified the date on which the lease could be brought to an end.

Dun & Bradstreet Software Services (England) Ltd v Provident Mutual Life Assurance Association [1998] 2 EGLR 175

A landlord was estopped from disputing the validity of break notices on the ground that the notices been served by the tenant's parent company given that the landlord had given an unequivocal assurance to the tenant that the notices were acceptable.

Garston v Scottish Widows' Fund [1998] 1 WLR 1583

A break notice was valid even though it incorrectly identified the date upon which the lease would determine.

Lemmerbell Ltd v Britannia LAS Direct Ltd [1998] 3 EGLR 67

A break notice was invalid because it was stated to have been served by a company that was not the tenant.

Havant International Holdings v Lionsgate (H) Investment [2000] 2 L&TR 297

A break notice, which was purportedly served under a right that was personal to the tenant, was held to be valid even though it was expressed to be served by a company that was not the tenant.

Brown & Root Technology Ltd v Sun Alliance [2001] Ch 733

Between the completion of the assignment of a lease and the registration of the assignee as the lessee a break notice was validly served by the assignor.

Blunden v Frogmore Investments Ltd [2002] EWCA Civ 573, [2002] L&TR 31

A break notice was validly served by attaching it to demised premises that had been damaged by a bomb even though the tenant had been required to vacate the premises and so there was no prospect that the notice would come to the tenant's attention.

Trafford MBC v Total Fitness (UK) Ltd [2002] EWCA Civ 1513, [2003] 2 P&CR 2

A break notice was valid notwithstanding an internal inconsistency.

Procter & Gamble Technical Centres Ltd v Brixton plc [2003] 2 EGLR 24

A tenant's break notice was invalid on the ground that it was expressed to be served by a company that was not, in fact, the tenant.

Royal Bank of Canada v Secretary of State for Defence [2003] EWCA Civ 7982, [2004] 1 P&CR 28

A break notice was validly served without prejudice to an earlier notice.

Peer Freeholds Ltd v Clean Wash International Ltd [2005] EWHC 179 (Ch), [2005] 1 EGLR 47

A tenant's break notice, expressed to expire on 22 August 2004, was held to have validly exercised a right to determine the lease on 7 November 2004.

Disrepair notice

Hughes v Metropolitan Railway Co [1887] 2 App Cas 439

The operation of a landlord's notice requiring the tenant to repair demised premises was suspended when the tenant – with the concurrence of the landlord – postponed the repair works during negotiations for the surrender of the lease.

Notice to quit

Doe d Cox v Roe (1803) 3 Esp 185

A notice to quit served in respect of demised premises consisting of a public house called *The Bricklayer's Arms* was valid even though it was stated to refer to 'the premises which you hold of me ... commonly called or known by the name of *The Waterman's Arms*'.

Doe d Macartney v Crick (1805) 5 Esp 196

A notice to quit can be given orally.

Doe d Aslin v Summersett (1830) 1 B&Ad 135

A notice to quit served by one of two joint tenants was valid.

Rees d mears v Perrot (1830) 4 C&P 230

After the tenant's death a notice to quit was validly served on his widow, who had remained in possession.

Doe d Kindersley v Hughes (1840) 7 M&W 139

A notice to quit was valid even though it had not been served by all of the joint tenants.

Alford v Vickery (1842) Car & M 280

A notice to quit was valid even though it had not been served by all of the joint tenants.

Bird v Defonville (1846) 2 C&K 415

A notice to quit can be given orally.

Doe v Timothy (1847) 2 Car & K 351

A notice to quit was valid which was stated to expire 'at the expiration of the present year's tenancy'.

Pearse v Boulton (1860) 2 F&F 133

A person who, on behalf of the landlord, was entrusted to collect the rent was not authorised to accept service from the tenant of a notice to quit.

Tayleur v Wildin (1868) LR 3 Exch 303

An agreement between the landlord and tenant for the withdrawal of a notice to quit results in the creation of a new tenancy.

Jones v Phipps (1868) LR 3 QB 567

A notice to quit was valid even though it had been served by an agent in his own name.

Tanham v Nicholson (1871) LR 5 HL 561

A notice to quit was validly served on the daughter of a tenant even though the daughter did not pass the notice on to the tenant (who was mentally incapable).

Sidebotham v Holland [1895] 1 QB 378

A notice to quit was valid which stated that it expired on the anniversary of the commencement of the term.

London School Board v Peters (1902) 18 TLR 509

Service on a servant was effective.

Wordsley Brewery Co v Halford (1903) 90 LT 89

A notice to quit was invalid because it had been served after the grant by the landlord of a concurrent tenancy which had operated as an assignment of the term for the duration of the concurrent term.

May v Borup [1915] 1 KB 830

A notice to quit was valid even though it was stated to expire 'at the earliest possible moment' and it stated that, in specified circumstances, it would be cancelled.

Norfolk County Council v Child [1918] 2 KB 805

A notice to quit served by a landlord was valid even though it was sent under cover of a letter which stated that the notice was intended to terminate the tenancy on a specified date 'unless [the landlord] see sufficient reason in the meantime to change [its] mind'.

Phipps and Coy (Northampton and Towcester Breweries) Ltd v Rogers [1925] 1 KB 14

A tenancy which could be brought to an end by three months' notice to quit to expire 'on any one of the days appointed as special transfer sessions by the justices for the district in which the premises are situate' was not determined by a notice to quit 'on the earliest day on which your tenancy can be brought to an end'.

Farrow v Orttewell [1933] 1 Ch 480

An assignee of a landlord's interest, who had served a notice to quit before completion, was estopped from disputing the validity of the notice to quit because the tenant had relied upon that notice by vacating the demised premises and selling his stock.

Hawtrey v Beaufront Ltd [1946] 1 KB 280

A notice to quit was valid even though it had been addressed to the directors of the tenant company.

Re Swanson's Agreement, Hill v Swanson [1946] 2 All ER 628

A tenant was estopped from disputing the validity of a notice to quit on the ground that it was expressed to expire on a date before which the tenancy could be brought to an end because she should be taken to have represented that she would act on the basis that the notice had not contained the error.

Lemon v Lardeur [1946] 1 KB 613

A notice to quit was invalid because it was stated to have been served by the landlord's husband.

W Davis (Spitalfields) Ltd v Huntley [1947] 1 All ER 246

A notice to quit was valid that stated that 'we must give three months' notice to terminate the lease' without identifying the date of the expiry of the notice.

Thompson v McCullough [1947] 1 KB 447

A notice to quit served by an assignee of the landlord's freehold interest was invalid because it was served before completion of the assignment and the vesting of the legal estate in the assignee.

Lowenthal v Vanhoute [1947] 1 KB 342

A landlord had not waived his entitlement to contend that a notice to quit had determined a tenancy by serving a second notice to quit.

Addis v Burrows [1948] 1 All ER 177

A notice to quit was valid which was stated to expire 'after the end of one half year from the service of the notice'.

Harrowby (Earl) v Snelson [1951] 1 All ER 140

A notice to quit was validly served on the widow of the deceased tenant, who was in possession, even though, because the tenant had died intestate, the tenancy had vested in the President of the Probate, Divorce and Admiralty Division.

Egerton v Rutter [1951] 1 KB 472

A notice to quit was validly served on a son and daughter of the deceased tenant, who were in possession, even though, because the tenant had died intestate, the tenancy had vested in the President of the Probate, Divorce and Admiralty Division.

Chez Auguste v Cottat [1951] 1 KB 292

A notice 'to quit and deliver up possession of ... the premises ... on Monday, October 3, 1949 or at the expiration of the current period of your tenancy, which shall expire next after the service upon you of this notice' did not bring to an end (what was) a yearly tenancy because the notice presupposed the existence of a weekly tenancy.

London County Council v Agricultural Food Products Ltd [1955] 2 QB 218

A notice to quit required to be signed 'by the valuer of the council' would be properly signed by someone else in the name of the valuer, even if the letters 'p.p.' were not added to show that the signature was by proxy.

Bathavon Rural District Council v Carlile [1958] 1 QB 461

A notice to quit to determine a weekly tenancy running from Monday to Sunday was invalid on the ground that it was stated to expire at noon on Monday.

Stylo Shoes Ltd v Prices Tailors Ltd [1960] 1 Ch 396

A notice to quit had been validly served, pursuant to the *Landlord and Tenant Act 1927*, s 23(1), by sending it by ordinary post, given that the notice was delivered to the tenant's place of business.

Lower v Sorrell [1963] 1 QB 959

A 'waiver' of a notice to quit results in the creation of a new tenancy.

Chapman v Honig [1963] 2 QB 502

A notice to quit was valid even though it was served by the landlord in a vindictive attempt to punish the tenant for giving evidence against him.

Harmond Properties Ltd v Gajdzis [1968] 1 WLR 1858

A notice to quit was valid even though it was stated to be served 'on behalf of your landlord Mr R P Harvey', whereas Mr Harvey was a director of the landlord who had been acting as a general agent in relation to the letting.

Lord Newborough v Jones [1975] 1 Ch 90

A notice to quit was validly served, pursuant to the *Agricultural Holdings Act 1948*, s 92 by pushing the notice under the bottom of the side or back door of the demised premises, even if the tenant was correct in saying that the notice had slipped beneath some linoleum and did not come to the attention of the tenant.

Elsden v Pick [1980] 1 WLR 898

A tenant waived any entitlement to dispute the validity of a notice to quit on the ground that it was short because he had agreed with his landlord that the notice would, notwithstanding that 'deficiency', be valid.

Greenwich LBC v McGrady (1982) 81 LGR 288

A notice to quit was valid even though it had been served only one of two joint tenants.

Datnow v Jones [1985] 2 EGLR 1

A landlord was estopped from serving a notice to quit on a tenant of a farm as a result of an agreement that the tenant would be safeguarded against future encroachment on his farm for the purpose of afforestation.

Hammersmith and Fulham LBC v Monk [1992] 1 AC 478

A notice to quit was valid even though it had been served by only one of the two joint tenants.

Divall v Harrison [1992] 2 EGLR 64

Following the death of the landlord and the grant of probate, a notice to quit was invalid on the ground that it was stated to be served on behalf of the residuary beneficiary of the landlord's estate.

John v George (1995) 71 P&CR 375

A landlord had become estopped from serving a notice to quit.

Wandsworth London Borough Council v Attwell [1996] 1 EGLR 57

A notice to quit was not validly served by leaving at copy at the demised premises.

Crawley BC v Ure [1996] 1 All ER 724

A joint tenant serving a notice to quit did not thereby act in breach of trust.

Osei-Bonsu v Wandsworth LBC [1999] 1 WLR 1011

A notice to quit was valid even though it was served, not on the person in whom the reversion immediately expectant upon the lease was vested (being a tenant under a concurrent tenancy), but upon the freeholder (who was the original landlord).

Hackney LBC v Snowden (25 July 2000, unreported)

A landlord had waived the requirement, contained in the *Protection from Eviction Act 1977*, s 5(1) that notices to quit in respect of premises let as a dwelling must be given not less than four weeks before the date on which it is stated to take effect.

Notting Hill Housing Trust v Brackley [2001] EWCA Civ 601, [2001] 3 EGLR 12

A joint tenant did act in breach of trust by serving a notice to quit to determine a joint tenancy.

Rent review notices

Davstone (Holdings) Ltd v Al-Rifai [1976] 32 P&CR 18

The proposed rent stated in a trigger notice served by a landlord was not required to be a rent capable of qualifying as the full yearly market value as defined in the rent review provisions.

Dean and Chapter of Chichester v Lennards Ltd (1977) 35 P&CR 309

A landlord's notice triggering a rent review was valid even though it had failed to comply with a requirement that such a notice should specify the proposed rent.

United Scientific Holdings Ltd v Burnley BC [1978] AC 904

Time is not usually of the essence in respect of the timetable in rent review machinery, including deadlines for the service of rent review notices.

Amalgamated Estates Ltd v Joystretch Manufacturing Ltd [1981] 1 EGLR 96

The proposed rent stated in a trigger notice served by a landlord was not required to be a bona fide and genuine pre-estimate of the open market rent.

Armherst v James Walker Goldsmith & Silversmith Ltd [1983] 1 Ch 305

Mere delay on the part of the landlord in serving a notice triggering a rent review will not disentitle the landlord from serving such a notice.

Shirlcar Properties Ltd v Heintz [1983] 1 EGLR 125

A letter from a landlord was held not to have operated as a valid trigger notice under rent review provisions because it was stated to be 'subject to contract'.

Norwich Union Life Assurance Society v Tony Waller Ltd [1984] 1 EGLR 126

A letter headed 'without prejudice' was held not to be a valid notice to trigger a rent review.

Sheridan v Blaircourt Investments Ltd [1984] 1 EGLR 139

A letter from a tenant headed 'without prejudice and subject to contract' was held not to constitute a valid counter-notice on a rent review.

Taylor Woodrow Property Co Ltd v Lonrho Textiles Ltd (1985) 52 P&CR 28

A landlord's notice triggering a rent review was held to be valid even though it failed to comply with a requirement that such a notice refer the tenant to the terms of the rent review clause.

British Rail Pension Trustee Co Ltd v Cardshops Ltd [1987] 1 EGLR 127

A letter from a tenant was held to constitute a valid counter-notice containing the tenant's proposed new rent even though the letter was headed 'subject to contract'.

Phipps-Faire Ltd v Malbern Construction Ltd [1987] 1 EGLR 129

Time was not of the essence for a deadline for the service of a tenant's counter-notice.

Cordon Bleu Freezer Food Centres Ltd v Marbleace Ltd [1987] 2 EGLR 143

A firm of surveyors were held not to have had authority from a landlord to serve a rent review trigger notice.

Commission for the New Towns v Levy [1990] 2 EGLR 121

A landlord's notice triggering a rent review was invalid on the ground that it failed to comply with a requirement that such a notice should specify the proposed rent.

Royal Life Insurance v Phillips [1990] 2 EGLR 135

A letter had operated as a notice triggering a rent review even though it was headed 'without prejudice' and 'subject to contract'.

Patel v Earlspring Properties Ltd [1991] 2 EGLR 131

A tenant's counter-notice was valid even though it did not comply with a requirement to specify the rent which the tenant was willing to pay.

EAE (RT) Ltd v EAE Properties Ltd 1994 SLT 627

A rent review notice was validly served by fax.

Central Estates Ltd v Secretary of State for the Environment [1995] 72 P&CR 482

Time was of the essence for the service of a trigger notice given that the same timetable was set for the rent review and also for the tenant's right to determine the tenancy by serving a break notice.

Tudor Evans (Swansea) Ltd v Longacre Securities Ltd (31 July 1997, unreported)

A rent review trigger notice served by the landlord's surveyors was invalid because it contained the following fraudulent statement: 'Please be advised now that, having considered carefully the size and corner location of the subject property, and the terms of your tenancy ... that we determine the market rental value as at [the relevant date] to be the [specified sum].'

Fox & Widley v Guram [1998] 1 EGLR 91

A trigger notice did not have to contain a genuine pre-estimate of the market rent.

Fifield v W&R Jack Ltd [2001] L&TR 4

The landlord waived a right to complain that a tenant's counter-notice was served out of time when it treated the counter-notice as valid and negotiated over the new rent.

Starmark Enterprises Ltd v CPL Distribution Ltd [2001] EWCA Civ 1252, [2002] Ch 306

Time will be of the essence in respect of a deadline for the service of a tenant's counter-notice if there is a 'deeming provision' providing that, if a counter-notice is not served by that date, the rent shall be the rent proposed in the landlord's notice triggering the rent review.

WX Investments Ltd v Begg [2002] EWHC 925 (Ch), [2002] 3 EGLR 47

A trigger notice had been validly served by recorded delivery, pursuant to section 196(4) of the Law of Property Act 1925, at the time when delivery would 'in the ordinary course' have been effected, even though, as a matter of fact, there was no available recipient at that time.

Arundel Corpn v Khokher [2003] EWCA Civ 1784

A rent review trigger notice had not been effectively served at the tenant's 'last known address' because the landlord's solicitor had been informed about a change of address.

Lancecrest Ltd v Asiwaju [2005] EWCA Civ 117, [2005] 1 EGLR 40

In holding that a tenant's counter-notice to a landlord's rent review trigger notice was valid the Court of Appeal held that, when determining the validity of a notice, the actual recipient's response to the notice should be ignored.

Warborough Investments Ltd v Central Midlands Estates Ltd [2006] EWHC 2622 (Ch), [2007] L&TR 10

Pursuant to a provision in a lease enabling notices to be 'left ... on the demised premises' (which consisted of a supermarket), a landlord validly served a notice triggering a rent review by handing the notice to an employee of a subtenant who was seated behind a 'customer services desk'.

Maurice Investments Ltd v Lincoln Insurance Services Ltd [2006] EWHC 376 (Ch)

A letter stated to be served 'without prejudice' and 'subject to contract' was held not to constitute a valid notice to trigger a rent review.

White v Riverside Housing Association Ltd [2007] UKHL 20, [2007] L&TR 22

A rent review clause in an assured tenancy agreement entitling the landlord to increase the rent annually with effect from the first Monday in June each year entitled the landlord to increase the rent on any date from and including the first Monday in June.

INCREASE OF RENT AND MORTGAGE INTEREST (RESTRICTIONS) ACT 1920

Section 3

Fredco Estates Ltd v Bryant [1961] 1 All ER 34

A notice to increase the rent, which was signed in a firm of surveyors' own name, was held to be valid on the ground that it was well known to the tenant that the firm was the landlord's agent.

AGRICULTURAL HOLDINGS ACT 1923

Section 12

Howson v Buxton (1928) 97 LJKB 749

A valid notice had been served under s 12 even though it had been served by only one of the two joint tenants.

Sharpley v Manby [1942] 1 KB 217

A notice had been validly served, pursuant to the provisions of s 53 of the Act, because the landlord sent the notice in the post and the post office had delivered the notice to the demised premises.

Section 146

Cannon Brewery Co Ltd v Signal Press Ltd (1929) 139 LT 382

A section 146 notice was validly served pursuant to the Law of Property Act 1925, s 196 when the notice was handed to the forewoman of the tenant's business.

Blewett v Blewett [1936] 2 All ER 188

A section 146 notice is invalid unless it is served on all of the joint tenants.

BL Holdings Ltd v Marcolt Investments Ltd [1979] 1 EGLR 97

The service of a counter-notice claiming the benefit of the Leasehold Property (Repairs) Act 1938 did not waive defects in the section 146 notice, nor create an estoppel preventing the tenant from subsequently relying upon those defects.

Old Grovebury Manor Farm Ltd v W Seymour Plant Sales & Hire Ltd (No 2) [1979] 3 All ER 504

A section 146 notice was invalid because it was served on the original tenant rather that the current tenant who had taken an assignment of the lease.

Van Haarlam v Kasner (1992) 64 P&CR 214

A section 146 notice was properly served by posting it through the letter box of the demised premises, even though the tenant did not receive the notice because, as the landlord was aware, he was in prison.

Akici v LR Butlin Ltd [2005] EWCA Civ 1296, [2006] L&TR 1

A section 146 notice was ineffective for the purposes of a purported forfeiture on the ground of an unlawful parting with possession because it was not a notice 'specifying the particular breach complained of'.

AGRICULTURAL HOLDINGS ACT 1948

Section 23

Elsden v Pick [1980] 1 WLR 898

A notice to quit served by a tenant was valid, even though it was stated to expire less than 12 months after it had been served, because the tenant had agreed with the landlord that, notwithstanding short service, the notice would be treated as being valid.

Section 24

Jones v Lewis (1973) 25 P&CR 375

A notice requiring a tenant to remedy disrepair was invalid on the ground that it was addressed to only one of the two joint tenants.

Newman v Keedwell (1977) 35 P&CR 393

A counter-notice to a notice to quit was invalid because it had been served by only one of two joint tenants.

Section 70

Hallinan (Lady) v Jones [1984] 2 EGLR 20

A notice had not been validly served under s 70 because, although it had been sent to the tenant by recorded delivery, it had been returned by the Post Office undelivered.

HOUSING REPAIRS AND RENTS ACT 1954

Section 23

Lazarus Estates Ltd v Beasley [1956] 1 QB 702

A notice to increase the rent payable by a statutory tenant would be invalid if a declaration relating to the value of works of repair that had been undertaken by the landlord was made fraudulently.

LANDLORD AND TENANT ACT 1954

Section 4

Galinski v McHugh (1988) 57 P&CR 359

A notice proposing a statutory tenancy was properly served on the tenant's solicitor.

R (on the application of Morris) v London Rent Assessment Committee [2002] EWCA Civ 276, [2002] 2 EGLR 13

A section 4 notice was invalid because it had mis-identified the tenant.

Section 25

Tennant v London County Council (1957) 55 LGR 421

A section 25 notice was properly signed by an agent of the landlord.

Stylo Shoes Ltd v Prices Tailors Ltd [1960] 1 Ch 396

A section 25 notice was validly served by sending the notice by ordinary post to a previous business address given that the post office had redirected the notice to the tenant's current business address.

Barclays Bank Ltd v Ascot [1961] 1 WLR 717

The omission of notes from the prescribed form of a section 25 notice did not invalidate the notice because those notes would have been irrelevant to the particular recipient.

Rostron v Michael Nairn & Co Ltd [1962] EGD 284

In relation to a tenancy vested in a husband and wife, a section 25 notice was not validly served on the wife as a result of having been sent by registered post and delivered to the husband.

Price v West London Investment Building Society Ltd [1964] 1 WLR 616

A section 25 notice was validly served by sending it by registered post to the tenant's business address.

Stidolph v American School in London Educational Trust Ltd (1969) 20 P&CR 802

The requirement for a signature on a section 25 notice could be satisfied by a signature on a covering letter under which the notice was served.

Sun Alliance & London Assurance Co Ltd v Hayman [1975] 1 WLR 177

A notice was 'substantially to the like effect' as a prescribed notice even though it was in a form that had been superseded.

Tegerdine v Brooks (1978) 36 P&CR 261

A section 25 notice, which stated that the landlord would not oppose an application by the tenant for a new tenancy, was not invalidated by virtue of having omitted information relating to the situation in which a landlord had stated that he would oppose such an application.

Gatwick Investments Ltd v Radviojevic [1978] CLY 1768

Following the bankruptcy of the tenant, a section 25 notice was required to be served on the trustee in bankruptcy.

Harris v Black (1983) 46 P&CR 366

An application to require one of two joint tenants to join in the service of a counter-notice was dismissed.

Italia Holdings SA v Bayadea [1985] 1 EGLR 70

A section 25 notice was validly served at the demised premises, being a hotel.

Morrow v Nadeem [1986] 1 WLR 1381

A section 25 notice was invalid on the ground that it had misidentified the landlord.

Morris v Patel (1987) 281 EG 419

A section 25 notice that had adopted a form of the prescribed form that had been replaced was nevertheless held to be in a form 'substantially to the like effect' as the current prescribed form.

Pearson v Alyo [1990] 1 EGLR 114

A section 25 notice was invalid on the ground that it was stated to be served by only one of the two joint landlords.

Smith v Draper [1990] 2 EGLR 70

A section 25 notice was invalid because it had been served by two of the three joint landlords.

Lex Services plc v Johns [1990] 1 EGLR 92

A section 25 notice had been properly served by recorded delivery even though the tenant claimed not to have received the notice.

Yamaha-Kemble Music (UK) Ltd v ARC Properties Ltd [1990] 1 EGLR 261

A section 25 notice was held to be invalid on the ground that it had incorrectly identified the landlord as a subsidiary company of the landlord.

Bridges v Stanford [1991] 2 EGLR 265

A section 25 notice was valid even though it mis-identified the tenant.

M&P Enterprises (London) Ltd v Norfolk Square Hotels Ltd [1994] 1 EGLR 129

Where the reversion had been severed the landlord was nevertheless required to serve a single section 25 notice in respect of the whole of the demised premises.

Keepers and Governors of the Free Grammar School of John Lyon [1997] 1 EGLR 88

A tenant became estopped from disputing the validity of a section 25 notice by serving a counter-notice.

Sabella Ltd v Montgomery [1998] 1 EGLR 65

A section 25 notice was invalid because it omitted material contained on the prescribed form.

Wroe v Exmos Cover Ltd [2000] 1 EGLR 66

The service of a section 25 notice did not create an estoppel precluding the owner from contending that an occupier, in fact, held under a licence.

Barclays Bank v Bee [2001] EWCA 1126, [2002] 1 WLR 332

The landlord had failed to serve a valid notice when it had simultaneously served two inconsistent notices, one of which stated that the landlord would oppose an application by the tenant for a new tenancy, whilst the other notice stated that the landlord would not oppose such an application.

Beanby Estates Ltd v Egg Stores (Stamford Hill) Ltd [2003] EWHC 1252, [2003] 1 WLR 2064

A section 25 notice that had been served pursuant to the Landlord and Tenant Act 1927, s 23 was deemed to have been served on the date when it had been posted by recorded delivery.

CA Webber (Transport) Ltd v Railtrack plc [2003] EWCA Civ 1167, [2004] 1 WLR 320

Section 25 notices, served pursuant to the Landlord and Tenant Act 1927, s 23, were deemed to have been served on the date when they were posted by recorded delivery.

Shaws (EAL) Ltd v Pennycook [2004] EWCA Civ 100, [2004] Ch 296

A tenant was unable to withdraw a 'positive counter-notice' stating that he was willing to give up possession of the demised premises.

Section 26

Sidney Bolsom Investments Trust Ltd v Karmios [1956] 1 QB 529

A request for a new tenancy was valid even though it had not expressly stated the proposed term of the new lease.

Betty's Cafes Ltd v Phillips Furnishing Stores Ltd [1959] AC 20

A landlord, when serving a counter-notice, must honestly and truthfully state his ground for opposing an application for a new tenancy and establish that intention as existing at the date of the hearing.

Morris Marks v British Waterways Board [1963] 1 WLR 1008

A landlord's counter-notice could avail a subsequent entity who was the landlord at the date of the hearing.

Stile Hall Properties Ltd v Gooch [1979] 3 All ER 848

A tenant cannot, after he had missed the deadline for applying for a new tenancy, withdraw his 'section 26 notice'.

Hackney LBC v Hackney African Organisation (1998) 77 P&CR D18

A tenants' counter-notice was held to be valid even though it described only one of the four joint tenants as 'the tenant'.

Railtrack plc v Gojra [1998] 1 EGLR 63

A notice to terminate a tenancy was validly served on the landlord's agent.

Sun Life Assurance plc v Thales Tracs Ltd [2001] EWCA Civ 704, [2001] 1 WLR 1562

A section 26 notice served by a tenant and requesting a new tenancy was not invalidated on the ground that the tenant, when he served the notice, did not intend to take up a new tenancy.

Section 36(2)

Re 88, Berkeley Road [1971] 1 Ch 648

A notice severing a beneficial joint tenancy had been properly served at the property even though delivery of the notice had been accepted by the server of the notice, who had failed to pass the notice on to the recipient.

Kinch v Bullard [1999] 1 WLR 423

A notice severing a beneficial joint tenancy was properly served at the property by sending the notice to the property by ordinary post even though, after the notice had been posted through the letter box, the server of the notice had picked up the notice and destroyed it, thereby ensuring that it did not come to the attention of the recipient.

LEASEHOLD REFORM ACT 1967

Section 8

Bynlea Property Investment Ltd v Ramsay [1969] 2 QB 253

A leaseholder's notice purporting to exercise a right to acquire a long lease of a house was invalid because it contained an internal inconsistency in that it provided that the leaseholder had a 'desire to have the freehold or a long lease'.

Cresswell v Duke of Westminster [1985] 2 EGLR 151

A notice to exercise a right to purchase the freehold of a house was not invalidated by 'inaccuracies' in the particulars required to be set out in the notice.

Dymond v Arundel-Timms [1991] 1 EGLR 109

A notice to exercise a right to purchase the freehold of a house was held to be invalid because, in respect of the information relating to the tenant's occupation of the house, the tenant had sought deliberately to conceal or misrepresent the true position.

Wax v Viscount Chelsea [1996] 2 EGLR 80

A section 8 notice was invalid because it had been served by only one of the two joint tenants.

Speedwell Estates Ltd v Dalziel [2001] EWCA Civ 1277, [2002] 1 EGLR 55

A notice to exercise a right to purchase the freehold of a house was invalid on the ground that it failed to contain all of the prescribed information.

Earl Cadogan v Straus [2004] EWCA Civ 21, [2004] 2 EGLR 69

A notice to exercise the right to purchase a house was not invalidation on the ground that it had failed to refer to two earlier leases that had been surrendered.

AGRICULTURAL HOLDINGS (NOTICES TO QUIT) ACT 1977

Section 2(1)

Featherstone v Staples [1986] 2 All ER 461

A counter-notice served in response to a landlord's notice to quit was invalid because it had been served by only one of two joint tenants.

RENT ACT 1977

Section 24

Aristocrat Property Investments v Harounoff (1982) 2 HLR 102

In possession proceedings relying upon alleged arrears of rent, a landlord could not rely upon an estoppel to 'cure' defects in a notice that had purported to increase the rent because, to do so, would be to use an estoppel as 'a sword' to create a cause of action.

Schedule 15, case 19

Henry Smith's Charity Trustees v Kyriakou [1989] 2 EGLR 110

A notice under case 19 of Sch15 was properly served by leaving it at the place that was the furthest that a member of the public or postman could go to communicate to tenants residing at a property.

Schedule 15, case 11

Minay v Sentongo (1982) 45 P&CR 190

A notice not 'given' for the purposes of case 11 of Sch 15 if, although it was sent through the post, it was never received.

HOUSING ACT 1980

Section 16

Milne-Berry and Madden v Tower Hamlets LBC (1995) 28 HLR 225

A notice to complete was not invalid, even though it was incorrectly stated to have been served under the Housing Act 1980 rather than the Housing Act 1985, but the local authority had waived an entitlement to rely upon the notice by informing the tenant that the right to buy could proceed.

AGRICULTURAL HOLDINGS ACT 1986

Section 26

Rous v Mitchell [1991] 1 WLR 469

A notice to terminate an agricultural tenancy was invalid because it did not contain an honest statement of the reasons for giving the notice.

John v George (1995) 71 P&CR 375

An estoppel by convention precluded a landlord from relying upon a notice to quit stating that the land was required for a use other than agriculture which had the benefit of planning permission because the tenant had supported the planning application in reliance on a promise that the proceeds of sale would be applied for the construction of other buildings for the use of the tenant.

LANDLORD AND TENANT ACT 1987

Section 11A

Tudor v M25 Group Ltd [2003] EWCA Civ 1760, [2004] 1 WLR 2319

A notice seeking information about a disposal was not invalidated by virtue of non-compliance with the requirement, imposed by s 54(2) of the Act, to specify the addresses of the flats of which the leaseholders who had served the notice were qualifying tenants.

Section 12

Kay Green v Twinsectra Ltd [1996] 1 WLR 1587

A 'purchase notice' served by leaseholders under s 12 was not invalid even though it failed to comply with the requirements in sub-s (3), in particular that such a notice 'shall, where the estate or interest that was the subject matter of the disposal related to any property in addition to the premises to which this Part applied at the time of the disposal ... require the new landlord to dispose of that estate or interest only so far as relating to those premises'.

Section 16

Belvedere Court Ltd v Frogmore Ltd [1997] QB 858

A letter did not constitute a valid notice under s 16 because it did not expressly refer to s 16 and would not clearly be understood as a notice served under that provision.

Section 48

Rogan v Woodfield Building Services Ltd [1995] 1 EGLR 72

The requirement that a landlord provide the tenant with an address at which notices could be served on him was satisfied by the inclusion of the landlord's address in the lease itself.

Glen International Ltd v Triplerose Ltd [2007] EWCA Civ 388, [2007] 26 EG 164

A letter from a landlord's agent to the tenant's solicitor did not constitute a valid notice informing the tenant of an address at which notices could be served on him.

HOUSING ACT 1988

Section 8

Tadema Holdings Ltd v Ferguson (2000) HLR 866

A section 8 notice had been validly served on a tenant who, by virtue of his mental incapacity, was unable to understand, or to act upon, the notice.

Section 20

York v Casey [1998] 2 EGLR 25

Incorrectly identifying the expiry date of the term of the proposed tenancy did not invalidate the notice.

Ravenseft Properties Ltd v Hall [2001] EWCA Civ 2034, [2002] 1 EGLR 9

Mis-identifying the commencement or expiry dates of the term of the proposed tenancy, and certain other errors, did not invalidate a section 20 notice.

Yenula Properties Ltd v Naidu [2002] EWCA Civ 719, [2002] L&TR 9

A section 20 notice was validly served on the tenant's licensed conveyancer.

Osborn & Co Ltd v Dior [2003] EWCA Civ 281, [2003] HLR 45

Departures from the prescribed form did not invalidate notices.

Section 21

Lower Street Properties Ltd v Jones (1996) 28 HLR 877

A section 21 notice was valid which was stated to expire 'at the end of the period of your tenancy which will end after the expiry of two months from the service upon you of this notice'.

Fernandez v McDonald [2003] EWCA Civ 1219, [2003] 4 All ER 1033

A notice served under s 21(4) to obtain possession of a assured shorthold tenancy that was a periodic tenancy was invalid because it had failed to specify a date for possession that was 'the last day of a period of the tenancy'.

Notting Hill Housing Trust v Roomus [2006] EWCA Civ 407, [2006] 1 WLR 1375

A section 21 notice was valid which required the tenant to give up possession 'at the end of the period of your tenancy which will end after expiry of two months from the service upon you of the notice'.

Schedule 2A, para 1

Andrews v Cunningham [2007] EWCA Civ 762

A rent book, on the cover of which appeared the words 'Assured Tenancy', did not constitute a notice stating that an assured tenancy would not be an assured shorthold tenancy.

LEASEHOLD REFORM, HOUSING AND URBAN DEVELOPMENT ACT 1993

Section 13

Crean Davidson Investments Ltd v Earl Cadogan [1998] 2 EGLR 96

A notice to exercise right to collective enfranchisement was not invalidated by defects relating to the plan.

Sinclair Gardens Investments (Kensington) Ltd v Poets Chase Freehold Co Ltd [2007] EWHC 1776 (Ch), [2007] 49 EG 104

Leaseholders were entitled to serve a notice to exercise the right to collective enfranchisement immediately after the service of a purported notice that was invalid.

Section 21

9 Cornwall Crescent London Ltd v Kensington and Chelsea Royal London Borough Council [2005] EWCA Civ 324

The premium specified in a counter-notice served by a landlord did not have to reflect a proposal that the landlord considered to be realistic.

Section 42

Viscount Chelsea v Hirshorn [1998] 2 EGLR 90

A section 42 notice claiming to exercise an entitlement to a new lease was invalid on the ground that it had been signed by the tenant's solicitor rather than the tenant personally.

Cadogan v Morris [1999] 1 EGLR 59

A notice claiming to exercise an entitlement to a new lease was invalid because the proposed premium of £100 was not a proposal that the tenant considered to be realistic.

Keepers and Governors of John Lyon Grammar School v Secci (1999) 32 HLR 820

Notices claiming new leases were invalid because they failed to state a date for the service of a counter-notice that was not less than two months after the date of the service of the notices.

St Ermins Property Co Ltd v Tingay [2002] EWHC 1673, [2002] L&TR 6

A section 42 notice was invalid because it was served, not by the leaseholder personally, but by her son under a power of attorney.

City & Country Properties Ltd v Plowden Investments Ltd [2007] L&TR 15

A section 42 notice served by a company was invalid on the ground that it was signed only by a director of the company, rather than being under seal or signed by two directors of the company or by a director and the secretary of the company.

Section 45

Burman v Mount Cook Land Ltd [2002] 1 EGLR 61

A landlord's counter-notice was invalid on the ground that it failed to comply with an indispensable condition for the validity of such a notice that it contains a statement about whether or not the landlord admits that on the relevant date the tenant was entitled to a new lease.

Latifi v Colherne Court Freehold Ltd [2002] EWHC 2873, [2003] 1 EGLR 78

The leaseholder had waived the requirement that a counter-notice had to be served by the 'competent landlord'.

Lay v Ackerman [2004] EWCA Civ 184, [2003] 1 EGLR 139

A landlord's counter-notice was valid even though it had mis-identified the landlord by naming trustees of a non-existent trust.

Leasehold Reform (Collective Enfranchisement) (Counter-notices) (England) Regulations 2002, reg 4

7 Strathray Gardens Ltd v Pointstar Shipping & Finance Ltd [2004] EWCA Civ 1669, [2005] 1 EGLR 53

A failure to state that premises did not form part of an Estate Management Scheme did not invalidate a counter-notice.

LANDLORD AND TENANT (COVENANTS) ACT 1995

Section 17

Commercial Union Life Assurance Co Ltd v Moustafa [1999] 2 EGLR 44

A notice claiming arrears from the original tenant of a lease was validly served by recorded delivery even though it had been returned by the post office undelivered.

Appendix 2

MANNAI INVESTMENT CO LTD V EAGLE STAR LIFE ASSURANCE CO LTD

352   All England Law Reports   [1997] 3 All ER

Mannai Investment Co Ltd v Eagle Star Life Assurance Co Ltd   *a*

HOUSE OF LORDS

LORD GOFF OF CHIEVELEY, LORD JAUNCEY OF TULLICHETTLE, LORD STEYN, LORD
HOFFMANN AND LORD CLYDE   *b*

20 JANUARY, 21 MAY 1997

*Landlord and tenant – Lease – Option to determine – Lease for fixed term commencing
on 13 January containing break clause – Break clause providing for determination on
expiry of six months' notice on third anniversary of commencement of lease – Notice*   *c*
given expiring on 12 January – Whether notice valid.

By two leases dated 11 March 1992 the landlord demised office premises and a
car park to the tenant for fixed terms of ten years commencing on and
including 13 January 1992. Both leases contained a break clause enabling the
tenant to determine the lease 'by serving not less than six months notice in   *d*
writing ... such notice to expire on the third anniversary of the term
commencement date'. By letters dated 24 June 1994 the tenant purported to
give notice to determine the leases on 12 January 1995, although the third
anniversary of the commencement date was in fact 13 January 1995. On the
tenant's originating summonses, the judge held that the notices were effective   *e*
to determine the leases on 13 January 1995. The Court of Appeal allowed the
landlord's appeal on the ground that, in purporting to determine the leases on
12 January, the notices had not complied strictly with the terms of the leases
and were therefore not effective to determine them. The tenant appealed.

Held – (Lord Goff and Lord Jauncey dissenting) Where a tenant served a   *f*
notice purporting to exercise his contractual right to determine a lease, that
notice would be effective to do so notwithstanding the fact that it contained a
minor misdescription, provided that, construed against its contextual setting,
it would unambiguously inform a reasonable recipient how and when it was
to operate. In the instant case, having regard to the fact that the leases   *g*
commenced on 13 January and were determinable on the third anniversary of
the term of commencement, it would have been obvious to a reasonable
recipient that the notices purporting to determine the leases on 12 January
contained a minor misdescription and that the tenant sought to determine the
leases on 'the third anniversary of the term commencement', ie 13 January. It   *h*
followed that the notices were effective to determine the leases and the
tenant's appeal would accordingly be allowed (see p 369 *b* to p 370 *d*, p 373 *e j*
to p 374 *a c* to *e*, p 380 *f j*, p 381 *c d f g*, p 382 *j* to p 383 *a c* to *j* and p 384 *c*, post).

    Carradine Properties Ltd v Aslam [1976] 1 All ER 573 applied.

    Hankey v Clavering [1942] 2 All ER 311 overruled.

    Decision of the Court of Appeal [1996] 1 All ER 55 reversed.   *j*

Notes

For option to determine lease and notice to exercise option, see 27(1)
Halsbury's Laws (4th edn reissue) paras 116–118, and for cases on the subject,
see 31(1) *Digest* (2nd reissue) 274–275, 2289–2300.

Cases referred to in opinions

a *Antaios Cia Naviera SA v Salen Rederierna AB, The Antaios* [1984] 3 All ER 229, [1985] AC 191, [1984] 3 WLR 592, HL.
Cadby v Martinez (1840) 11 Ad & El 720, 113 ER 587.
Carradine Properties Ltd v Aslam [1976] 1 All ER 573, [1976] 1 WLR 442.
Delta Vale Properties Ltd v Mills [1990] 2 All ER 176, [1990] 1 WLR 445, CA.
b *Doe d Cox v Roe* (1802) 4 Esp 185, 170 ER 685, NP.
Doe d Duke of Bedford v Kightley (1796) 7 Term Rep 63, 101 ER 856.
Doe d Spicer v Lea (1809) 11 East 312, 103 ER 1024.
Fish, Re, Ingam v Rayner [1894] 2 Ch 83, CA.
Gardner v Ingram (1889) 61 LT 729, [1886–90] All ER Rep 258, DC.
Garston v Scottish Widows' Fund and Life Assurance Society [1996] 4 All ER 282,
c   [1996] 1 WLR 834, CA.
Germax Securities Ltd v Spiegal (1978) 37 P & CR 204, CA.
Hankey v Clavering [1942] 2 All ER 311, [1942] 2 KB 326, CA.
Heap v Ind Coope & Allsopp Ltd [1940] 3 All ER 634, [1940] 2 KB 476, CA.
Micrografix v Woking 8 Ltd [1995] 2 EGLR 32
d *National Society for the Prevention of Cruelty to Children v Scottish National Society for the Prevention of Cruelty to Children* [1915] AC 207, HL.
Norwegian American Cruises A/S (formerly Norwegian American Lines A/S) v Paul Mundy Ltd, The Vistafjord [1988] 2 Lloyd's Rep 343, CA.
Peel's Goods, Re (1870) LR 2 P & D 46.
e *Phipps (P) & Co (Northampton and Towcester Breweries) Ltd v Rogers* [1925] 1 KB 14, CA.
Prenn v Simmonds [1971] 3 All ER 237, [1971] 1 WLR 1381, HL.
Price v Mann [1942] 1 All ER 453, CA.
Reardon Smith Line Ltd v Hansen-Tangen, Hansen-Tangen v Sanko Steamship Co [1976] 3 All ER 570, [1976] 1 WLR 989, HL.
f *Sidebotham v Holland* [1895] 1 QB 378, [1891–4] All ER Rep 617, CA.
Sudbrook Trading Estate Ltd v Eggleton [1982] 3 All ER 1, [1983] 1 AC 444, [1982] 3 WLR 315, HL.
Sunrose Ltd v Gould [1961] 3 All ER 1142, [1962] 1 WLR 20, CA.

g ### Appeal
The tenant, Mannai Investment Co Ltd, appealed from the decision of the Court of Appeal (Nourse, Roch and Hobhouse LJJ) ([1996] 1 All ER 55, [1995] 1 WLR 1508) on 5 July 1995 reversing the decision of Judge Rich QC sitting as a judge of the High Court in the Chancery Division whereby, on originating summonses dated 4 October 1994 issued by the tenant he declared that two
h notices dated 24 June 1994 served by the tenant on the landlord, Eagle Star Life Assurance Co Ltd, purporting to determine on 12 January 1995 two leases of commercial premises dated 11 March 1992 were effective to determine the leases on 13 January 1995, being the date on which the tenant's right to determine arose pursuant to cl 7(13) of each lease. The facts are set out in the
j opinion of Lord Goff.

John Cherryman QC and *Kenneth Munro* (instructed by *Manches & Co*) for the tenant.
Nicholas Patten QC and *Thomas Leech* (instructed by *Nabarro Nathanson*) for the landlord.

Their Lordships took time for consideration.

a

21 May 1997. The following opinions were delivered.

LORD GOFF OF CHIEVELEY. My Lords, this appeal is concerned with the question whether a notice given by a tenant pursuant to a break clause in a lease was an effective notice. In fact, there were two leases with identical *b* break clauses, and two identical notices were given. For convenience, however, I will assume that there was only one.

The premises were in Jermyn Street in London. The lease was dated 11 March 1992, and was for a term of ten years from 13 January 1992. The respondent company, Eagle Star Assurance Co Ltd, was the landlord, and the appellant company, Mannai Investment Co Ltd, was the tenant. The relevant *c* clause was cl 7(13), which provided as follows:

'The Tenant may by serving not less than six months notice in writing on the Landlord or its solicitors such notice to expire on the 3rd anniversary of the term commencement date determine this Lease and *d* upon expiry of such notice this Lease shall cease and determine and have no further effect ...'

So the clause gave the tenant a single opportunity to bring the lease to an end. It so happened that the market for rents in this area had fallen, and the tenant decided to take advantage of this opportunity. It served the following notice *e* on the landlord: 'Pursuant to Clause 7(13) of the Lease we as Tenant hereby give notice to you to determine the Lease on 12th January 1995.' Unfortunately, however, the tenant made a mistake. The third anniversary of the term commencement date was not 12 January 1995 but 13 January 1995. The landlord has claimed that in the result the notice was ineffective. The Court of Appeal ([1996] 1 All ER 55, [1995] 1 WLR 1508), reversing the *f* decision of Judge Rich QC (sitting as an additional judge of the High Court in the Chancery Division), upheld the landlord's contention. It is from that decision that the tenant now appeals to your Lordships' House.

I should record at once that the judge held that the tenant was entitled to succeed on the basis that, because 12 and 13 January were contiguous dates, *g* there was a moment of time at which they coincided; and from this it followed that a notice expressed to determine the lease on 12 January was effective to do so on 13 January as required by the clause. In so holding, he invoked the authority of *Sidebotham v Holland* [1895] 1 QB 378, [1891–4] All ER Rep 617. But, as Nourse LJ pointed out in the Court of Appeal in the present case that *h* case provided no authority for the judge's conclusion (see [1996] 1 All ER 55 at 60–61, [1995] 1 WLR 1508 at 1514–1515). It was concerned with a notice to quit and deliver up possession by midnight. It related therefore to a notice to quit at a point of time which was held to be common to both dates, and not, as in the present case, a notice to take effect on a certain date. Here, a notice taking effect on a different, though contiguous date, could not be rendered *j* effective on the basis of *Sidebotham v Holland*. With that reasoning, I find myself in complete agreement. It follows that the central question in the appeal before your Lordships' House is whether the Court of Appeal was right to hold that the notice was in any event not an effective notice under the clause. To that question I now turn.

a   At first sight it seems unreasonable that the notice should not have been
effective. It was obvious that the tenant was trying to give an effective notice
under the clause, and that it had mistakenly assumed that the anniversary of
the term commencement date was not 13 January but 12 January 1995. As
Hobhouse LJ pointed out, the tenant had mistakenly read the clause as if it said
'to expire at the end of the third year of the term', when it did not do so (see
b   [1996] 1 All ER 55 at 62, [1995] 1 WLR 1508 at 1516). It is tempting therefore
to assist the tenant who has made a mistake of this kind, when it must have
been obvious to the landlord that the tenant intended to give an effective
notice under the clause. But the difficulty in the way of adopting this approach
is that, on the authorities, it is inconsistent with the agreement of the parties
as expressed in the clause.

c   An early authority in this line is *Cadby v Martinez* (1840) 11 Ad & El 720, 113
ER 587. In that case a tenant was entitled under a clause in his lease to
determine it by notice expiring on Michaelmas Day 1837. The tenant
mistakenly gave notice to quit and deliver up the premises on 24 June 1837.
The notice was expressed to be 'agreeably to the covenants of the lease'. It
d   was held that notice was not effective to determine the lease. Lord Denman
CJ said (11 Ad & El 720 at 726, 113 ER 587 at 590):

'We have heard the case argued, and are of opinion that the covenant to
pay rent during the whole term cannot be got rid of by any notice to quit
which is not in accordance with the proviso introduced into the lease for
e   the purpose. The cases that seemed to point the other way merely show
that, where there is no covenant, a notice describing the premises, so as
to be perfectly understood between the parties, will be sufficient: but in
none has a proviso or covenant in a deed been held to be satisfied by a
notice inconsistent with the terms of it.'

f   The reasoning in this brief judgment is clear and compelling. You start with
the position that, under the lease, the tenant has covenanted to pay rent for
the full term; but under a proviso in the lease the tenant may, by notice, rid
himself of the obligation under that covenant. However, to be effective for
that purpose, the notice must conform to the terms of the proviso. If on its
true construction the notice does not do so, it will not be effective for its
g   purpose, because the parties have agreed that only a notice conforming to the
terms of the proviso will be effective. The fact that the landlord realises that
the tenant intended to take advantage of his rights under the proviso, but has
only failed through some mistake to give the required notice, is irrelevant.
The simple fact is that the tenant has failed to use the right key which alone is
h   capable of turning the lock.

Nowadays, the leading case is *Hankey v Clavering* [1942] 2 All ER 311, [1942]
2 KB 326. The lease in question was for a term of 21 years from 25 December
1934. The break clause conferred on either party the right to determine the
lease at the expiration of the first seven years, by six calendar months' notice.
j   The landlord gave notice to the tenant's solicitors in the following terms:

'As I may have to be away for some time in the near future, I will be
obliged if you would accept the six months' notice to terminate your
client's lease which I am allowed to give on June 21, 1941. This would
mean that he would have to give up the cottage on December, 21 1941.'

This was obviously a mistake on the part of the landlord, because the six
months' notice should have expired on 25, not 21, December. At first instance,   *a*
Asquith J held that the notice could be saved on the basis that it had been
accepted as a good notice by the tenant's solicitors; but that solution was
rejected by the Court of Appeal on the facts. The Court of Appeal, which
consisted of two distinguished and very experienced Chancery lawyers, Lord
Greene MR and Lord Clauson, held that the notice was ineffective. They   *b*
regarded the point as so clear that they gave judgment ex tempore. Indeed,
Lord Clauson concluded his brief judgment ([1942] 2 KB 326 at 331, cf [1942]
2 All ER 311 at 314):

> '... I should have thought that, as a matter of construction, an argument
> other than that which leads to the result the Master of the Rolls has   *c*
> announced was quite untenable.'

Lord Greene MR introduced his judgment with the following passage
([1942] 2 KB 326 at 328, cf [1942] 2 All ER 311 at 312–313):

> 'This appeal raises a short point in connection with a break clause in a   *d*
> lease wherein the plaintiff was the lessor and the defendant was the lessee.
> By his letter of January 15, 1940, the plaintiff, on the face of it, was
> purporting to determine the lease by notice on December 21, 1941. The
> whole thing was obviously a slip on his part, and there is a natural
> temptation to put a strained construction on language in aid of people
> who have been unfortunate enough to make slips. That, however, is a   *e*
> temptation which must be resisted, because documents are not to be
> strained and principles of construction are not to be outraged in order to
> do what may appear to be fair in an individual case.'

He expressed his reasoning and conclusion as follows ([1942] 2 KB 326 at
329–330, cf [1942] 2 All ER 311 at 313–314):   *f*

> 'Notices of this kind are documents of a technical nature, technical
> because they are not consensual documents, but, if they are in proper
> form, they have of their own force without any assent by the recipient the
> effect of bringing the demise to an end. They must on their face and on a
> fair and reasonable construction do what the lease provides that they are   *g*
> to do. It is perfectly true that in construing such a document, as in
> construing all documents, the court in a case of ambiguity will lean in
> favour of reading the document in such a way as to give it validity, but I
> dissent entirely from the proposition that, where a document is clear and
> specific, but inaccurate on some matter, such as that of date, it is possible   *h*
> to ignore the inaccuracy and substitute the correct date or other particular
> because it appears that the error was inserted by a slip. By the clear
> wording of this notice the plaintiff purported to bring the lease to an end
> on December 21, 1941. In so doing he was attempting to do something
> which he had no power to do, and, however much the recipient might   *j*
> guess, or however certain he might be, that it was a mere slip, that would
> not cure the defect because the document was never capable on its face of
> producing the necessary legal consequence.'

The essential point made by Lord Greene MR therefore was that notices of
this kind are documents of a technical nature because they are not consensual

a documents; but, if they are in proper form, ie if they comply with the specification in the clause, they have of their own force the effect of bringing the demise to an end. It is necessary, therefore, to turn to the lease to ascertain what is required. Here the landlord had to give six months' notice of his desire to determine the demise at the expiration of the first seven years, which in fact expired on 25 December 1941. This he failed to do; and accordingly the notice

b was not effective. The facts that he had obviously meant to give an effective notice at the end of the first seven years, that he had simply made a mistake about the date, and that this may have been obvious to the other party, made no difference. The simple position was that the notice he gave did not conform to the agreed specification in the clause which gave the right to determine the lease, and so was not effective for that purpose.

c   It is, in my opinion, correct in principle that a notice under such a clause will only be effective if it conforms to the specification in the clause. The specification in the clause is contained in a document which has been agreed between the parties, and so prescribes the requirements with which the notice must comply if it is to achieve the desired effect. In the case before your

d Lordships, the notice must (1) be not less than six months notice, (2) be in writing, (3) be served on the landlord or its solicitors, (4) expire on the third anniversary of the term commencement date. It is plain that fulfilment of all four of these requirements is essential. It is with the fourth requirement that we are here concerned; and it is well established that this required that the notice should be so *expressed* as to expire on the relevant date. The position

e was made clear by another distinguished lawyer, Atkin LJ, in *P Phipps & Co (Northampton and Towcester Breweries) Ltd v Rogers* [1925] 1 KB 14 at 27. He there cited Lord Coleridge CJ as saying in *Gardner v Ingram* (1889) 61 LT 729 at 730, [1886–90] All ER Rep 258 at 260, that: 'Although no particular form need be followed, there must be plain, unambiguous words claiming to determine

f the existing tenancy at a certain time.' Atkin LJ continued: 'The date of determination must be the right date.'

    The principle is therefore clear. The agreement between the parties provides what notice has to be given to be effective to achieve the relevant result. The question in each case is: does the notice which was given, properly

g construed, comply with the agreed specification? If it does, it is effective for its purpose. If it does not, it is not so effective; and the mere fact that the person serving the notice plainly intended, and was trying, to give an effective notice under the clause, and that the recipient of the notice realised that he was doing so, makes no difference. This is because the notice, properly construed, did not comply with the agreement between the parties. The key

h does not fit the lock, and so the door will not open.

    I have been careful to use the expression 'properly construed'. This is because, although at first sight the notice given may not appear to comply with the agreed specification in the clause, nevertheless on examination it may transpire that, properly construed, it does in fact do so. This may occur where

j there is a latent ambiguity in the notice. A striking example is to be found in *Doe d Cox v Roe* (1802) 4 Esp 185, 170 ER 685 (which was cited in argument in *Cadby v Martinez*). There the landlord of a public house in Limehouse gave notice to quit 'the premises which you hold of me ... commonly called or known by the name of the Waterman's Arms'. On the evidence, the only property let by the landlord to the tenant was a public house called the

Bricklayer's Arms; moreover there was no public house in Limehouse called
the Waterman's Arms. The notice was held effective in respect of the tenancy   *a*
of the Bricklayer's Arms, the case being treated as one of latent ambiguity.
Another example occurs when a date is specified in the notice which, as is plain
from the face of the notice, was obviously stated in error for the true date
which the giver of the notice must have intended to specify. This will usually
occur nowadays through a simple typing error. In such a case, the date so   *b*
given can properly be construed as a reference to the true date. An example
of the application of this principle is to be found in *Carradine Properties Ltd v
Aslam* [1976] 1 All ER 573, [1976] 1 WLR 442. In that case, which was (like the
present) concerned with a break clause in a lease, the relevant date upon which
a notice given by either party under the clause might take effect was a date in
September 1975, but a notice given by the landlord in September 1974   *c*
specified a date in September 1973. It was plain from the face of the notice that
a date in 1973, which had already passed, could not conceivably have been
intended by him. It must have been a clerical error, and could properly be read
as intended to refer to 1975. In these circumstances Goulding J, applying
ordinary principles of construction, held the notice to be an effective notice to   *d*
determine the lease on 27 September 1975. He said ([1976] 1 All ER 573 at 577,
[1976] 1 WLR 442 at 446):

> 'In an option clause the requirement is that a party must strictly comply
> with the condition for its exercise. If the condition includes the giving of
> a particular notice, it seems to me that the logical first approach is to   *e*
> interpret the notice, looking at the words and applying legal principles to
> their construction, and then ask whether it complies with the strict
> requirements as to exercise of the option. If that is right, I think a
> benevolent approach could be applied in this case, as in the *Duke of
> Bedford's* case [*Doe d Duke of Bedford v Kightley* (1796) 7 Term Rep 63, 101
> ER 856], because reasonably read by a reasonable tenant the mistake is   *f*
> obvious on the face of it, and there is no doubt what the mistake was.
> *Therefore one interprets the notice as asserting an intention to determine in the
> year 1975.* It is true that if whoever made the mistake had typed 1976
> instead of 1973, the error would probably have been incurable because
> although the tenant might suspect there was a slip, it might be that the   *g*
> landlord did intend 1976, not knowing or understanding his rights under
> the lease. In such a case the tenant would be entitled to disregard the
> notice, but because a past date was given in the notice it is insensible and
> therefore an authority such as the *Duke of Bedford's* case is in point.' (My
> emphasis.)
                                                                                 h

The decision of Goulding J in that case was therefore made in accordance with
the principles I have stated. I should however mention that, in the report of
the case in [1976] 1 WLR 442 at 443, it is stated that, although the date upon
which a notice given by either party under the clause might take effect was 27
September 1975, the notice given by the landlord specified the date as 17   *j*
September 1973. Your Lordships were, however, informed that comparison
of this report with other reports of the case reveals that the date of
determination specified in the landlord's notice was, in fact, 27 September, not
17 September, so that the only error in the landlord's notice consisted of
specifying 1973 instead of 1975. I am satisfied that this must have been the

a case. If not, Goulding J would certainly have addressed the question of the effect of the error as to the day of the month; and, if he had done so, he would, consistently with the reasoning in his judgment, have held that on that ground the notice was ineffective.

It is, however, well settled that, under a clause such as the present which does not require that the date of expiry should be specified as such in the *b* notice but merely that the notice should be expressed to expire on the relevant date, it is enough that the notice should be so expressed to expire in accordance with the terms of the clause. This was made clear by Lord Coleridge CJ in *Gardner v Ingram* (1889) 61 LT 729 at 730, [1886–90] All ER Rep 258 at 260 in the passage I have already quoted. So if the tenant in the present case had given a notice expressed to determine the lease on the third *c* anniversary of the commencement date, that would have been a sufficient compliance with the specification in the clause. Furthermore, it is also well settled that, if the person giving the notice specifies the actual date but out of caution also specifies, in the alternative, the end of the period at which the notice is required under the clause to take effect, the alternative so given will *d* be effective to save the notice if the actual date so given should prove to have been mistaken. For obvious reasons, therefore, it is a commonplace for notices to quit to take this form, which avoids the trap into which the tenant fell in the present case. The position was stated clearly by A L Smith LJ in *Sidebotham v Holland* [1895] 1 QB 378 at 389, [1891–4] All ER Rep 617 at 622–623, a case to which I have already referred, when he said:

e

> 'I would point out that the plaintiff has only himself to blame for the difficulties he is in in this case. Had he added the words which are very ordinarily inserted in a notice to quit, "or at the expiration of the year of your tenancy, which shall expire next after the end of one half-year from *f* the service of this notice," and which are inserted to avoid such a point as that now taken, all would have been in order; but the words are not there. If the notice to quit in this case had been for 20 or 21 May or any later day I should have had no doubt but that it was a bad notice; and I own that the inclination of my opinion is that the present notice is bad because it does not expire upon the last day of some year of the tenancy; but, as Lord *g* Halsbury and Lindley L.J. are of opinion that, inasmuch as this was a full six months' notice given to quit upon the anniversary of the day upon which the tenancy commenced, it is good, though the tenancy expired at midnight the day before, I yield to what they say, and will not differ from them, and hold that this unmeritorious technicality must prevail; and I *h* content myself with expressing what I have said.'

That what I have said sets out the long-established law on this subject appears clearly from the judgments of Lindley LJ (with whom Lord Halsbury agreed) and A L Smith LJ in that case. This was the established law which was applied by the Court of Appeal in *Hankey v Clavering* [1942] 2 All ER 311, [1942] *j* 2 KB 326, and by the Court of Appeal in the present case. I wish to stress however that these principles have been evolved in the case of clauses in leases, such as notices under a break clause, options to purchase, and notices to quit, in which provision is regularly made as to the conditions to be fulfilled in respect of the relevant notice and, in particular, that the notice must be expressed so as to take effect on a certain date.

Before your Lordships Mr Cherryman QC, for the tenant, faced with the
relevant authorities, sought in the present case to distinguish *Hankey v*   *a*
Clavering, which was the authority held by the Court of Appeal to be decisive
against his client. He submitted that the date of determination specified by the
tenant in its notice was not an essential part of the notice and must give way
to the tenant's obvious intention, having regard to the express invocation by
the tenant of cl 7(13), that the notice should have the effect of expiring on the   *b*
third anniversary. But in my opinion that submission is contrary to the
judgment of Lord Greene MR in *Hankey v Clavering* itself. He treated it as
necessary that the person giving the notice should claim to determine the
tenancy at a certain time, and (as Atkin LJ said in the *Phipps* case [1925] 1 KB
14 at 27) that must be the right time. The fact that the tenant in the present
case expressly identified the clause in question as opposed to implicitly   *c*
referring to it (as in *Hankey v Clavering*) cannot, as I see it, make any difference.
If that were so, it would be enough for the person giving the notice simply to
invoke the clause without specifying any time at which the notice should take
effect. That would, however, be contrary to the construction which has for a
long time been placed upon clauses of this kind.   *d*

Mr Cherryman next relied upon a test stated by Goulding J in *Carradine*
Properties Ltd v Aslam [1976] 1 All ER 573 at 576, [1976] 1 WLR 442 at 444, to be
generally applicable, viz: '... is the notice quite clear to a reasonable tenant
reading it? is it plain that he cannot be misled by it?' These words have been
fastened upon to suggest that a broader test should be applied than is
recognised in the authorities, and have been cited in textbooks as having that   *e*
effect. Indeed, in *Micrografix v Woking 8 Ltd* [1995] 2 EGLR 32 Jacob J referred
to Goulding J as having 'distinguished the celebrated, much distinguished,
case of *Hankey v. Clavering* [1942] 2 KB 326' and stated (at 33) that '*Carradine* ...
is the modern approach'. I have to say, however, that this interpretation
reveals a complete misunderstanding of Goulding J's judgment in the   *f*
Carradine case which, read as a whole, demonstrates that he had no intention
of departing from the law as established in the previous authorities, including
Hankey v Clavering, by which he was bound. In his judgment, Goulding J
quoted at length from the judgment of Lord Greene MR in that case, and said
correctly ([1976] 1 All ER 573 at 577, [1976] 1 WLR 442 at 446):
                                                                         g

'In an option clause the requirement is that a party must strictly comply
with the conditions for its exercise. If the condition includes the giving of
a particular notice, it seems to me that the logical first approach is to
interpret the notice, looking at the words and applying legal principles to
their construction, and then ask whether it complies with the strict   *h*
requirements as to exercise of the option.'

Applying those principles, he was able to distinguish *Hankey v Clavering* on
the basis that, if the notice was reasonably read by a reasonable tenant, the
mistake (viz, specifying 1973) was obvious on the face of it and there was no
doubt what that mistake was, ie that the date 1973 must have been typed   *j*
instead of 1975 which the landlord had intended to specify. It is in this sense
that the test stated by Goulding J earlier in his judgment must be understood,
as was made plain when he went on to say that if, instead of the earlier date of
1973, the later date of 1976 had been typed for 1975, such a mistake would
probably have been incurable, because 'although the tenant might suspect

a there was a slip, it might be that the landlord did intend 1976, not knowing or understanding his rights under the lease' (see [1976] 1 All ER 573 at 577, [1976] 1 WLR 442 at 446). Having regard to the reasoning of Goulding J in his judgment, the suggestion that the test earlier stated by him constituted a departure by him from the well-established authorities by which he was bound is, frankly, untenable. Moreover, it is also plain from his judgment that, in
b considering the question whether the notice, on its true construction, complied with the clause in the lease, he was entitled to have regard to the terms of the lease; indeed, it is difficult to see how he could otherwise have considered that question. In this respect, the decision is well summarised in the headnote to the report.

In the *Micrografix* case the tenants gave a notice determining the lease on 23
c March 1995 when under the relevant clause they could only have done so on 23 June 1995. Jacob J held that, as the landlords knew that the date of determination could only be 23 June 1995, they would not have been misled, and the notice should therefore be treated as an effective notice to determine the lease on the correct date, viz 23 June 1995. In my opinion that decision was
d contrary to the long-established line of authority, including *Hankey v Clavering*, by which Jacob J was bound. It failed to give effect to the underlying principle that the notice must, on its true construction, conform to the agreed specification in the applicable clause, failing which it will not under the contract be effective for its purpose. On its true construction it could not be read as a notice taking effect on 23 June 1995, because there was no reason to
e believe that the landlords must have intended to give a notice on that date; on the contrary, in all probability they gave the wrong date as a result of a mistaken view of their rights. I wish to add that the invocation of Goulding J's test by the Court of Appeal in *Germax Securities Ltd v Spiegal* (1978) 37 P & CR 204 reveals no such error, because (as Buckley LJ pointed out (at 206)) the
f mistaken date in that case was not in the operative part of the notice.

Mr Cherryman also relied upon the decision of the Court of Appeal in *Delta Vale Properties Ltd v Mills* [1990] 2 All ER 176, [1990] 1 WLR 445, in which the test propounded by Goulding J in the *Carradine* case was referred to in the judgment of Slade LJ (see [1990] 2 All ER 176 at 183, [1990] 1 WLR 445 at 454). That case was concerned with the meaning and effect of notices to complete
g served by a vendor on a purchaser of land. Under the contract it was provided that, upon service of such a notice, the transaction should 'be completed within 15 working days of service and in respect of such period time shall be of the essence'. The notices however substituted a period of 28 days for the period of 15 days. The purchaser, lacking the necessary funds, failed to
h complete within the period of 28 days; then, having obtained the necessary funds a few days later, sought specific performance of the contract. The vendor claimed that he had rescinded the contract on the purchaser's failure to comply with the notice to complete. The question at issue was whether that notice was effective. The Court of Appeal held that it was. Slade LJ said
j that there was only one sense in which any reasonable recipient would have read it, viz that the vendor would not exercise the rights conferred by the contract (to rescind if the purchaser did not complete within 15 days), provided that the purchaser completed within 28 days (see [1990] 2 All ER 176 at 184, [1990] 1 WLR 445 at 455). Bingham LJ, who reached the same conclusion, said:

'The authorities show that a notice will be invalid and ineffective unless
it gives the precise notice which the contract requires and leaves the
recipient in no reasonable doubt as to the effect of the notice.' (See [1990]
2 All ER 176 at 186, [1990] 1 WLR 445 at 457.)

I can see nothing in the judgments in this case which detracts from the
principles which I have already stated.

In the end Mr Cherryman was forced to submit in his reply that *Hankey v
Clavering* should be overruled. In doing so, he was faced with the dual
handicap, first, that no such argument had been foreshadowed in his printed
case, and second, that he was in truth inviting your Lordships to overrule not
merely *Hankey v Clavering* itself but the long line of authority which had
preceded it. Even so, I have considered with some care whether your
Lordships should accept this submission. In doing so I have, as previously
stated, recognised that, on occasion, the recipient of a notice under, for
example, a break clause in a lease may, as here, treat it as ineffective because
it does not comply with the contractual specification, even though he must
have been aware that the giver of the notice intended to comply with the
clause and only failed to do so through a mistake on his part. I am, however,
driven to state that there are formidable obstacles in the way of Mr
Cherryman's submission.

The suggestion is that a more relaxed approach be adopted to the
construction of notices of this kind, so that, if it is clear that the giver of the
notice intended to comply with the provisions of the clause, he should be held
to have done so, despite an erroneous choice of the date on which the notice
is to take effect. It was submitted that, provided that this test is expressed in
sufficiently strict terms, so that the recipient is left in no reasonable doubt that
the giver of the notice intended to comply with the clause, this approach
should not lead to any undue uncertainty in its application. This latter
argument I do not find persuasive. There is a wide range of possible errors,
and there are bound to be cases on the borderline in which there is doubt
whether the intention is sufficiently clear. More fundamentally, however, it
seems to me that the adoption of such a test in truth requires that a new
meaning should be given to clauses of this kind, so that they are read as
requiring no more than that the giver of the notice should express a clear
intention to exercise his rights under the clause, instead of requiring that the
date on which it is to take effect must be expressly identified, either as such or
with reference to the terms of the clause.

I have no doubt that this may indeed be the meaning properly to be
attributed to many contractual provisions conferring a right exercisable upon
notice. But the difficulty in the way of so holding in the case of clauses in
leases, such as the break clause in the present case, is that for well over a
century a different construction has been placed upon them. Innumerable
leases, many of them still in force, must have been drafted on the
understanding that they bear the well-known meaning established in the
authorities. It follows that, quite apart from the element of uncertainty to
which I have referred, the step which your Lordships are being invited to take
would have a retrospective effect. In these circumstances I am most reluctant
to depart from the established meaning unless I am persuaded that there is
very good reason to do so.

a   In considering this question, I start from the position not only that the established meaning is clear and well known, but also that the trap which the tenant fell into in the present case is easily avoided by adopting the familiar stratagem of invoking, as an alternative to the specified date, a date identifiable by reference to the terms of the clause itself. In these circumstances I am driven to wonder how often it occurs that, among the numerous notices of

b   this kind which are given each year, mistakes of this kind are made. I simply do not know; though I cannot help suspecting that such cases are very few. If they were more frequent than I suspect, it would be surprising if there was not a greater move for such clauses to be drafted in different terms, or even for the legislature to require that such clauses should be read as having a different effect. In these circumstances I find myself responding to the submission

c   made by Mr Patten QC, in his admirable argument on behalf of the respondent landlords, that it is inadvisable for the judges to disturb this well-settled branch of the law. After all, the number of notices given each year under leases must be very great. Their effect, if challenged, will ordinarily fall to be considered in the county court. At present, the applicable law is clear and well settled, and

d   Mr Patten informed your Lordships that disputes were rare. In these circumstances the change in the law now proposed would not, in my opinion, be justified.

   For these reasons, I would dismiss the appeal.

e   **LORD JAUNCEY OF TULLICHETTLE.** My Lords, cl 7(13) of each lease empowered the tenant to terminate the lease by serving not less than six months notice 'to expire on the 3rd anniversary of the term commencement date [to] determine this Lease *and upon expiry of such notice* this Lease shall cease and determine ...' The words emphasised (by me) refer to the expiry of the period of not less than six months which must be contemporaneous with

f   the termination of the lease. It is agreed that the third anniversary expired on 13 January 1995. However the notices, although stated to be pursuant to cl 7(13) bore to determine the leases on 12 January, the day before a notice given in accordance with that provision could expire. The question is whether the reference to 12 instead of 13 January is fatal to the validity of the notices.

g   The Court of Appeal ([1996] 1 All ER 55, [1995] 1 WLR 1508) reversing the decision of the judge, held that it was.

   Notices terminating a tenancy are technical documents because they are effective without the consent of the receiver. It is therefore essential that they conform to the statutory or contractual provisions under which they are

h   given. In *Cadby v Martinez* (1840) 11 Ad & El 720 at 726, 113 ER 587 at 590 Lord Denman CJ observed that a covenant in a lease 'cannot be got rid of by any notice to quit which is not in accordance with the proviso introduced into the lease for the purpose'. This proposition was expressly approved more than 100 years later in *Hankey v Clavering* [1942] 2 All ER 311 at 314, [1942] 2 KB 326 at 330 by Lord Greene MR. Mr Cherryman QC for the tenants in his opening

j   speech accepted this proposition but argued that properly construed the notices did accord with cl 7(13) of the lease inasmuch as the specific reference thereto predominated over the subordinate and unnecessary reference to the date 12 January. The notices would have been perfectly good if the words '12 January 1995' had been omitted. My Lords, I reject this contention. Clause 7(13) required that the notice be expressed to expire in accordance with the

provisions thereof. This could be achieved either by reference to the correct
date or by repeating the formula 'to expire on ...' in the clause. This was the *a*
form of notice which the tenants had agreed to serve but which in the event
they did not. The notice contains within itself a specific date upon which the
tenancy is to determine. Is that date to be construed as another date because
of the reference to the empowering provisions of cl 7(13) or are those
provisions to be construed as authorising notices which do not strictly *b*
conform to what has been agreed? In *Hankey v Clavering* the Court of Appeal
had to determine the validity of a landlord's notice to quit which purported to
terminate a tenancy some four days before the break clause in the lease
permitted this to be done. In terms of the lease termination thereof could
properly take place on 25 December 1941 whereas the notice was in, inter alia,
the following terms: *c*

> 'As I may have to be away for some time in the near future, I will be
> obliged if you would accept the six months' notice to terminate your
> client's lease which I am allowed to give on June 21, 1941. This would
> mean that he would have to give up the cottage on December 21, 1941.'
>   *d*

In accepting that the date in the notice was obviously a slip Lord Greene MR
rejected the temptation to put a strained construction on the document in
order to aid someone who had made an unfortunate slip. He said ([1942] 2 KB
326 at 329–330, cf [1942] 2 All ER 311 at 313–314):

> 'Notices of this kind are documents of a technical nature, technical *e*
> because they are not consensual documents, but, if they are in proper
> form, they have of their own force without any assent by the recipient the
> effect of bringing the demise to an end. They must on their face and on a
> fair and reasonable construction do what the lease provides that they are
> to do. It is perfectly true that in construing such a document, as in *f*
> construing all documents, the court in a case of ambiguity will lean in
> favour of reading the document in such a way as to give it validity, but I
> dissent entirely from the proposition that, where a document is clear and
> specific, but inaccurate on some matter, such as that of date, it is possible
> to ignore the inaccuracy and substitute the correct date or other particular
> because it appears that the error was inserted by a slip. By the clear *g*
> wording of this notice the plaintiff purported to bring the lease to an end
> on December 21, 1941. In so doing he was attempting to do something
> which he had no power to do, and, however much the recipient might
> guess, or however certain he might be, that it was a mere slip, that would
> not cure the defect because the document was never capable on its face of *h*
> producing the necessary legal consequence. The authority for that
> proposition is *Cadby* v. *Martinez* ...'

I take from these observations the proposition that if a notice to quit is ex
facie clear and specific as to a matter such as the subjects to which it relates or
the date upon which it is to operate it matters not that consideration of the *j*
empowering provision demonstrates a discrepancy between it and the notice.
The case of ambiguity to which Lord Greene MR referred was one appearing
on the face of the notice and not one which was only apparent from a
consideration of the lease. Indeed it was implicit in the notice in that case that
it was given in pursuance of the landlord's contractual powers with which it

a did not accord. However, the conflicting terms of the lease did not save it. Furthermore, I can see no reason for construing cl 7(13) as permitting non-conforming notices.

It was argued that the specific reference to cl 7(13) distinguished this case from *Hankey v Clavering*. I disagree. If it were appropriate to read into an otherwise clear and specific notice a contractual power for the purpose of

b substituting a correct for an incorrect date Lord Greene MR would no doubt have done so, given his observation as to the court endeavouring to give validity to a document. I see no difference in principle between an implied reference to a contractual provision and an express one. If *Hankey v Clavering* is still good law then the notice given by this tenant was ineffective.

I turn to consider whether the law has, as Mr Cherryman submitted, during

c the last 50 years developed a more flexible attitude to notices to quit which contained inaccuracies. In *Carradine Properties Ltd v Aslam* [1976] 1 All ER 573, [1976] 1 WLR 442 Goulding J held that a notice by landlords correctly dated 6 September 1974, to determine a lease on 27 September 1973 would be interpreted as a notice to determine on 27 September 1975, a date which

d accorded with the provisions of the break clause. The judge after referring to the need for a party to comply strictly with the requirement for the exercise of an option or break clause continued ([1976] 1 All ER 573 at 577, [1976] 1 WLR 442 at 446):

e 'If the condition includes the giving of a particular notice, it seems to me that the logical first approach is to interpret the notice, looking at the words and applying legal principles to their construction, and then ask whether it complies with the strict requirements as to exercise of the option. If that is right, I think a benevolent approach could be applied in this case, as in the *Duke of Bedford's* case [*Doe d Duke of Bedford v Kightley*

f (1796) 7 Term Rep 63, 101 ER 856], because reasonably read by a reasonable tenant the mistake is obvious on the face of it, and there is no doubt what the mistake was. Therefore one interprets the notice as asserting an intention to determine in the year 1975. It is true that if whoever made the mistake had typed 1976 instead of 1973, the error would probably have been incurable because although the tenant might

g suspect there was a slip, it might be that the landlord did intend 1976, not knowing or understanding his rights under the lease.'

In this passage the judge was contrasting the situation where it was apparent from the face of the notice that the date of determination must be mistaken

h because it had already passed with one where the date of determination had yet to come and where it could not therefore be seen from the notice itself that the date was inserted in error. Mr Cherryman argued that the judge was correct in relation to the first situation but wrong in relation to the second. In my view the distinction drawn by Goulding J was entirely logical. In the first situation, which was the case before him, it only required a glance at the notice

j to see that the date of determination must be a mistake. This was not the position in *Hankey v Clavering*. In the second situation there was nothing within the four corners of the notice which showed that 1976 was a mistake. This was the position in *Hankey v Clavering*.

In *Delta Vale Properties Ltd v Mills* [1990] 2 All ER 176, [1990] 1 WLR 445 a contract for sale of property provided, inter alia, for service of a completion notice requiring the transaction to be completed within 15 days. The seller served such a notice requiring completion within 28 days and the buyers *a* challenged its validity. The Court of Appeal held that the notice was valid since a reasonable reader thereof could only have concluded that the notice was intended to be one conforming to the empowering provision and that the sellers were giving him 28 days instead of 15 to complete. This was not a case of a party serving a notice which he was not empowered to serve but rather of *b* a party exercising forbearance in the strict compliance with a contractual term in his favour by giving, as he was entitled to do, a longer period of notice than was required. The case is no support for the tenant's argument that 13 January should be substituted for 12 January. In *Micrografix v Woking 8 Ltd* [1995] 2 EGLR 32 the provisions of a lease entitled tenants to give not less than 12 months notice of their intention to determine the lease on 23 June 1995. In *c* January 1994 they sent a letter stating that they were enclosing a notice determining the lease on 23 March 1995, which notice stated the date of determination as 23 March 1994. Jacob J in holding that the notice was valid because the landlords would not have been misled by the pair of wrong dates and would have seen exactly what the tenants intended, observed that *d* *Carradine Properties Ltd v Aslam* [1976] 1 All ER 573, [1976] 1 WLR 442 was the modern approach to construction of documents which was more in favour of making them work than in the past. After referring to Goulding J's second situation, he stated (at 33):

'That was an obiter observation at a point in time up to which the rather *e* stricter view of Lord Greene had prevailed. In 1995 I rather think that a court faced with an obvious slip would construe the document without the slip.'

My Lords I consider that Jacob J was in error in placing so much reliance on the understanding of the landlord. Lord Greene MR in the passage from *f* *Hankey v Clavering* [1942] 2 All ER 311 at 313–314, [1942] 2 KB 326 at 329–330, to which I have already referred emphasised that even certainty by a recipient that a date was a slip would not cure the defect and this view was echoed in the Court of Appeal in this case by Nourse LJ (see [1996] 1 All ER 55 at 59, [1995] 1 WLR 1508 at 1513). In *Delta Vale Properties Ltd v Mills* [1990] 2 All ER *g* 176 at 184, [1990] 1 WLR 445 at 455, Slade LJ accepted that the absence of confusion or prejudice on the part of the recipient was irrelevant. Their Lordships were referred to no other case in which this approach had been questioned nor the stricter approach of Lord Greene MR in *Hankey v Clavering* [1942] 2 All ER 311 at 313–314, [1942] 2 KB 326 at 329–330, doubted. The *h* *Micrografix* case [1995] 2 EGLR 32 was the only case cited in argument in which the court had construed a specific date as other than that stated and in which the error did not, as in the *Carradine* case, proclaim itself from the face of the notice. I consider that it was wrongly decided.

Hankey v Clavering is a case of considerable authority, which has stood unchallenged and been applied for more than 50 years. Mr Cherryman only *j* sought to challenge it with no great enthusiasm in the last speech. I am not persuaded that there is any good reason for departing from the principles enunciated by Lord Greene MR. It would be tempting to say that where a notice is disconform to that stipulated in the relevant empowering provision due to a slip which was obvious to any reasonable receiver thereof it may be a construed so as to conform. However, I can see considerable difficulties arising out of the application of such a principle. On one view it could be said that the giver of a notice empowered by a contractual provision always intends to comply with that provision, thus however far such notice departed from what was contractually required it could be construed to conform with such requirements. On another view it could be argued that a notice which

b departed substantially from what was required cannot have been intended to conform but was intended to depart from contractual requirements or given in ignorance thereof. Where is the line to be drawn between defective notices which can and those which cannot be construed so as to conform? Such possibilities would create inevitable uncertainties which as Mr Patten QC, for the landlord, submitted would be likely to lead to increased litigation. There

c will, of course, be cases where an unintended slip in the drafting of a notice will result in hardship to the giver thereof but he will only have himself to blame for not complying with the terms of the empowering provision. Against this, however, must be measured the advantage to the recipient of certainty inasmuch as a date in a notice is to be read as stated unless it is

d obvious from the face of the notice that it must be mistaken.

Applying Lord Greene MR's principles to this case, the tenant had no power under cl 7(13) to determine the lease on 12 January from which it follows that its notice was ineffective.

My Lords, I have had the advantage of reading in draft the speech of my noble and learned friend, Lord Goff of Chieveley with whose reasoning I am

e in entire agreement. I would therefore dismiss the appeal.

LORD STEYN. My Lords, the short but not uncomplicated question is whether notices given by a tenant to a landlord purportedly under a right to determine reserved in terms of leases for fixed terms were effective to

f determine the leases.

The landlord is Eagle Star Life Assurance Co Ltd. The tenant is Mannai Investment Co Ltd. There are two leases both dated 11 March 1992. The demised property consists of office premises and car parking space in London, SW1. The two leases demised the office premises and the car parking space in each case 'FOR the term of TEN YEARS subject to the provisions of Clause 7(13)

g hereof from and including the 13th day of January 1992 ...' Clause 7(13) of each lease provided as follows:

> 'The Tenant may by serving not less than six months notice in writing on the Landlord or its solicitors such notice to expire on the 3rd
h anniversary of the term commencement date determine this Lease and upon expiry of such notice this Lease shall cease and determine and have no further effect ...'

Under each lease the term granted included 13 January as the first day of the term. The 'term commencement date' in cl 7(13) was not defined in either

j lease. But it is common ground that by reason of the words 'from and including 13 January 1992' it was that date. Accordingly, it was agreed that the third anniversary of the 'term commencement date' was 13 January 1995.

By two letters dated 24 June 1994 and served on the landlord more than six months before 13 January 1995 the tenant gave notice to the landlord in respect of each lease as follows: 'Pursuant to Clause 7(13) of the Lease we as

Tenant hereby give notice to you to determine the Lease on 12th January 1995.'

a

The tenant contended that the leases were determined by the notices. The landlord claimed that the notices did not comply with the right reserved under cl 7(13) and that the notices were ineffective in law.

By an originating summons the tenant sought a declaration that the notices effectively determined the leases. The matter came before Judge Rich QC, *b* sitting as a judge of the High Court in the Chancery Division. Relying on *Sidebotham v Holland* [1895] 1 QB 378, [1891–4] All ER Rep 617 Judge Rich held that the notices were good inasmuch as they did not take effect until that moment of time which was both the last moment of 12 January and the first of 13 January, so that they did determine the leases on 13 January. The landlord appealed to the Court of Appeal ([1996] 1 All ER 55, [1995] 1 WLR *c* 1508).

Two issues were debated in the Court of Appeal. The first was whether, despite the erroneous reference in the notices to 12 rather than 13 January, the notices were nevertheless as a matter of construction sufficiently clear to be effective: this was described as the construction point. The second issue was *d* whether the notices were saved by what was called the special rule in *Sidebotham v Holland*. The Court of Appeal decided both issues against the tenant. The Court of Appeal held that the notices did not determine the leases.

On the appeal to your Lordship's House counsel for the tenant again *e* advanced both arguments. The point of construction is one of substance. Despite a lucid argument by junior counsel for the tenant your Lordships were of the view, which I shared, that the argument based on *Sidebotham v Holland* was plainly wrong and did not find it necessary to call on counsel for the landlord to reply on this issue. As Nourse LJ trenchantly explained in the Court of Appeal *Sidebotham v Holland* is no authority for the proposition that *f* in respect of a lease for a fixed term a notice served on one day can be treated as a notice served on the next (see [1996] 1 All ER 55 at 61, [1995] 1 WLR 1508 at 1515). That disposed of this point. I turn therefore to the construction of the notices.

On reflection I have come to the conclusion that the question of the *g* construction of the notices should be answered by holding that the notices were effective to determine the leases.   I will first summarise my analysis of the problem before I explain why I feel unable to accept the attractively presented arguments of counsel for the landlord.

The reasons for my conclusion can be stated in the form of numbered *h* propositions:

(1) This is not a case of a contractual right to determine which prescribes as an indispensable condition for its effective exercise that the notice must contain specific information. After providing for the form of the notice ('in writing'), its duration ('not less than six months') and service ('on the Landlord or its solicitors'), the only words in cl 7(13) relevant to the content of the *j* notice are the words 'notice to expire on the 3rd anniversary of the term commencement date determine this Lease'. Those words do not have any customary meaning in a technical sense. No terms of art are involved. And neither side has suggested that anything should be implied into the language. That is not surprising since the tests governing the implication of terms could

a not conceivably be satisfied. The language of cl 7(13) must be given its ordinary meaning. A notice simply expressed to determine the lease on third anniversary of the commencement date would therefore have been effective. The principle is that that is certain which the context renders certain: see *Sunrose Ltd v Gould* [1961] 3 All ER 1142, [1962] 1 WLR 20.

b (2) The question is not how the landlord understood the notices. The construction of the notices must be approached objectively. The issue is how a reasonable recipient would have understood the notices. And in considering this question the notices must be construed taking into account the relevant objective contextual scene. The approach in *Reardon Smith Line Ltd v Hansen-Tangen, Hansen-Tangen v Sanko Steamship Co* [1976] 3 All ER 570, [1976]
c 1 WLR 989, which deals with the construction of commercial contracts, is by analogy of assistance in respect of unilateral notices such as those under consideration in the present case. Relying on the reasoning in Lord Wilberforce's speech in the *Reardon Smith* case [1976] 3 All ER 570 at 574–575, [1976] 1 WLR 989 at 996–997, three propositions can be formulated. First, in respect of contracts and contractual notices the contextual scene is always
d relevant. Secondly, what is *admissible* as a matter of the rules of evidence under this heading is what is arguably relevant. But admissibility is not the decisive matter. The real question is what evidence of surrounding circumstances may ultimately be allowed to influence the question of interpretation. That depends on what meanings the language read against the objective contextual scene will let in. Thirdly, the inquiry is objective: the
e question is what reasonable persons, circumstanced as the actual parties were, would have had in mind. It follows that one cannot ignore that a reasonable recipient of the notices would have had in the forefront of his mind the terms of the leases. Given that the reasonable recipient must be credited with knowledge of the critical date and the terms of cl 7(13) the question is simply
f how the reasonable recipient would have understood such a notice. This proposition may in other cases require qualification. Depending on the circumstances a party may be precluded by an estoppel by convention from raising a contention contrary to a common assumption of fact or law (which could include the validity of a notice) upon which they have acted: see *Norwegian American Cruises A/S (formerly Norwegian American Lines A/S) v Paul*
g *Mundy Ltd, The Vistafjord* [1988] 2 Lloyds Rep 343. Such an issue may involve subjective questions. That is, however, a different issue and not one relevant to this appeal. I proceed therefore to examine the matter objectively.

h (3) It is important not to lose sight of the purpose of a notice under the break clause. It serves one purpose only: to inform the landlord that the tenant has decided to determine the lease in accordance with the right reserved. That purpose must be relevant to the construction and validity of the notice. Prima facie one would expect that if a notice unambiguously conveys a decision to determine a court may nowadays ignore immaterial errors which would not have misled a reasonable recipient.

j (4) There is no justification for placing notices under a break clause in leases in a unique category. Making due allowance for contextual differences, such notices belong to the general class of unilateral notices served under contractual rights reserved, e g notices to quit, notices to determine licences and notices to complete (see *Delta Vale Properties Ltd v Mills* [1990] 2 All ER 176 at 183, [1990] 1 WLR 445 at 454). To those examples may be added notices

under charterparties, contracts of affreightment, and so forth. Even if such
notices under contractual rights reserved contain errors they may be valid if *a*
they are 'sufficiently clear and unambiguous to leave a reasonable recipient in
no reasonable doubt as to how and when they are intended to operate': see the
Delta case [1990] 2 All ER 176 at 183, [1990] 1 WLR 445 at 454 per Slade LJ and
adopted by Stocker and Bingham LJJ and *Carradine Properties Ltd v Aslam* [1976]
1 All ER 573 at 576, [1976] 1 WLR 442 at 444. That test postulates that the *b*
reasonable recipient is left in no doubt that the right reserved is being
exercised. It acknowledges the importance of such notices. The application
of that test is principled and cannot cause any injustice to a recipient of the
notice. I would gratefully adopt it.

(5) That brings me to the application of this test. The facts are simple.
Crediting a reasonable recipient with knowledge of the terms of the lease and *c*
third anniversary date (13 January), I venture to suggest that it is obvious that
a reasonable recipient would have appreciated that the tenant wished to
determine the leases on the third anniversary date of the leases but wrongly
described it as 12 January instead of 13 January. The reasonable recipient
would not have been perplexed in any way by the minor error in the notices. *d*
The notices would have achieved their intended purpose.

That brings me to the contrary reasoning of the Court of Appeal in this case,
and the submission of counsel for the landlord. Central to both was the
proposition that *Hankey v Clavering* [1942] 2 All ER 311, [1942] 2 KB 326
precluded such a conclusion. Given the importance ascribed to this decision I
must embark on what Cardozo J once described as a gruesome autopsy. In *e*
Hankey v Clavering there was a lease for a term of 21 years from 25 December
1934. The lease provided, inter alia, that if either party should desire to
determine the lease after seven or fourteen years he could do so by giving to
the other party six months' notice. The landlord gave notice to the tenant as
from June 1941, which purported to terminate the lease on 21 December 1941. *f*
On 8 March 1940 the landlord's solicitors acknowledged the notice as
'properly served upon us'. The tenant refused to give up possession of the
premises. The landlord brought an action for possession. Mr Denning KC
submitted that the landlord attempted to terminate the tenancy on 21
December whereas he was only entitled to terminate it on 25 December. In
these circumstances, he said, that the defect could not be cured by showing *g*
that the other party understood what was meant. Mr Blanco White KC argued
that if a notice can be understood by a reasonable person it is a good notice.
The judge decided in favour of the landlord on the effect of the
correspondence. The matter came before a two judge Court of Appeal. It was
disposed of by ex tempore judgments. Lord Greene MR gave the principal *h*
judgment; Lord Clauson added nothing of substance. The Court of Appeal
ruled that the judge had misinterpreted the correspondence. Turning to the
construction of the notice, Lord Greene MR said ([1942] 2 KB 326 at 329–330,
cf [1942] 2 All ER 311 at 313–314):

'Notices of this kind are documents of a technical nature, technical *j*
because they are not consensual documents, but, if they are in proper
form, they have of their own force without any assent by the recipient the
effect of bringing the demise to an end. They must on their face and on a
fair and reasonable construction do what the lease provides that they are
to do. It is perfectly true that in construing such a document, as in

a construing all documents, the court in a case of ambiguity will lean in favour of reading the document in such a way as to give it validity, but I dissent entirely from the proposition that, where a document is clear and specific, but inaccurate on some matter, such as that of date, it is possible to ignore the inaccuracy and substitute the correct date or other particular because it appears that the error was inserted by a slip. By the clear

b wording of this notice the plaintiff purported to bring the lease to an end on December 21, 1941. In so doing he was attempting to do something which he had no power to do, and, however much the recipient might guess, or however certain he might be, that it was a mere slip, that would not cure the defect because the document was never capable on its face of producing the necessary legal consequence.'

c
Lord Greene MR said that his ruling was based on *Cadby v Martinez* (1840) 11 Ad & El 720, 113 ER 587, which he described of as 'a case of the highest authority in these matters'. Lord Denman CJ said in that case:

d '... the covenant to pay rent during the whole term cannot be got rid of by any notice to quit which is not in accordance with the proviso introduced into the lease for the purpose.' (See 11 Ad & El 720 at 726, 113 ER 587 at 590.)

It goes without saying that any judgment of Lord Greene MR is entitled to great respect. But one must put the case in context. First, in relying on *Cadby*

e *v Martinez* Lord Greene MR was founding his proposition on a case which with the benefit of hindsight seems far from conclusive on the point. Lord Denman CJ's judgment contains no reasoning at all; it is purely conclusionary. A century and a half later it is sometimes necessary to consider the force of reasoning in decided cases. *Cadby v Martinez* does not enable one to do so. In

f any event, Lord Denman CJ's conclusion is in such absolute terms as to be of little value. It is not supported in this case by the judgment in the Court of Appeal or by the submissions of counsel for the landlord: it is conceded that some errors in a notice can be ignored. The real question is: What errors can be overlooked? Taking due account of what Lord Greene MR thought of *Cadby v Martinez* in 1942, I incline to the view that the persuasive force of this

g precedent must be regarded as slight. Secondly, it is noteworthy that Lord Greene MR does not expressly pose an objective test. He dismisses the reaction of the recipient ('however much the recipient might guess'). The law has moved on. The test is entirely objective. Thirdly, Lord Greene MR did not expressly deal with the position where the notice contains an error which

h proves wholly immaterial and incapable of causing any confusion. The second and third matters detract from the force of reasoning in *Hankey v Clavering*. Lord Greene MR was not considering the issues as they have to be faced in this case. But there is a fourth point to be taken into account. *Hankey v Clavering* was decided more than half a century ago. Since then there has been a shift from strict construction of commercial instruments to what is sometimes

j called purposive construction of such documents. Lord Diplock deprecated the use of that phrase in regard to the construction of private contracts as opposed to the construction of statutes: see *Antaios Cia Naviera SA v Salen Rederierna AB, The Antaios* [1984] 3 All ER 229 at 233, [1985] AC 191 at 201. That is understandable. There are obvious differences between the processes of interpretation in regard to private contracts and public statutes. For a

perceptive exploration of the differences in the context of US law, see Robert
S Summers 'Statutes and Contracts as Founts of Formal Reasoning' in Cane
and Stapleton (editors) *Essays for Patrick Atiyah* (1991) p 71ff. It is better to
speak of a shift towards commercial interpretation. About the fact of the
change in approach to construction there is no doubt. One illustration will be
sufficient. In *Antaios Cia Naviera SA v Salen Rederierna AB* [1984] 3 All ER 229
at 233, [1985] AC 191 at 201, Lord Diplock in a speech concurred in by his
fellow Law Lords observed:

> '... if a detailed semantic and syntactical analysis of words in a
> commercial contract is going to lead to a conclusion that flouts business
> common sense, it must be made to yield to business common sense.'

In determining the meaning of the language of a commercial contract, and
unilateral contractual notices, the law therefore generally favours a
commercially sensible construction. The reason for this approach is that a
commercial construction is more likely to give effect to the intention of the
parties. Words are therefore interpreted in the way in which a reasonable
commercial person would construe them. And the standard of the reasonable
commercial person is hostile to technical interpretations and undue emphasis
on niceties of language. In contradistinction to this modern approach Lord
Greene MR's judgment in *Hankey v Clavering* [1942] 2 All ER 311, [1942] 2 KB
326 is rigid and formalistic. Nowadays one expects a notice to determine
under a commercial lease to be interpreted not as a 'technical document' but
in accordance with business common sense: see *Micrografix v Woking 8 Ltd*
[1995] 2 EGLR 32. After all, there is no reason whatever why such a document
must be drafted by a lawyer. Qualitatively, the notices are of the same type as
notices under charterparties and contracts of affreightment. Such notices,
even if they entail the exercise of important options, are habitually drafted by
commercial men rather than lawyers. It would be a disservice to commercial
practice to classify such notices as technical documents and to require them to
be interpreted as such. Nowadays one must substitute for the rigid rule in
Hankey v Clavering the standard of a commercial construction.

It is, however, also important to note that the decision in *Hankey v Clavering*
caused surprise even in 1942. There was a case note on *Hankey v Clavering*
(1943) 59 LQR 17 bearing the initials R E M. The author of the note was a
great authority on the field of landlord and tenant. He later became Sir Robert
Megarry, Vice Chancellor of the Chancery Division. He was clearly surprised
at the decision. He drew attention to Lord Greene MR's decision in *Price v
Mann* [1942] 1 All ER 453. In that case the question was whether under the
Landlord and Tenant (War Damage) Act 1939 a notice to avoid disclaimer
given by the landlord, requiring the tenant to retain the lease on the terms set
out in s 10, was invalid because s 10 was irrelevant and by mistake inserted for
s 11. The Court of Appeal held that the notice was good. Lord Greene MR
said (at 454):

> 'Reading this document as a whole, it seems to me perfectly manifest
> that a person who received it, and who had that familiarity with the
> provisions of the Act which a recipient of such a document must be
> presumed to have, could not possibly be under any illusion as to what it
> was intended to be and what its legal consequences were.'

a   Mr Megarry observed (at p 18):

> 'But for the line of authority governing notices to quit, it would have
> occasioned little surprise to some had the words used by the Master of the
> Rolls in the two cases been interchanged. Read literally, both notices
> purported to do something which they could not do, yet read as a whole,
> neither was at all likely to mislead the recipient ... The distinction may be
b
> that in *Price v. Mann* the reference to the precise section of the Act was
> unnecessary whereas in *Hankey v. Clavering* the insertion of the date was
> essential to the validity of a notice cast in the form employed. If this is not
> the case, perhaps all that can be said is that in *Price v. Mann* each member
> of the Court of Appeal could use the words of MacKinnon, L.J., and say to
c
> himself "The law as it stands does permit me to give effect to
> common-sense and decency" (*Heap v. Ind Coope & Allsopp, Ltd.* ([1940] 3
> All ER 634 at 637, [1940] 2 KB 476 at 484), whereas in *Hankey v. Clavering*
> the hand of stare decisis was writ large.'

Lord Greene MR's observation in *Price v Mann* is much closer to the modern
d   standard of commercial construction than *Hankey v Clavering*.

Counsel for the tenant invited the House in his case and in his reply to say
that *Hankey v Clavering* was wrongly decided. I am content to say that it no
longer represents the law. Like Lord Hoffmann I would hold that the correct
test for the validity of a notice is that posed by Goulding J in *Carradine
e   Properties Ltd v Aslam* [1976] 1 All ER 573 at 576, [1976] 1 WLR 442 at 444, viz:
'... is the notice quite clear to a reasonable tenant reading it? is it plain that he
cannot be misled by it?'

It is necessary to turn briefly to other arguments advanced by counsel for
the landlord. He argued that the tenant's construction argument must fail
because the tenant's error may have been due to a mistaken legal view. He
f   said that it may not have been a case of a mistaken insertion of a date but the
tenant may have intended to refer to the 12th. This reveals a contradiction in
the landlord's argument. Counsel for the landlord accepted that the test is an
objective one: How would a reasonable recipient have understood the notice?
But then he invited your Lordships to speculate that the tenant's error was due
g   to a mistake of law rather than a typing or clerical error. That argument, if
accepted, would drive a juggernaut through the objective test. Speculation
about the subjective intention of the tenant is irrelevant. The only question is
how a reasonable recipient would have understood the notice.

Counsel also argued that as a matter of legal logic a process of interpretation
h   can never permit one to substitute 13 January for 12 January. Why should that
be so? If a contract contains a termination date linked to an intended
three-year period, which is variously expressed in the contract as 12 January
and 13 January, why should the court not as a matter of interpretation be able
to select the date which best matches the contractual intent? The same
reasoning must apply to unilateral documents such as contractual notices. It
j   is surely permissible in all cases satisfying the test that no reasonable recipient
of the notice could be misled. Counsel's argument is based on too formalistic
a formulation of the question to be decided. The question is not whether 12
January can *mean* 13 January: it self-evidently cannot. The real question is a
different one: Does the notice construed against its contextual setting
unambiguously inform a reasonable recipient how and when the notice is to

operate *under the right reserved*? As Lord Hoffmann has observed we no longer confuse the meaning of words with the question of what meaning in a particular setting the use of words was intended to convey.

That brings me to counsel's argument that, if the notices are treated as valid, there will be great deal of confusion and unnecessary litigation. Experience teaches that 'floodgates' arguments need to be examined with an initial scepticism. In this case the predictions of counsel are unrealistic. Those arguments must be judged on the basis that the test posed above is accepted. That test can only be satisfied where the reasonable recipient could be left in no doubt whatever. It is in accord with business common sense that in cases where that simple and straightforward test is satisfied the notices should be treated as valid.

That brings me to my conclusion. I do not accept the extreme argument of counsel for the tenant that whenever a notice to determine refers to a break clause, and whatever the other circumstances of the case, the notice must be valid. That goes too far. One can easily conceive of much weaker cases where the test posed above could not be satisfied. But in the present case it would have been obvious to a reasonable recipient that the notices contained a minor misdescription and that the notices conveyed that the tenant sought to determine the leases on 'the 3rd anniversary of the term commencement', ie 13 January. I end this judgment with the words with which in 1903 Sir Leslie Stephen concluded a famous series of lectures: 'I hope I have not said anything original.'

It follows that I would allow the appeal.

LORD HOFFMANN. My Lords, the appellant was tenant under two 10-year leases of offices in Jermyn Street, each of which contained in cl 7(13) a right to terminate at the end of the third year in the following terms:

> 'The Tenant may by serving not less than six months notice in writing on the Landlord or its solicitors such notice to expire on the 3rd anniversary of the term commencement date determine this Lease and upon expiry of such notice this Lease shall cease and determine and have no further effect ...'

After the grant of the leases the market rents of offices in the West End fell sharply. On 24 June 1994 the tenant served on the landlord two notices, each of which read as follows: 'Pursuant to Clause 7(13) of the Lease we as Tenant hereby give notice to you to determine the Lease on 12th January 1995.' It is agreed that the third anniversary of the commencement date was actually 13 January 1995. The question is whether notwithstanding this mistake the notices were effective to terminate the leases.

This might seem a straightforward question, particularly when it is remembered that such notices, operating, as they do, unilaterally to alter the rights of the parties, must comply strictly with the terms of the lease. The Court of Appeal ([1996] 1 All ER 55, [1995] 1 WLR 1508) held that the notice was ineffective on the simple ground that '12 January' could not mean '13 January'. In so doing, they followed (as in my view they were bound to do) the decision of the Court of Appeal in *Hankey v Clavering* [1942] 2 All ER 311, [1942] 2 KB 326 which in turn had followed the decision of the Court of Queen's Bench in *Cadby v Martinez* (1840) 11 Ad & El 720, 113 ER 587. In that *a* case, the notice said Midsummer instead of Lady Day. It seemed obvious to Lord Denman CJ that there was no way in which it could be construed to refer to Lady Day and he merely observed that 'in [no case] has a proviso or covenant in a deed been held to be satisfied by a notice inconsistent with the terms of it' (see 11 Ad & El 720 at 726, 113 ER 587 at 590).

b And yet, my Lords, the case is by no means straightforward. The clause does not require the tenant to use any particular form of words. He must use words which unambiguously convey a particular meaning, namely an intention to terminate the lease on 13 January. In *Hankey v Clavering*, where the notice to quit said '21 December' instead of '25 December', Lord Greene MR said ([1942] 2 All ER 311 at 313, 314, [1942] 2 KB 326 at 328, 330): '... the whole thing [was] obviously a slip' on the part of the landlord but that the *c* notice was invalid 'however much the recipient might guess, or however certain he might be' that it was a mere slip. So even if the recipient was certain that the landlord actually wanted to terminate his tenancy on the right date, which was 25 December, so that the necessary intention was unambiguously communicated, the notice was bad. One is bound to be left with a feeling that *d* something has gone wrong here. Common sense cannot produce such a result; it must be the result of some rule of law. If so, what is that rule and is it correct?

I propose to begin by examining the way we interpret utterances in everyday life. It is a matter of constant experience that people can convey their meaning unambiguously although they have used the wrong words. We *e* start with an assumption that people will use words and grammar in a conventional way but quite often it becomes obvious that, for one reason or another, they are not doing so and we adjust our interpretation of what they are saying accordingly. We do so in order to make sense of their utterance: so that the different parts of the sentence fit together in a coherent way and also *f* to enable the sentence to fit the background of facts which plays an indispensable part in the way we interpret what anyone is saying. No one, for example, has any difficulty in understanding Mrs Malaprop. When she says 'She is as obstinate as an allegory on the banks of the Nile', we reject the conventional or literal meaning of allegory as making nonsense of the sentence and substitute 'alligator' by using our background knowledge of the *g* things likely to be found on the banks of the Nile and choosing one which sounds rather like 'allegory'.

Mrs Malaprop's problem was an imperfect understanding of the conventional meanings of English words. But the reason for the mistake does not really matter. We use the same process of adjustment when people have *h* made mistakes about names or descriptions or days or times because they have forgotten or become mixed up. If one meets an acquaintance and he says 'And how is Mary?' it may be obvious that he is referring to one's wife, even if she is in fact called Jane. One may even, to avoid embarrassment, answer 'Very well, thank you' without drawing attention to his mistake. The message *j* has been unambiguously received and understood.

If one applies that kind of interpretation to the notice in this case, there will also be no ambiguity. The reasonable recipient will see that in purporting to terminate pursuant to cl 7(13) but naming 12 January 1995 as the day upon which he will do so, the tenant has made a mistake. He will reject as too improbable the possibility that the tenant meant that unless he could terminate on 12 January, he did not want to terminate at all. He will therefore understand the notice to mean that the tenant wants to terminate on the date on which, in accordance with cl 7(13), he may do so, i e 13 January.

Why, then, do cases like *Hankey v Clavering* arrive at a different answer? I want first to deal with two explanations which seem to me obviously inadequate. First, it is sometimes said that the examples which I have given from ordinary life are concerned with what the speaker meant to say. He may subjectively have intended to say something different from what he actually said and it may be possible, by the kind of reasoning which I have described, to divine what his subjective intentions were. But the law is not concerned with subjective intentions. All that matters is the objective meaning of the words which he has used.

It is of course true that the law is not concerned with the speaker's subjective intentions. But the notion that the law's concern is therefore with the 'meaning of his words' conceals an important ambiguity. The ambiguity lies in a failure to distinguish between the meanings of words and the question of what would be understood as the meaning of a person who uses words. The meaning of words, as they would appear in a dictionary, and the effect of their syntactical arrangement, as it would appear in a grammar, is part of the material which we use to understand a speaker's utterance. But it is only a part; another part is our knowledge of the background against which the utterance was made. It is that background which enables us, not only to choose the intended meaning when a word has more than one dictionary meaning but also, in the ways I have explained, to understand a speaker's meaning, often without ambiguity, when he has used the wrong words.

When, therefore, lawyers say that they are concerned, not with subjective meaning but with the meaning of the language which the speaker has used, what they mean is that they are concerned with what he would objectively have been understood to mean. This involves examining not only the words and the grammar but the background as well. So, for example, in *Doe d Cox v Roe* (1802) 4 Esp 185, 170 ER 685 the landlord of a public house in Limehouse gave notice to quit 'the premises which you hold of me ... commonly called ... the Waterman's Arms'. The evidence showed that the tenant held no premises called the Waterman's Arms; indeed, there were no such premises in the parish of Limehouse. But the tenant did hold premises of the landlord called the Bricklayer's Arms. By reference to the background, the notice was construed as referring to the Bricklayer's Arms. The meaning was objectively clear to a reasonable recipient, even though the landlord had used the wrong name. We therefore will in due course have to answer the question: if, as long ago as 1802, the background could be used to show that a person who speaks of the Waterman's Arms means the Bricklayer's Arms, why can it not show that a person who speaks of 12 January means 13 January?

The immediate point, however, is that the fact that the law does not have regard to subjective meaning is no explanation of the way *Hankey v Clavering* was decided. There was no need to resort to subjective meaning: the notice would objectively have been understood to mean that the landlord wanted to terminate the tenancy on the day on which he was entitled to do so.

I pass on to a second explanation which also seems to me inadequate. Lord Greene MR said that because such notices have unilateral operation, the conditions under which they may be served must be strictly complied with a (see [1942] 2 All ER 311 at 313–314, [1942] 2 KB 326 at 329–330). I have already said that this principle is accepted on both sides. But, as an explanation of the method of construction used in *Hankey v Clavering*, it begs the question. If the clause had said that the notice had to be on blue paper, it would have been no good serving a notice on pink paper, however clear it might have been that the tenant wanted to terminate the lease. But the condition in cl 7(13) related

b solely to the meaning which the notice had to communicate to the landlord. If compliance had to be judged by applying the ordinary techniques for interpreting communications, there was strict compliance. The notice clearly and unambiguously communicated the required message. To say that compliance must be strict does not explain why some other technique of interpretation is being used or what it is.

c   A variation of this explanation is to say that the language of the notice must be strictly construed. But what does it mean to say that a document must be 'strictly' construed, as opposed to the normal process of ascertaining the intentions of the author? The expression does not explain itself. If it operates merely by way of intensification, so that the intention must be clear,

d unambiguous, incapable of misleading, then I think that the notice in this case satisfied the test at that level. Likewise, as Lord Greene MR acknowledged when he said that the whole thing was obviously a slip, did the notice in *Hankey v Clavering*. So the concept of strict construction does not explain the decision.

e   A more promising clue to the explanation is Lord Greene MR's statement, in two places, that the notice must 'on its face' comply with the terms of the lease. What does 'on its face' mean? Clearly, the face of the document is being contrasted with the background, in law sometimes called the 'extrinsic evidence', against which the language is ordinarily construed. But Lord Greene MR cannot have meant that the document must always be read

f without any background, because (even if, which I doubt, it were conceptually possible to interpret the use of language without the aid of any background) cases like the *Cox* case show that some background, at least, can be used. It appears, therefore, that Lord Greene MR is referring to some principle whereby background can be used to show that a person who speaks of the Waterman's Arms means the Bricklayer's Arms, but not that a person who

g speaks of 12 January means 13 January. What principle is this?

   It is, I think, to be found in an old rule about the admissibility of extrinsic evidence to construe legal documents. In its pure form, the rule was said to be that if the words of the document were capable of referring unambiguously to a person or thing, no extrinsic evidence was admissible to show that the

h author was using them to refer to something or someone else. An extreme example is in *Re Peel's Goods* (1870) LR 2 P & D 46, in which the testator appointed 'Francis Courtenay Thorpe, of Hampton ... Middlesex' to be his executor. There was a Francis Courtenay Thorpe of Hampton, Middlesex. He was however only 12 years old and his father Francis Corbet Thorpe, of

j Hampton, Middlesex, was an old friend of the testator. Lord Penzance said (at 47) that these facts were inadmissible: 'The testator makes use of a description which applies in fact to one person, and not to any other.' A variation on this rule was *Re Fish, Ingham v Rayner* [1894] 2 Ch 83, in which the testator left his residuary estate to his 'niece Eliza'. He had no niece called Eliza but his wife had an illegitimate grandniece called Eliza, to whom the evidence of their

relationship showed that he must have intended to refer, and also, as it
happened, a legitimate grandniece called Eliza. The Court of Appeal said that   *a*
the estate went to the legitimate grandniece and that evidence of the
relationship between the testator and the illegitimate grandniece was
inadmissible. Lindley LJ said (at 85):

> '... where the person most nearly answering the description is the
> legitimate grandniece of the testator's wife ... no evidence can be   *b*
> admitted to prove that her illegitimate grandniece was intended.'

On the other hand, if there was no one to whom the description accurately
applied, there was said to be a 'latent ambiguity' and evidence of background
facts which showed what the testator must have meant, notwithstanding that
he had used the wrong words, was admitted.   *c*

Let us compare this rule with ordinary common sense interpretation of
what people say. If someone has gone to great pains, well in advance, to
secure tickets for himself and a friend for a Beethoven concert at the Royal
Festival Hall by a famous visiting orchestra on 13 January and says to the
friend a week earlier 'I'll see you at the Festival Hall concert on 12 January' it   *d*
will be obvious that he is referring to the concert on 13 January. According to
the old rules of construction, the law will agree if there is no concert at the
Festival Hall on 12 January. In that case there is a latent ambiguity. But if
there is a concert on that date (Stockhausen, say, played by a different
orchestra) he will be taken to have referred to that concert.

This extraordinary rule of construction is, as it seems to me, the only   *e*
explanation for the decisions in *Hankey v Clavering* [1942] 2 All ER 311, [1942]
2 KB 326 and *Cadby v Martinez*. The *Cox* case was distinguished by counsel in
Cadby's case (1840) 11 Ad & El 720 at 723, 113 ER 587 at 589 as involving a
latent ambiguity: there was no Waterman's Arms in Limehouse, so evidence
that the landlord would have been understood by a reasonable tenant as   *f*
intending to refer to the Bricklayer's Arms was admissible. But Midsummer
1837, or 21 December 1941 (in *Hankey v Clavering*) or 12 January 1995 (in this
case) are all real dates to which the notices could have referred. Therefore
evidence of background which showed that a reasonable recipient would have
understood the person giving the notice as having intended to refer to a
different date had to be disregarded. The effect is that apart from the   *g*
exceptional case in which the date is obviously impossible on the face of the
notice (as in *Carradine Properties Ltd v Aslam* [1976] 1 All ER 573, [1976] 1 WLR
442) the intention which the notice would convey as to date has to be
determined without regard to the terms of the lease (or anything else) as
background. There is an artificial assumption that the reasonable recipient   *h*
does not know what would be the correct date. On this basis, the
interpretation of the notices as referring to the wrong dates and therefore
being invalid is, of course, inescapable.

It is clear that this rule of construction has been applied to the interpretation
of notices for at least 200 years and it is hardly surprising that Lord Greene MR   *j*
and Lord Clauson felt obliged to apply it in *Hankey v Clavering* and that the
Court of Appeal applied it in this case. It is, however, highly artificial and
capable of producing results which offend against common sense. Lord
Penzance began his decision that the testator had appointed a 12-year-old boy
as his executor by saying ((1870) LR 2 P & D 46):

a
'If I am at liberty to look at the facts stated on the affidavits, I may possibly have no difficulty in deciding that the person meant is the father, but the question is, whether I am at liberty to do so.'

In *Re Fish* [1894] 2 Ch 83 at 84, Lindley LJ began his judgment by saying: 'This is one of those painful cases in which it is probable that the testator's

b intention will be defeated' and A L Smith LJ said (at 86) that if he could have admitted the evidence about the testator's relationship with his wife's illegitimate grandniece he would gladly have done so.

I think that the rule is not merely capricious but also, for reasons which I need not develop at length, incoherent. It is based upon an ancient fallacy which assumes that descriptions and proper names can somehow inherently

c refer to people or things. In fact, of course, words do not in themselves refer to anything; it is people who *use* words to refer to things. The word 'allegory' does not mean a large scaly creature or anything like it, but it is absurd to conclude, as judges sometimes do, that this is not an 'available meaning' of the word in the interpretation of what someone has said. This is simply a

d confusion of two different concepts; as we have seen, a person can use the word 'allegory', successfully and unambiguously, to refer to such a creature.

Even in its natural habitat, the construction of wills, the rule has not been (and, I think, cannot be) applied with any consistency. In *National Society for the Prevention of Cruelty to Children v Scottish National Society for the Prevention of*

e *Cruelty to Children* [1915] AC 207 this House refused to accept that a gift to the 'National Society for the Prevention of Cruelty to Children' should go to the society of that name, which had its head office in Leicester Square. It relied upon the background facts that, as Earl Loreburn said, the testator was 'a Scotsman living in Scotland' who had made a 'Scotch will' to construe the will as intended to refer to the 'Scottish National Society for the Prevention of

f Cruelty of Children' (see [1915] AC 207 at 211–214). Earl Loreburn refused to accept that there was 'a rigid rule' that 'once a persona is accurately named in a will' there is not to be 'any further inquiry or consideration in regard to the person who is to take the benefit'. The true rule, he said, was that 'the accurate use of a name in a will creates a strong presumption against any rival

g who is not the possessor of the name'. This demotes the rule to the common sense proposition that in a formal document such as a will, one does not lightly accept that people have used the wrong words. I doubt whether anyone would dissent from this principle, which would present no obstacle to a conclusion that the tenant in this case must have used the wrong words.

h   If your Lordships are to follow this path, it will be necessary to say that *Hankey v Clavering* and the older cases which it followed are no longer good law. It would be wrong, I think, to distinguish them on narrow grounds and leave them as wrecks in the channel, causing uncertainty and litigation in the future. Furthermore, the old rule of construction has been applied not only to notices exercising break clauses but also to notices to terminate periodic

j tenancies (see *Doe d Spicer v Lea* (1809) 11 East 312, 103 ER 1024). In his admirable submissions on behalf of the landlord, Mr Patten QC warned that a departure from the old rule would cause great uncertainty in the daily construction of notices to quit in county courts throughout the land. I confess that this prospect has caused me some anxiety and I think that it must be given serious consideration.

The rule as applied to wills, which restricts the use of background in aid of construction, reflects a distrust of the use of oral evidence to prove the background facts. The people who could give evidence about the background to a will would in most cases be members of the family interested in the outcome of the case and until 1843, persons with an interest in the litigation were not even competent witnesses. No doubt the exclusion of background makes, in a somewhat arbitrary way, for greater certainty in the sense that there is less room for dispute about what the background was and the effect which it has upon the intention to be attributed to the testator. But, as the cases mournfully show, this certainty is bought at the price of interpretations which everyone knows to be contrary to the meaning which he intended.

There are documents in which the need for certainty is paramount and which admissible background is restricted to avoid the possibility that the same document may have different meanings for different people according to their knowledge of the background. Documents required by bankers' commercial credits fall within this category. Article 13(*a*) of the Uniform Customs and Practice for Commercial Credits (1993 revision) says (echoing Lord Greene MR's phrase in *Hankey v Clavering*) that the documents must 'upon their face' appear to be in accordance with the terms and conditions of the credit. But the reasons of policy which require the restriction of background in this case do not apply to notices given pursuant to clauses in leases. In practice, the only relevant background will be, as in this case, the terms of the lease itself, which may show beyond any reasonable doubt what was the intention of the person who gave the notice. There will be no question of the parties not being privy to the same background—both of them will have the lease—and no room for dispute over what the relevant background is.

In the case of commercial contracts, the restriction on the use of background has been quietly dropped. There are certain special kinds of evidence, such as previous negotiations and express declarations of intent, which for practical reasons which it is unnecessary to analyse, are inadmissible in aid of construction. They can be used only in an action for rectification. But apart from these exceptions, commercial contracts are construed in the light of all the background which could reasonably have been expected to have been available to the parties in order to ascertain what would objectively have been understood to be their intention: see *Prenn v Simmonds* [1971] 3 All ER 237 at 239, [1971] 1 WLR 1381 at 1383. The fact that the words are capable of a literal application is no obstacle to evidence which demonstrates what a reasonable person with knowledge of the background would have understood the parties to mean, even if this compels one to say that they used the wrong words. In this area, we no longer confuse the meaning of words with the question of what meaning the use of the words was intended to convey. Why, therefore, should the rules for the construction of notices be different from those for the construction of contracts? There seems to me no answer to this question. All that can be said is that the rules for the construction of notices, like those for the construction of wills, have not yet caught up with the move to common sense interpretation of contracts which is marked by the speeches of Lord Wilberforce in *Prenn v Simmonds* and *Reardon Smith Line Ltd v Hansen-Tangen, Hansen-Tangen v Sanko Steamship Co* [1976] 3 All ER 570, [1976] *a* 1 WLR 989. The question is therefore whether there is any reason not to bring the rules for notices up to date by overruling the old cases.

There can, I think, be no question of anyone having acted in reliance on the principle of construction used in *Hankey v Clavering*. The consequence of such a construction is only to allow one party to take an unmeritorious advantage of another's verbal error, an adventitious bonus upon which no one could

b have relied. In this respect, the case for rejecting the old authorities is at least as strong as it was in *Sudbrook Trading Estate Ltd v Eggleton* [1982] 3 All ER 1, [1983] 1 AC 444, in which this House overruled cases going back to the early nineteenth century on the construction of contracts for sale at a valuation.

Nor do I think that a decision overruling the old cases will create uncertainty as to what the law is. In fact I think that the present law is

c uncertain and that only a decision of this House, either adopting or rejecting the *Hankey v Clavering* rule of construction, will make it certain. So, for example, in *Carradine Properties Ltd v Aslam* [1976] 1 All ER 573 at 576, [1976] 1 WLR 442 at 444, Goulding J said that the test for the validity of a notice was: '... is the notice quite clear to a reasonable tenant reading it? is it plain that he

d cannot be misled by it?' and he went on to say that the reasonable tenant must be taken to know the terms of the lease. This test was approved by the Court of Appeal in *Germax Securities Ltd v Spiegal* (1978) 37 P & CR 204 at 206 and, as will be apparent from what I have already said, I think that it was the right test to adopt. It is, however, absolutely impossible to reconcile the application of such a test with the decision in *Hankey v Clavering*, in which no reasonable

e tenant who knew the terms of the lease could possibly have mistaken the landlord's meaning. It is therefore not surprising that in *Micrografix v Woking 8 Ltd* [1995] 2 EGLR 32, Jacob J felt free to dismiss *Hankey v Clavering* as 'much distinguished' and to ignore it, or that Rattee J in *Garston v Scottish Widows' Fund and Life Assurance Society* [1996] 4 All ER 282, [1996] 1 WLR 834 should be

f puzzled as to why the Court of Appeal in this case considered, as I think rightly, that they were bound by *Hankey v Clavering*.

In my view, therefore, the House should say unequivocally that the test stated by Goulding J in *Carradine Properties Ltd v Aslam* was right and that *Hankey v Clavering* and the earlier cases should no longer be followed. The notice should be construed against the background of the terms of the lease.

g Interpreted in this way, the notice in the present case was valid and I would therefore allow the appeal.

LORD CLYDE. My Lords, the question in this appeal is whether the two letters dated 24 June 1994 and sent by the appellant tenant to the respondent

h landlord qualify as effective notices to determine the leases to which each letter respectively referred. Their validity as notices has to be tested against the terms of the power under which they were served. It is accepted that the two cases are for present purposes indistinguishable and that the relevant terms of the power were set out in cl 7(13) and were as follows:

j
'The Tenant may by serving not less than six months notice in writing on the Landlord or its solicitors such notice to expire on the 3rd anniversary of the term commencement date determine this Lease and upon expiry of such notice this Lease shall cease and determine and have no further effect ...'

The substance of the power is expressed by the words 'The Tenant may ... determine this Lease'. The method of its exercise is specified by the intervening words. The tenant must give six months' notice; the notice must be in writing; the notice must be served on the landlord or its solicitors. The sub-clause also states that the notice is to expire on the third anniversary of the term commencement date. The significance of that statement is that the period of six months is to terminate on that date. This regulates the time for the giving of the notice. The third anniversary marks the end of the period prior to which a notice under cl 7(13) must be given. But it is not required that the notice should include mention of the date of the intended determination of the lease. That date is prescribed by cl 7(13) where it states that the lease shall determine on expiry of the notice.

Where a notice of termination complies precisely and unambiguously with the provision which empowers the sending of the notice then its validity should be unquestioned. Where the terms of the notice do not altogether accord with the provisions of the contract that may or may not render the notice unenforceable. The problem then may come to be one of finding a fair and reasonable construction of the notice. But there can be cases where the validity of the notice cannot be saved by any construction and will have to be regarded as bad.

In some cases it may be obvious from the notice by itself that an error has been made. In *Carradine Properties Ltd v Aslam* [1976] 1 All ER 573, [1976] 1 WLR 442 an expressed intention to determine the lease at a date in 1973 was obviously incorrect in a notice served in 1974. In other cases the discrepancy can only be seen from a study of the terms of the lease. One would need to be aware of the provisions of the lease in such a case to appreciate that the permitted date was inaccurately stated. I see no reason in principle why in each of these kinds of case, provided of course that the wording is not absolutely clear and unambiguous, a notice should not be equally open to construction with a view to its possible validation.

In the present case the two letters in my view satisfy the formal and technical requirements of cl 7(13). But they go further and call for a determination of each lease one day before the day which the sub-clause identified as the date for the determination of the notice and for the determination of the lease. As I have mentioned that was not a formal requisite of the notice. Each notice proclaims at the outset that it is given 'Pursuant to Clause 7(13)'. This was a precise reference to the particular provision under which the notices were each being sent, as distinct from some general reference to the agreement between the parties. But it is evident from a consideration of that clause that there is a discrepancy between the date there indicated for the termination of the lease and the date stated in the notice. Whether that inaccuracy in the notice is fatal or not depends on the proper construction of the notices. The formulation propounded by Goulding J in the *Carradine* case [1976] 1 All ER 573 at 576, [1976] 1 WLR 442 at 444, was 'is the notice quite clear to a reasonable tenant reading it? is it plain that he cannot be misled by it?' *Delta Vale Properties Ltd v Mills* [1990] 2 All ER 176, [1990] 1 WLR 445 concerned a vendor's notice to complete which was in condition 23 of the conditions of sale, but I see no reason why any different principle of construction should apply. Slade LJ observed ([1990] 2 All ER 176 at 183, [1990] 1 WLR 445 at 454):

a   'In my judgment, notices to complete served under condition 23, if they
    are to be valid, must be sufficiently clear and unambiguous to leave a
    reasonable recipient in no reasonable doubt as to how and when they are
    intended to operate.'

The standard of reference is that of the reasonable man exercising his common
sense in the context and in the circumstances of the particular case. It is not
b an absolute clarity or an absolute absence of any possible ambiguity which is
desiderated. To demand a perfect precision in matters which are not within
the formal requirements of the relevant power would in my view impose an
unduly high standard in the framing of notices such as those in issue here.
While careless drafting is certainly to be discouraged the evident intention of
c a notice should not in matters of this kind be rejected in preference for a
technical precision.

The test is an objective one. In circumstances where an estoppel might arise
the actual understanding of the recipient may be relevant, but in general the
actual understanding of the parties is beside the point. That the test is an
objective one was recognised in *Micrografix v Woking 8 Ltd* [1995] 2 EGLR 32.
d It was held there that the landlords would not have been misled by the
references to a wrong date both in the notice to terminate the lease and in the
covering letter. Each document was expressly written pursuant to the
particular break clause in the lease. The recipients would have observed the
errors because they would be familiar with the terms of the lease and would
e have known that the only date of determination had to be 23 June 1995. They
would know that there was no requirement to specify any date in the notice.
They would see that the tenant wanted to leave. It was held that the notice
was valid.

In my opinion a like view should be taken in the circumstances of the
present case. The notices were expressed to be 'Pursuant to Clause 7(13)'. It
f is plain from that that the tenant intended to invoke that clause. It is also plain
that the tenant wished to determine the tenancy and that clause is the only
clause under which the tenant could achieve that result. The landlord would
be expected to know the terms of the lease and the date on which the lease fell
to be determined under that clause. He would also be expected to know that
g there was no formal requirement for the tenant to specify in the notice the
date of termination of the lease. There was no evident reason why the tenant
should specify 12 January rather than 13 January. The close proximity of the
13th makes it the more evident that it was erroneous and that the date
intended was the date which the parties had agreed for a determination of the
tenancy under cl 7(13). While there is a discrepancy evident in the notices
h between the reference to the clause and the statement of the date it seems to
me that the notices were sufficiently clear and unambiguous. No reasonable
landlord would in my view be misled by the statement of a date which in the
context of a clear intention to invoke cl 7(13) was inaccurate. The landlord
would in my view recognise that in each case the reference to 12 January was
j to be read as a reference to 13 January and I would so construe the notices.

In *Hankey v Clavering* [1942] 2 All ER 311, [1942] 2 KB 326 the court refused
to disregard a slip even although the intention of the notice was sufficiently
clear from its terms and the recipient could not reasonably misunderstand it.
In my view that was too strict and too technical an approach. Counsel for the
tenant sought to restrict the decision in *Hankey*'s case to circumstances where

the insertion of the date of termination is an essential requirement of a notice.
I am, however, not persuaded that the decision in *Hankey's* case rested on the $\quad a$
understanding that the specification of the date was an essential. I note that
the corresponding provisions in the *Carradine* case and in the *Micrografix* case
were not dissimilar and indeed in the latter case one element in the decision
was the consideration that there was no requirement to specify a date. While
to a considerable extent the cases in this field may turn upon their own $\quad b$
circumstances I do not consider that the decision reached in the *Hankey* case
was sound and in my opinion it should be overruled. In the circumstances of
the present case I take the view that the notices were valid and effective. I
agree with your Lordships that the argument based on *Sidebotham v Holland*
[1895] 1 QB 378, [1891–4] All ER Rep 617 is without merit. But for the reasons
which I have explained I would allow the appeal. $\quad c$

Appeal allowed.

Celia Fox   Barrister.

d

e

f

g

h

j

INDEX

References are to paragraph numbers.

Agent
notices identifying as server — 3.62, 3.63,
3.64, 3.65
Agents
managing agents — 5.21
service by — 5.4
sub-agents — 5.8
signatures of — 3.16, 3.17, 3.18
tenant, of
service on — 7.48

Break clauses — 1.23
interpretation — 1.24, 2.5
post-Mannai Investment — 2.11, 2.12
misidentification of server, and — 3.57,
3.58, 3.59
Break notices
date of expiry — 3.37
Business tenancy
fraudulent statements, and — 3.5

Capacity
service of notice, and — 5.25
Companies
service by — 5.4
Contractual notices
requirements — 1.17
omissions, and — 1.18
oral notification — 1.19
validity, and — 1.17
Counter-notice
notice requirements, and — 1.16
Covering letters
interpretation of notices, and — 2.30
signatures in — 3.15

Date of expiry of notice
specification of — 3.34
break notices — 3.37
licences — 3.35
multiple dates — 3.39
notices to quit — 3.36
orders for possession — 3.38
Deadlines for service of notices — 3.28
rent review notices — 3.29
delay — 3.33
late service, effect — 3.31
rebuttal of presumption — 3.32

Deadlines for service of notices—*continued*
rent review notices—*continued*
rule of equity — 3.30
usual rule — 3.28
Death
tenant, of
service of notice to quit — 3.45

Email
methods of service — 7.69
Estoppel — 4.1
convention, by — 4.1
disentitlement from reliance on
effective notice — 4.3
limitations on — 4.14
creating cause of action, and — 4.14
public policy — 4.15
loss of right to serve notice — 4.2
promissory — 4.1
representation, by — 4.1
suspension of operation of notice — 4.4
validity of notice, loss of right to
dispute — 4.5
defective contents — 4.9, 4.10
incorrect date of expiry — 4.8
recipient, by — 4.5
server, by — 4.11, 4.12, 4.13
service after contractual
deadline — 4.7
service by wrong person — 4.6

Fax
methods of service — 7.69
Formal requirements
example of — 1.26, 1.27, 1.28, 1.29
requirements to convey particular
meaning distinguished — 1.30, 1.31
types of — 1.25
Fraud
methods of service, and — 7.5
Fraudulent statements — 3.3
business tenancy, under — 3.5
case law — 3.4, 3.6
invalidation — 3.3
proposals and requests, and — 3.9

Human rights
methods of service, and — 7.3

Inaccuracy
  defective contents   4.9, 4.10
  identification of server   3.54
  intention to exercise right, and   2.34
  particulars, in   1.40, 1.41, 1.42
  recipient, misidentification of   3.66
  substance of notice, and   1.33
  type of requirement, and   1.30
    requirement to convey
      particular meaning   1.31
Inconsistencies
  validity of notice, and   3.26
    factual background   3.27
Indirect service   5.27
Interpretation of notices   2.1
  contractual and statutory   2.19
    common approach   2.19
    Mannai Investment approach   2.20
    test for   2.19
  Mannai Investment v Eagle Star   2.2
  objective contextual scene   2.28, 2.29
    covering letters   2.30
    non-factual background   2.33
    rent demands and prior
      litigation   2.32
    types of notice   2.31
  obvious mistake, significance   2.21
    test for   2.22
  post-Mannai Investment   2.13, 2.14, 2.15,
      2.16
  reappraisal of   2.1
  reasonable recipient   2.1
    application of test   2.17, 2.18
    doubt, and   2.23
    recipient's interpretation   2.25, 2.26,
      2.27
    server's interpretation   2.24
  traditional approach   2.6, 2.7, 2.8, 2.9
  types of 'defect'   2.34, 2.36, 2.37, 2.38
    prescribed forms, and   2.35

Joint owners
  service of notices   3.46
    Agricultural Holdings Act
      1923, s 12   3.51, 3.52
    exception to general rule   3.48
    general rule   3.46
    notice to quit   3.48, 3.49, 3.50
    subsequent ratification   3.47
  services of notices
    identity of recipient   3.53
Joint tenants
  service of notices, and   3.51, 3.52

Last-known place of abode or business
  leaving notice at   7.18
Legal proprietors   3.40
  service of notices, and   3.40
    owner of interest   3.43
  validity of notices, and   3.41

Licences
  notice terminating
    date of expiry   3.35

Managing agents
  service of notice on   5.21
Mandatory requirements   1.8
  written notice as   3.1
Mannai Investment   2.2
  decision in   2.10
    application of 'reasonable
      recipient test'   2.17, 2.18
    interpretation of break clauses   2.11,
      2.12
    interpretation of notices   2.13, 2.14,
      2.15, 2.16
  facts   2.2, 2.3
  law before   2.4
    interpretation of break clauses   2.5
    interpretation of notices   2.6, 2.7, 2.8,
      2.9
  types of 'defect'   2.34
Methods of service   6.2
  Agricultural Holdings Act 1986,
    s 93   7.51
    agents and servants, service on   7.63
    change of landlord   7.64
    delivering to recipient   7.53
    leaving at recipient's proper
      address   7.54, 7.55, 7.56, 7.57
    methods of service under   7.52
    recorded delivery   7.58, 7.59, 7.60,
      7.61, 7.62
    registered post   7.58, 7.59, 7.60, 7.61,
      7.62
    text   7.51
  Agricultural Tenancies Act 1995,
    s 36   7.65
    methods of service under   7.66, 7.67
    text   7.65
  at recipient's last known address   6.3
  by post   6.2
  Companies Act 2006   7.68
    authorised methods   7.68
    electronic form   7.69
  Landlord and Tenant Act 1927,
    s 23   7.32
    agent of tenant, on   7.48
    application   7.33
    Interpretation Act 1978, s 7,
      and   7.49, 7.50
    landlord predecessor in title, on   7.46
    leaving at last known place of
      abode   7.35, 7.36, 7.37, 7.38,
      7.39, 7.40
    personal service   7.34
    recorded delivery   7.41, 7.42, 7.43,
      7.44, 7.45
    registered post   7.41, 7.42, 7.43, 7.44,
      7.45
    scope   7.47
    text   7.32

Methods of service—*continued*
  Law of Property Act 1925, s 196   7.10
    affixed or left at demised or
      mortgaged premises 7.25, 7.26,
                         7.27
    extension of operation of   7.13
    instrument affecting property,
      meaning   7.14
    leaving notice at last known
      place of abode or
      business   7.18, 7.19, 7.20, 7.21,
                   7.22, 7.23, 7.24
    left at office or counting house
      of mine   7.25, 7.26, 7.27
    methods authorised by   7.18
    recorded delivery 7.28, 7.29, 7.30, 7.31
    registered post 7.28, 7.29, 7.30, 7.31
    'required'   7.16
    'required or authorised' by   7.12
    serving and giving, distinction   7.15
    text   7.10
    type of notice provisions   7.17
    types of notice   7.11
  legislation   7.70
  statutory provisions   7.1
    human rights   7.3
    purpose of   7.2
    scope   7.4
    use as 'engine of fraud' 7.5, 7.6, 7.7,
                   7.8, 7.9
Mines
  methods of service, and   7.25

Notice
  valid
    fraud, and   3.3
    requirements   1.1
Notice to quit
  date of expiry of notice   3.36
  given orally   3.2
  joint owners, and   3.48, 3.49, 3.50
  misidentification of server   3.60
  service
    death of tenant, following   3.45
    service prior to creation of tenancy   3.42
Notices
  interpretation   2.1
  withdrawal   4.16
Notices served 'subject to contract' or
  'without prejudice'   3.21
  case law   3.22, 3.24, 3.25
  misuse of   3.23
  subject to contract, meaning   3.21
Notices served without prejudice to
  earlier notice   3.19, 3.20

Obvious mistake
  interpretation of notices, and   2.21
Omission
  irrelevant material, of   1.36
    prejudiced recipient, and   1.38
  substance of notice, and   1.33

Omission—*continued*
  type of requirement, and   1.30
    requirement to convey
      particular meaning   1.31
Oral notice
  notice to quit   3.2
Oral notification
  validity   1.19
Order for possession
  specification of date, and   3.38

Particulars
  inaccuracies in   1.40
    case law   1.42
    pariculars, meaning   1.41
    partial   1.41
Personal service
  methods of service   7.34
Post
  methods of service   6.2, 7.28, 7.29, 7.30,
      7.31, 7.41, 7.42, 7.43, 7.44, 7.45,
         7.58, 7.59, 7.60, 7.61, 7.62
Predecessor in title
  service upon   7.46
Prescribed forms   1.32
  adoption of superseded version   1.39
  court's approach   1.33
    misidentification of landlord   1.34
    misidentified dates   1.35
    purpose of notice, and   1.33
  departure from
    compliance, and   1.32
  omission of irrelevant material   1.36
    identification of material   1.37
    prejudiced receipient, and   1.38
  reasonable recipient, and   2.35
  statutory requirements   1.32
Prior litigation
  interpretation of notices, and   2.32
Proposals and requests   3.7, 3.11
  interpretation of provisions   3.7
  propose, meaning   3.10
  rent review trigger notice   3.9
  server's state of mind, and   3.8
Public policy
  waiver and estoppel, and   4.15
Purchase notice
  notice requirements, and   1.14

Reasonable recipient test
  application   2.17, 2.18
  doubt, and   2.23
  objective contextual scene, and   2.28
  recipient's interpretation of notice,
    and   2.25, 2.26, 2.27
  server's interpretation of notice,
    and   2.24
Recipient
  identification   3.40
    establishing identity   3.44
    joint owners   3.53

Recipient—*continued*
  incapable of understanding notice,
    service on 5.24
  last known address 6.3
  misidentification of 3.66
    case law 3.68, 3.69
    conveyance of meaning, and 3.67
    requirements 3.66
  same person as server, and 5.28
  service of notice on 5.10
  validity of notice, loss of right to
    dispute 4.5
Recorded delivery
  methods of service 7.28, 7.29, 7.30, 7.31,
    7.41, 7.42, 7.43, 7.44, 7.45, 7.58,
    7.59, 7.60, 7.61, 7.62
Registered post
  methods of service 7.29, 7.30, 7.31, 7.41,
    7.42, 7.43, 7.44, 7.45, 7.58, 7.59,
    7.60, 7.61, 7.62
  mthods of service 7.28
Rent collectors
  acceptance of service by 5.23
Rent demands
  interpretation of notices, and 2.32
Rent review notices
  deadline for service 3.29, 3.30, 3.31, 3.32,
    3.33
Rent review trigger notice 3.9
Requests
  proposals, and 3.7
Requirements to convey particular
    meaning 1.21
  formal requirements distinguished 1.30,
    1.31

Section 20 notice
  purpose 1.35
Section 25 notice
  validity 1.6
Section 26 notice
  withdrawal 4.17
Servants
  service of notice on 5.22
  service on 7.63
Server
  identification 3.40
    establishing identity 3.44
  misidentification
    service by agents, and 5.6
  misidentification of 3.54
    break clauses 3.57, 3.58, 3.59
    case law 3.56, 3.61
    interpretation of provisions 3.55
    notice to quit 3.60
  notices identifying agent as 3.62, 3.63,
    3.64, 3.65
  same person as recipient and 5.28
  validity of notice, loss of right to
    dispute 4.11, 4.12, 4.13

Service of notice
  agent of recipient, on 5.14
    authorising 5.14
    failure to pass to recipient 5.15
    managing agents 5.21
    rent collectors 5.23
    servants 5.22
    solicitors 5.16, 5.17, 5.18, 5.19, 5.20
  agents, by 5.4
    authorisation for 5.4
    case law 5.5, 5.7
    misidentification of server, and 5.6
    sub-agents 5.8
  common law, at 5.1
    proving service 5.2
    requirements 5.1
  contractual deadline, after 4.7
  contractual provisions, pursuant to 6.1
    displacement of common law,
      and 6.4, 6.5
  indirect 5.27
  legal proprietor 3.41
  loss of right to 4.2
  methods of 6.2
  presumed sequence for 5.13
  recipient incapable of
    understanding, on 5.24
    mental disorders 5.26
    validity 5.25
  recipient or his agent, on 5.10
    must be received by recipient 5.10,
      5.11, 5.12
  same person as server and recipient 5.28
  wrong person, by 4.6
    retrospective validation 5.9
Service of notices
  joint owners 3.46
Signatures 3.13
  agents, of 3.16, 3.17, 3.18
  covering letters, in 3.15
  meaning 3.14
Solicitors
  service of notice on 5.16, 5.17
    authorising 5.18
    implied authority 5.19
    ostensible authority 5.20
Statutory notices 1.5
  requirements 1.5
    failure to comply with 1.5
    flexible approach 1.9
    mandatory and directory
      distinguished 1.8
    necessity 1.7
    non-compliance, effect 1.6
    'rigid characterisation' 1.9
Statutory requirements 1.8
Sub-agents
  service by 5.8

Tenant
  death
    service of notice to quit 3.45

Tenants
   joint 3.51, 3.52
Trigger notice
   delay in serving 3.33

Valid notice 1.1
   deadline for service 3.28
   inconsistencies, and 3.26
   legal proprietor 3.41
   loss of right to dispute 4.5
   prescribed forms 1.32
   requirements 1.1
      consequences of invalidity 1.12
      'defects' 1.4
      determination 1.10
      directory 1.5
      example of 1.14, 1.15, 1.16
      formal requirements 1.20, 1.25, 1.26, 1.27, 1.28, 1.29
      function of statutory 1.13
      identification of 1.1
      inaccuracy or omission 1.30, 1.31
      interpretation of provisions 1.4
      mandatory 1.5
      non-compliance with statutory 1.12
      omitted information 1.12
      statutory notices 1.5
      statutory, scope 1.2
      substance of statutory requirement 1.11
      to convey particular meaning 1.21, 1.22, 1.23, 1.24

Valid notice—*continued*
   requirements—*continued*
      two-stage approach 1.1
      types of 1.20
      upholding notices that achieve their purpose 1.3
   server's motivation, and 3.12
      relevance 3.12
   specification of date of expiry 3.34

Waiver 4.1
   disentitlement from reliance on effective notice 4.3
   limitations on
      public policy 4.15
   loss of right to serve notice 4.2
   meaning 4.1
   suspension of operation of notice 4.4
   validity of notice, loss of right to dispute 4.5
      defective contents 4.9, 4.10
      incorrect date of expiry 4.8
      recipient, by 4.5
      service after contractual deadline 4.7
      service by wrong person 4.6
Withdrawal of notices 4.16
   capability 4.16
   'countermanding' notices 4.18
   section 26 notice 4.17
Written notice
   requirements 3.1